Some Early Bahá'ís
of the West

SOME EARLY BAHÁ'ÍS
OF THE WEST

by

O. Z. WHITEHEAD

GEORGE RONALD
OXFORD

George Ronald
46 High Street, Kidlington, Oxford

12/97

ISBN 0 85398 065 9 (cased)
ISBN 0 85398 067 5 (paper)

Set in Great Britain by
Santype Ltd.
and printed by Billing & Sons Ltd.
Guildford and London

Contents

v

Illustrations

Introduction and Acknowledgements

EXCEPT FOR QUEEN MARIE OF RUMANIA, the first crowned head to proclaim the Revelation of Bahá'u'lláh, the believers mentioned in this book all recognized His Station during the lifetime of His son, the Centre of His Covenant, 'Abdu'l-Bahá, who left this life on 28th November 1921. Apart from the Hand of the Cause George Townshend, who only corresponded with 'Abdu'l-Bahá, the other believers had the even more precious experience of meeting Him, either in America or Europe or, for the majority of them, during a pilgrimage to the Holy Land. Fired by their overwhelming devotion to 'Abdu'l-Bahá, Whom they called the Master, they served Him with unquestioning obedience, and received in return His love and trust.

In June 1963 the Hand of the Cause A. Q. Faizi visited Ireland. The morning after his arrival in Dublin I was privileged to spend some time alone with him. Since he knew that I had come to live there only a few weeks before in order to help in the promotion of the Bahá'í Faith, he was obviously anxious to encourage me in any way that he could. I told him that, besides being a professional actor, I had also made some attempts to write, but always on subjects not directly related to the Faith. I also informed him that I had known some of the early believers. "Why don't you write your impressions of them?" he asked me. Mr. Faizi assured me that knowledge of the early believers was already of great interest to the Bahá'ís and that it would be the same to all humanity in the future.

When Mr. Faizi again made a visit to Ireland in January 1966, he asked me, "Have you done any writing as I suggested?" I described a little the contents of my work so far. He advised me again: "Write down every Bahá'í experience that you have. Before long people will want to know about Bahá'ís, no matter how obscure they may be. One line that anyone writes could be very important."

Some months later I sent Mr. Faizi four short impressions, and from then on, every time that I sent him an impression or even rough notes, he replied with a letter that inspired me to continue writing.

Adib Taherzadeh also read my first impressions with much interest and gave me constructive suggestions for future work. Stimulating letters from Marzieh Gail, as well as delightful conversations with Doris Holley, have equally helped me to write these essays.

Thanks to the efforts of Mrs. Evelyn Hardin, Miss Charlotte Linfoot, and Mr. William Geissler, twelve of these essays first appeared in the American 'Bahá'í News.' They have all been revised and some of them have been expanded.

I want to express my heartfelt thanks to Mr. Paul Haney for material about Charles and Mariam Haney, to Mrs. Alice Dudley for letters that she had received from Mariam, to Mr. David Hofman for his personal statement concerning George Townshend, to Dr. Edris Rice-Wray and Mrs. Muriel Ives Newhall for their letters about Howard and Mabel Ives, to Mr. Donald Kinney for information about Edward and Carrie Kinney, and to Miss Ethel Revell for her letter about Isabella Brittingham, and my deep gratitude to my publishers, particularly to Mr. Mark Hofman for his careful editing of this volume. My thanks go also to the Audio-Visual Department of the Bahá'í World Centre, which has supplied many of the photographs.

Two books especially have provided me with numerous details, *The Priceless Pearl* by Rúḥíyyih Rabbaní and *'Abdu'l-Bahá* by H. M. Balyuzi, and I am grateful to both of these authors.

In many cases, quotations from Tablets of 'Abdu'l-Bahá have been taken from old translations, the only ones available, in which the translators' knowledge of English was imperfect. Also, many other texts quoted were published before a uniform system of transliteration for Bahá'í writings had been adopted. In these cases, quotations are in accordance with the original texts.

Foreword

HISTORY TEACHES US MANY LESSONS. It is incumbent upon us
to listen carefully to its warning calls. How very often
historians reach turning-points in the story of Mankind where
they long to have even one sentence, anecdote or description
of an event in the words of the people of the time. Sometimes
they find themselves in an eternal darkness which envelops
them, with no way out.

Now we are living in the early days of our Faith; and we,
as Bahá'ís, should cultivate in our midst a strong sense of
history. The very early adherents of the Faith, in the thick
of the battles of life and in its death throes, could scarcely
find a moment of peace to write the history of their time.
Though we regret the gaps existing in the chapters of the
history of our Faith, it is not too late to redress the losses
which we so bitterly suffer.

Some years ago when I had the joy of meeting Zebby
Whitehead in Ireland, he expressed his desire to undertake
the writing of the biographies of some of the early believers
in the United States and the West. Then I learned that he
had started to fulfil this challenge; and most fortunately he
continued to write with an unabated energy. I feel sure that
present and future students of history will benefit greatly from
these essays written with much love and purity of heart. The
details will throw much light on events in the history of the
Cause in America and elsewhere in the West. May the writer
receive abundant blessings from on high.

Faizi

12th June 1976

To all those who serve
the Cause of Bahá'u'lláh

Thornton Chase

SOON AFTER I BECAME A MEMBER of the Bahá'í community in Los Angeles on 1st July 1950, I heard that Thornton Chase was not only the first believer in the United States of America, but also in the Western world. I often wondered what sort of a man he was. What indefinable quality did he have that enabled him to recognize the Station of Bahá'u'lláh before anyone else in such a large part of the planet?

I had heard the distinguished old believer, Willard Hatch, at that time Secretary of the Spiritual Assembly, say, "Thornton Chase and I were friends." One morning I telephoned him and said, "Mr. Hatch, may I come to see you? I want to hear more about Thornton Chase." "Well, bless your heart," Mr. Hatch answered warmly. "The Spiritual Assembly has invited me to say a few words about him at his grave in Inglewood on the afternoon of September 30th, the anniversary of his passing, when 'Abdu'l-Bahá wished the friends to meet there." "What was Mr. Chase's profession?" I asked directly.

"He was an insurance salesman, but he had one of the best baritone voices that I have ever heard." Despite my obvious encouragement, Mr. Hatch said no more about him.

The cemetery in Inglewood, a suburb of Los Angeles, is composed of lawnlike stretches of lowlands and only a few trees, with a view of distant hills. Since the anniversary took place on a weekday only a few of the believers were able to attend it. Helped by a cane, Mr. Hatch got out of a car in which an old friend had driven him to the cemetery and, with much dignity, limped to the side of the grave. He sat down on a chair that someone had placed there for him.

Stockily built, he had a strong face with few lines and full of character. His hair was white. He looked his age, about seventy.

The other believers gathered around the grave. The stone is of simple design and lies upon the ground. The quotation on the grave is from the Master: "This is the illumined resting-place of the holy soul, Thornton Chase, who is shining in the horizon of eternal life ever like a star."

Mr. Hatch spoke in a plain, direct, and forceful manner. I can remember a few sentences of his short address. "Thornton Chase was living in Chicago when he came into the Cause there in 1894. He was an insurance salesman and travelled from place to place for his work. Towards the end of his life he became more and more interested in the Faith and less and less interested in his work. The number of years that he was a Bahá'í is not important. That he was the first Bahá'í in the Western world and that he served the Cause faithfully until his passing is extremely important."

After the talk, during prayers, I was privileged to read the following one by 'Abdu'l-Bahá:

O Thou kind Lord! This gathering is turning to Thee. These hearts are radiant with Thy love. These minds and spirits are exhilarated by the message of Thy glad-tidings. O God! Let this American democracy become glorious in spiritual degrees even as it has aspired to material degrees, and render this just government victorious. Confirm this revered nation to upraise the standard of the oneness of humanity, to promulgate the Most Great Peace, to become thereby most glorious and praiseworthy among all the nations of the world. O God! This American nation is worthy of Thy favors and is deserving of Thy mercy. Make it precious and near to Thee through Thy bounty and bestowal.

Always moving, this prayer seemed particularly so at that moment when I thought of many tragic events, including two catastrophic wars that had afflicted the United States of America since the passing of Thornton Chase, all coming about because of man's disobedience to Bahá'u'lláh.

I felt in the group not only a deep realization of the spiritual blindness that still existed among the people, but also a heartfelt belief that through the Revelation of Bahá'u'lláh

2

this country was going to achieve what 'Abdu'l-Bahá fervently prayed that it would. A strong atmosphere of peace seemed to fill this holy spot.

Thornton Chase was born in Springfield, Massachusetts, on 22nd February 1847. His childhood home, according to his close friend Carl Scheffler, was "a large, rather ornate white frame dwelling, located at the intersection of two sharply converging streets."[1] Besides serving as a Captain in the Civil War, Thornton Chase went to Brown University. He was fond of fishing, had a love of music and a magnificent singing voice. Carl Scheffler thought that at one time his friend might have sung in opera. Always deeply interested in religion, and not content with partial acceptance of any prevailing doctrine or sect of which there were many always springing up, he was "convinced that this undoubtedly was 'The Day of God,'"[2] and he was determined to spare no pains to discover what God had brought to mankind.

A few years before he heard of the Bahá'í Revelation, he became a follower of the great Swedish mystic of the eighteenth century, Emanuel Swedenborg. But not content with those noble teachings, which have satisfied many brilliant, highly constructive people, Mr. Chase still looked for what he thought must be a greater light that God had already unveiled to the world.

According to Carl Scheffler, Thornton Chase heard of the Bahá'í Faith in the following manner. William F. James, a friend of Mr. Chase's, told him of a man he had met who had said that God "walked upon the earth."[3] Mr. Chase wanted to meet this man without delay. As a result he was taken to see Dr. Ibráhím Khayru'lláh, who had made this overwhelming statement.

Shortly before his passing Mr. Chase wrote about this meeting somewhat differently. "In the month of June, 1894, a gentleman in Chicago desired to study Sanskrit, in order to further pursue his search into ancient religious teachings. While seeking an instructor he met a Syrian who had come to Chicago from Egypt a short time before, and who told him of the Bahá'í Movement .... As the statements of the life and teachings of BAHA'O'LLAH and his son, Abbas Effendi, the 'Greatest Branch', otherwise known as Abdul-Baha, accorded with the declarations of numerous sacred prophecies, and with the agelong expectations of mankind, it was deemed of value to investigate those claims as far as possible. Other seekers for truth became attracted to the study of these matters, with the result that five accepted the teachings as true during the year 1894."[4]

During those early years many people showed an interest in the Faith, and even asked to be enrolled in the community. But a large portion of them had only a superficial understanding of what the Faith meant. As a result, when Dr. Ibráhím Khayru'lláh, who up to that time had recieved high praise for his teaching from 'Abdu'l-Bahá, blinded by self-love and ambition turned against Him and broke the Covenant of God for this day, more than a few left the Faith in doubt and confusion. This tragic and heart-breaking event in no way affected those like Thornton Chase who truly believed.

In the same article, Thornton Chase mentioned the arrival in the United States during 1900 of two fine teachers, Mírzá Asadu'lláh and Mírzá Ḥasan-i-Khurásání, and their most effective efforts; and a little later the coming of Mírzá Abu'l-Faḍl, "a scholar and historian, famous in the Orient for his learning and sincerity, one who had given up a position of the highest honor in Persia, as President of the Royal College of Teheran [the School of Ḥakím-Háshim], to embrace the Bahai Cause, which resulted in his imprisonment for three years in Persian dungeons."[5]

Mr. Chase stressed the enormous service that these teachers had given in bringing an entirely correct knowledge of the Bahá'í Writings to those who were already believers and to the sincere seekers of truth. Many who had mixed up the Faith with occult and psychic experiments and held views based on superstition and imagination left the Faith. Others, through the instruction of these great teachers, became "deeply confirmed in their belief, and clung to it as the most valuable instruction possible for man to obtain."[6]

His position with the Union Mutual Life Insurance Society made it necessary for Mr. Chase to travel a great deal. At first in each city that he visited he planted seeds for the Faith.

When the people in these cities began to investigate it seriously and some to join the community, he was able to teach and deepen them.

John Bosch, who emigrated from Switzerland in 1879, accepted the Faith on 29th May 1905. "He bought all the available pamphlets, mostly by Thornton Chase,"[7] records Marzieh Gail, who has also given a delightful report of the following incident between the two gentlemen (including some quotations from John Bosch):

In those days Thornton Chase had an important insurance position in Chicago, with a salary of $750 a month which diminished every year because the Faith meant more to him than his business. Whenever he was coming to San Francisco he wired John; they would stop at different hotels, but dined together. 'He was very tall—about six feet two. He always ate two or three ice creams after supper; he always dug a big bite right out of the middle of it to start with. Around eleven o'clock, he used to say, "Now, John, I guess it's about time to take you home."' Arm in arm, they would go to John's hotel, talking steadily about the Cause. They would sit in the parlor. 'About one o'clock I used to say, "Now, Mr. Chase, I guess it's about time to take you home." We used to wonder what the policeman on the beat thought about us. One night we brought each other home till four in the morning.'[8]

Never feeling that he had sufficient knowledge of the Cause, Mr. Chase was always trying to find out more. Despite the absence of much authentic material he could explain clearly aspects of the Cause that others found difficult to understand. As the Master gradually unfolded the Administrative Order, Mr. Chase eagerly received each new piece of information. He entirely appreciated the great importance of the Spiritual Assembly and did all that he could to uphold its authority. Many, not realizing why such an institution should exist, left the Faith. The serious problems and turmoil that the early communities went through in no way interfered with his constant and inspiring service.

In April 1907, Mr. Chase made a pilgrimage to 'Akká together with Mr. Arthur S. Agnew, Mr. Agnew's wife and son, and Mr. Scheffler. Mr Chase described this journey in a short book called *In Galilee*, long out of print.

After first staying for four days in Haifa at the Catholic Hospice of the Little Child and later at the Hotel Pross, during which time they had the precious experience of visiting the Shrine of the Báb, Mr. Chase and Mr. Scheffler took the beautiful drive along the coast of the Mediterranean to 'Akká. At the entrance to the house where 'Abdu'l-Bahá lived, three Persian gentlemen led them to the room where they were invited to stay, next to the room of 'Abdu'l-Bahá. Within a few minutes (Mr. Chase wrote), "Some one said, 'The Master!'—and he came into the room with a free, striding step, welcomed us in a clear, ringing voice—'Mahrhabba! Mahrhabba!' (Welcome! Welcome!)—and embraced us with kisses as would a father his son, or as would brothers after a long absence ....

"He bade us be seated on the little divan; he sat on the high, narrow bed at one side of the room, drew up one foot under him, asked after our health, our trip, bade us be happy, and expressed his happiness that we had safely arrived. Then, after a few minutes, he again grasped our hands and abruptly left us."[9]

During the five days that Mr. Chase and Mr. Scheffler spent in the prison house, they saw the Master several times each day, once in His room, sometimes in their or someone else's room, and at meals in company with other believers.

Mr. Chase pointed out, "Each conversation started with some simple reference to a natural thing, the weather, food, a stone, tree, water, the prison, a garden or a bird, our coming, or some little act of service, and this base would be woven into a parable and teaching of wisdom and simplicity, showing the oneness of all Spiritual Truth, and adapting it always to *the life*, both of the individual and of mankind."[10]

In one of the most moving passages in his book Mr. Chase has written of 'Abdu'l-Bahá, "And, as each hungry pilgrim comes to that prison house, that banquet hall of heavenly gifts, he takes him in his arms and draws him to his breast with such sincerity and enthusiasm of love that the petty cares, thoughts and ambitions of the world vanish away, and one is at peace and in happiness because he has reached home and found love there."[11]

On the Sabbath of their pilgrimage the two friends had the unforgettable experience of going to see the photograph of Bahá'u'lláh. Mr. Chase wrote, "It is a majestic face, that of a strong, powerful, stern man, yet filled with an indescribable sweetness."[12]

Soon after they had returned to their room the Master visited them there. On this occasion as on several others He spoke of His love for them and expressed the hope that when they returned home the effect on them of their experience in the Holy Land would bring happiness to the believers in the United States of America and increase their understanding. Mr. Scheffler has remarked that, in spite of Mr. Chase's deep understanding, he still had many wrong conceptions that 'Abdu'l-Bahá gently corrected. Mr. Chase responded to His love like a devoted son.

Because of troubles that enemies of the Cause were constantly stirring up, the Master felt obliged to cut short the visit of the two friends. In the morning of their last day in the prison house 'Abdu'l-Bahá stressed to them the great importance of unity among all the believers, explained that only with it could the Faith progress. During lunch he added that the building of the Temple in America should help to achieve this unity.

Mr. Chase has described his last meeting with the Master. "Soon after the noon meal Abdul-Baha met me in the little upper court. He embraced this servant, and, moving away a few feet, he turned, looked steadily and pronounced a promise that is a precious memory and hope."[13] Mr. Scheffler has informed us that as they walked down the old stone steps that led out of the prison house, Mr. Chase said to him, "The Master has assured me that I will return to this place soon. This reconciles me to this unbearable departure."[14]

After leaving 'Akká the friends visited the Shrine of Bahá'u'lláh, which Mr. Chase described as "the culmination of our pilgrimage."[15] They then went to rest in the Garden of the Riḍván where Bahá'u'lláh used to sit, and returned to spend the night again in the Hospice of the Little Child in Haifa.

Shortly after Thornton Chase's return from the Holy Land,

the company for which he worked transferred him to California. According to the Hand of the Cause, H. M. Balyuzi, the company decided to do this in the hope that Mr. Chase would spend more time in working for the company and less time in service to the Faith. The contrary took place, since his professional work still took him from city to city. As Mr. Balyuzi wrote, "A secretary in an office which he had to visit from time to time, spoke in later years of the electrifying presence of Thornton Chase. She recalled that whenever he came into the room, people felt elated; joy wafted in with him; his face radiated light."[16]

In 1919 his now famous book *The Bahá'í Revelation* was published. It is also out of print. Most valuable at that time, when there was a scarcity of Bahá'í Holy Writings translated into English and of reliable works on the Faith, this book still has great human and historic interest. Like *In Galilee*, it enables us to look into the mind and heart of the first believer in the West and to understand a little how he taught the Faith. Without unnecessary words, he wrote a most moving and persuasive explanation of the Bahá'í Revelation that no one, however great his gifts might be, would have been able to write without deep study, exceptional understanding, and passionate belief.

The book contains a short history of the Faith, starting with the declaration of the Báb in 1844, briefly describes His Dispensation, and then gives an outline of the life of Bahá'u'lláh, and of 'Abdu'l-Bahá. At the conclusion of this history, Mr. Chase has assured the reader that 'Abdu'l-Bahá, the Servant of God, is spreading the divine Word that His Father Bahá'u'lláh revealed to all parts of the planet and that "the fearless lovers of Truth"[17] are embracing His Cause.

In a most moving chapter, 'The Gift of God', he forcefully wrote, "Age after age, through all history, One has appeared, who gave to man the Word of God, divine instruction how to live and what to do to attain a higher and heavenly station, to overcome former conditions and rise to a manner of life which should be permanent, sinless, perfect and valuable."[18] In a later passage he explained, "Sometimes the effect is sudden, in the twinkling of an eye. Sometimes a great grief or disappointment is the cause of his awakening, because such experiences drive man, as it were, to God for relief from despair."[19]

In the chapter entitled 'The Succession of Divine Revelations', after pointing out that "toward the end of the 18th Century and in the nineteenth the world was in deep spiritual darkness,"[20] and commenting on the widespread materialism that has exalted man and turned him away from God, he most joyfully concluded that God has sent Bahá'u'lláh, the Glory of God, to rid mankind of this deep spiritual darkness, and that "this Great Light has shone forth with such brilliancy"[21] that the entire planet is becoming enlightened.

In a later chapter, 'The Fullness of Time', he stated, "There is nothing so blinding to man as the pride of intellect, the exaltation of success. One may as well deny the influence of the sun in the growing of a tree as to ignore the power of the Spirit, the divine light, in the growth of scientific knowledge." The intent of the natural man is to rule or ruin, and power without the fear of God means ruin.[22]

In a most moving chapter, 'What Shall I Do to Be Saved?', he made many beautiful observations about Faith, Prayer, and Obedience. "Faith is not an intellectual yielding to argument through being convinced that certain statements are correct, but it is rather from a hunger of the soul, a knowledge of personal helplessness and the perception of a possible Mighty Helpfulness .... Prayer, in its essence, is the abandonment of the personal will in favor of the Will of God. And such prayer God answers, because it is in agreement with his Law and can be answered."[23] "Man is always a servant; he obeys something; how much better for him to serve the Wise One, the True One, the Beautiful One, instead of his own ignorance and greed!"[24]

In a chapter entitled "The Bahá'í Revelation Makes All Things New', he most clearly wrote, "Old doctrines and beliefs are being tested in the courts of modern judgment, for this is the Day of Judgment, and the chaff of false teachings is being cast into the fires of ridicule and rejection. On the one side are scholarly efforts to destroy both wheat and tares together to make way for new material philosophies; on the other are anxious hearts looking for the Truth of the Eternal God and lifting their eyes to the hills to behold the coming of their Helper and their Lord."[25]

In a published letter called *What Is Truth?* after first stating that "Truth is single like light,"[26] he has logically explained how through false imaginings and misconceptions only a fragment of truth remains, not sufficient to transform the lives of men, and has given an example of what happened to the teachings of Jesus Christ, when through opposition, hatred and denial, they became divided through the establishment of many cults and sects.

Several weeks before his passing, Thornton Chase wrote a poem about 'Abdu'l-Bahá. At the Master's suggestion, the editors published it in 'The Star of the West.' Composed of nine verses that show a most powerful love for Him, the poem concludes with this verse:

> Thou Lion of the Tribe of Judah!
> Thou Lamb of the Sacrificial Love!
> Thou Baptizer of Evanescence!
> Thou Sum of Spiritual and Human Perfections!
> Thou MYSTERY OF GOD!

A most touching prayer follows this poem including these words: "Teach us to serve. Guide us in the paths of Knowledge and Wisdom. Unite us in mutual purpose and aim, and grant us the favor of Thy personal Presence and Voice."[27] These two pieces of work are dated 9th August 1912.

The next day John Bosch sent a telegram to the Master, then in Dublin, New Hampshire, begging Him to visit California, and included Thornton Chase's name among the signatories. Mr. Chase, however, felt that the Bahá'ís, himself included, were not worthy of the Master's visit. "John, don't you think it's too soon? The Bahá'ís aren't ready." "Well, I'm ready for Him," said John.[28]

After an illness of several weeks, Thornton Chase died on 30th September in Los Angeles. With the exception of those Tablets which he had sent to the archives in Chicago, Thornton Chase left all of his papers and books to John

Bosch. Unfortunately Mrs. Chase burned some fifteen hundred of her husband's letters before John could get to Los Angeles.[29] When, upon His arrival in San Francisco on 4th October 1912, the Master heard that Thornton Chase had died, He said, "This revered personage was the first Bahá'í in America. He served the Cause faithfully and his services will ever be remembered throughout ages and cycles."[30]

'Abdu'l-Bahá made a special trip to Los Angeles so that he might visit Thornton Chase's grave. On Saturday October 18th, at one o'clock in the afternoon, He arrived at Inglewood Cemetery, together with about twenty-five of the local Bahá'ís. The Master walked silently to the grave, and after He had scattered flowers over it, He stood at the head of the grave, turned towards the East, raised His Hands to heaven and chanted a most beautiful prayer. In this prayer the Master referred to Thornton Chase's rising to serve the Faith, his pilgrimage to 'Akká, his return to the United States, and his proclamation of the Faith there until his passing, and concluded the prayer with these words: "Submerge him in the ocean of Thy lights."[31]

After the prayer the Master said some words in most high praise of Thornton Chase. Among other remarks He said, "This is a personage who will not be forgotten. For the present his worth is not known, but in the future it will be inestimably dear. His sun will be ever shining, his star will ever bestow the light."[32]

In a talk that He gave that evening in Los Angeles about Mr. Chase, the Master said, "As many times as possible—at least once a year—you should make it a point to visit his tomb, for his spirit will be exhilarated through the loyalty of the friends, and in the world of God will it be happy. The friends of God must be kind to one another, whether it be in life or after death."[33] On Sunday October 20th, in Los Angeles, the Master concluded his final talk there with these beautiful words of assurance: "For I loved Mr. Chase very much indeed. His heart was pure. He had no other aim except service to the Cause; he had no other thought except the thought of the Kingdom. Therefore he was very near to me, and at the threshold of BAHA'O'LLAH he was accepted. The Blessed

Perfection has invited him to His Kingdom. At this very moment he is submerged in the Sea of His Bounty."[34]

On His way east in Cincinnati, Ohio, the Master spoke again to a group of Bahá'ís about the great character of Thornton Chase and his distinguished services to the Cause of God.

In an article entitled 'At The Grave of Thornton Chase', Willard Hatch has described a meeting there on 19th October 1924. He has informed us that it was a joyful meeting, "made so by the perfect assurance of all in the immortality of the soul,"[35] and in their happiness at the great spiritual station attained by Mr. Chase. Thornton Chase "had foretold the year of his passing .... Speaking of the troubles of this life he is reported to have said that they were like mosquitoes—annoying at the time but swept away by the Power of the Spirit."[36]

In the not too distant future, when man's present spiritual blindness has been at least partially healed, historians will certainly honour Thornton Chase. Undeterred by the conflicting voices, false ideals and worldly ambitions of those around him, he not only became the first in the entire Western world to recognize his Lord, but despite serious upheavals and countless misunderstandings in the Bahá'í community itself, remained as the Master has described him, 'Steadfast' until his passing.

No one now living can correctly estimate the great importance of what he accomplished. We can only read what 'Abdu'l-Bahá and the Guardian in perfect knowledge have written about him.

Phoebe Hearst and Robert Turner

OF GENTLE, ARISTOCRATIC background, Phoebe Apperson Hearst was born in Franklin, Missouri in 1842. Her parents has social position. They were prosperous owners of slaves. At the age of seventeen, after she had gained some knowledge of French, she became a school teacher.

Two years later, in 1862, she eloped with rough, but kindly George Hearst, a man of forty-one. Possessed of considerable wealth, he settled with his wife in his native city of San Francisco, where he had large business interests. In 1863 William Randolph Hearst, her only child, was born.

Extremely beautiful, Mrs. Hearst was firm, determined, and unusually generous. She had a fine moral sense. Although strong and generous like his wife and highly principled in business, Mr. Hearst soon discovered that his marriage was not completely satisfying. This unhappy situation brought Mrs. Hearst closer to her son. She became a possessive mother, and spoilt him. Her son's biographer has written, "Although she was conventionally God-fearing, she found her chief faith in secular self-improvement and her religion in the upbringing of her child."[1]

In the spring of 1873, when her husband was living some distance from the city, taking care of his mining interests, she leased out their large house on Chestnut Street and left for Europe with her son and his tutor, Thomas Barry. While travelling in Dublin, she wrote in her diary, "The poorer classes are so *terribly* poor, Willie wanted to give away all his money and clothes, too, and really I felt the same way, if we could have relieved even half of them."[2] In Rome, characteristically, she succeeded in arranging an audience with Pope Pius IX. "He was so kind and lovely, spoke altogether in French, asked where we came from," she wrote to her husband. "When he came to Willie, he placed his hand on his head, and blessed him ...." (7th February 1874)[3]

On their return from Europe, she found that her husband had suffered a serious financial reverse. As a result, while he remained away from the city in order to recoup his mining interests, she and her son lived in a modest boarding house. But Mr. Hearst had a genius for business. It did not take him long to revive his fortunes and to become much richer than before.

At this time Mrs. Hearst began her philanthropic work in earnest. Without any sectarian bias she not only gave away enormous sums of money, but also unsparingly devoted her time and energy to worthy causes. She helped in the foundation of the first Homeopathic Hospital in San Francisco, named after Dr. Hahnemann, the developer of that medical science. As well as contributing to orphanages and to a children's hospital, she established seven kindergartens. Several years later Mrs. Sarah B. Cooper, President of the Golden Gate Kindergarten Association, wrote to her: "Your seven kindergartens are a beacon light guiding the little ones to the port of peace—may we all reach the port of peace at last."[4]

In 1886 the Governor of California appointed George Hearst a Senator and the Hearsts moved to Washington, D.C. While there, she established more kindergartens, helped the Polyclinic Hospital, and did much to relieve the suffering caused by an earthquake in Charleston, South Carolina. In their house in Washington, D.C. at 1400 New Hampshire Avenue she gave big receptions, often in aid of some charity or a struggling artist. In February 1891 Senator Hearst died peacefully leaving his widow, then forty-eight, in control of an enormous fortune.

She returned to San Francisco for a short time, but the new responsibilities recently thrust upon her, combined with the problems that a number of grasping people created for her, led to the breakdown of her health. After resting for some months in the country, she returned to Washington and lived there during the next nine years except for frequent visits to San Francisco and occasional trips to Europe. She built the National Cathedral School for Girls in Washington, and was a co-founder of the Parent-Teacher Association in 1897.

* * *

Some time before 1898, Lua Getsinger (whom 'Abdu'l-Bahá had called Livá, meaning 'Banner of the Cause') visited San Francisco. During this trip she called on Mrs. Hearst and spoke to her about the Bahá'í Faith. Even without access to the facts it is not hard to imagine the thrilling scene that ensued. In a sketch, Louis G. Gregory has informed us that Robert Turner, her Negro butler, held a position of some responsibility in her household; he described him as "faithful, dependable, and wise."[5] Robert Turner let Mrs. Getsinger into the house and showed her into a finely furnished sitting-room. After giving her a gracious welcome, Mrs. Hearst asked her guest to sit down next to her on the sofa. When he had served the tea, Robert stood near to them. In a most moving manner, Mrs. Getsinger spoke to them both about the Bahá'í Faith. Surely on this occasion and those that followed Robert listened eagerly to Mrs. Getsinger and as a result did all that he could to learn about the Faith.

In *God Passes By* Shoghi Effendi has referred to the fact that an American Negro, Robert Turner, was "the first member of his race to embrace the Cause of Bahá'u'lláh in the West."[6]

Deeply moved by what she had heard, in 1898 Mrs. Hearst decided to visit 'Abdu'l-Bahá in the Holy Land. She generously invited others to go along with her and made up a party which consisted of Lua Getsinger and her husband, Dr. Ibráhím Khayru'lláh, a Syrian doctor who had been teaching the Cause in Chicago for four years, his wife, and Robert Turner. In Paris Mrs. Hearst added to the party her two nieces, Miss Pearson and Ann Apperson, another American, May Ellis Bolles, as well as two English believers, Mrs. Thornburgh and her daughter Miriam Thornburgh-Cropper. In Egypt, Dr. Khayru'lláh's daughters and their grandmother joined this historic party. Because of the serious dangers that constantly threatened 'Abdu'l-Bahá, the fifteen pilgrims made the journey to Haifa in three separate groups. Each group travelled from Port Said in a small, uncomfortable boat; for one of them, the outbreak of a storm did not make the journey easier. The first group, which included Lua Getsinger and Mrs. Thornburgh-Cropper, arrived in 'Akká on 10th December 1898. Mrs. Thornburgh-Cropper has recorded that as they went upstairs, "Someone went before us with a small piece of candle, which cast strange shadows on the walls of this silent place. Suddenly the light caught a form that at first seemed a vision of mist and light. It was the Master which the candle-light had revealed to us. His white robe, and silver, flowing hair, and shining blue eyes gave the impression of a spirit, rather than of a human being. We tried to tell Him how deeply grateful we were at His receiving us. 'No,' He answered, 'you are kind to come.' This was spoken in very careful English. Then He smiled and we recognized the Light which He possessed in the radiance which moved over His fine and noble face."[7]

The second group, which included May Bolles, Miss Pearson, Ann Apperson, Mrs. Thornburgh and Robert Turner, arrived in Haifa on the 16th February 1899. The Hand of the Cause Louis Gregory has recorded one account of Robert Turner's first meeting with 'Abdu'l-Bahá. "At sight of the Master he dropped upon his knees and exclaimed: 'My Lord! My Lord! I am not worthy to be here!'"[8] 'Abdu'l-Bahá raised him to his feet, and embraced him like a loving father.

A few days later the whole party visited 'Abdu'l-Bahá again in 'Akká, and May Bolles described this meeting. "On the morning of our arrival, after we had refreshed ourselves, the Master summoned us all to Him in a long room overlooking the Mediterranean. He sat in silence gazing out of the window, then looking up He asked if all were present. Seeing that one of the believers was absent, he said, 'Where is Robert?' .... In a moment Robert's radiant face appeared in the doorway and the Master rose to greet him, bidding him be seated, and said, 'Robert, your Lord loves you. God gave you a black skin, but a heart white as snow.'"[9]

When the Master led the party into the Most Holy Tomb and even into its innermost chamber, Robert was, of course, present. He, of no worldly importance, and brought along at least partly to serve Mrs. Hearst, was so greatly affected by the Master's most loving welcome and understanding treatment, that he became deeply convinced by Him of the Reality of God's Cause for this day. The Master assured him that "if he remained firm and steadfast until the end, he would be a door through which a whole race would enter the Kingdom." [10]

A year after her pilgrimage, Mrs. Hearst wrote to a friend, ".... Those three days were the most memorable days of my life ...." Shortly afterwards, in another letter she described the Master in these words: ".... I must say He is the Most Wonderful Being I have ever met or ever expect to meet in this world. Although He does not seek to impress one at all, strength, power, purity, love and holiness are radiated from His majestic, yet humble, personality, and the spiritual atmosphere which surrounds Him and most powerfully affects all those who are blest by being near Him, is indescribable .... I believe in Him with all my heart and soul ...." [11]

Mrs. Hearst had done an unforgettable service for the Bahá'í Cause in bringing the first pilgrimage of believers from a Christian background and from the West, to meet 'Abdu'l-Bahá and to visit the Most Holy Tomb.

As Shoghi Effendi has pointed out, "The return of these God-intoxicated pilgrims, some to France, others to the United States, was the signal for an outburst of systematic and sustained activity, which, as it gathered momentum, and spread its ramifications over Western Europe and the states and provinces of the North American continent, grew to so great a scale that 'Abdu'l-Bahá Himself resolved that as soon as He should be released from His prolonged confinement in 'Akká, He would undertake a personal mission to the West." [12]

After she had returned to her home in Washington, D.C., Mrs. Hearst gave a reception there for prominent educators of the Negro race. Mr. Gregory felt that she did this ".... prompted no doubt by her experiences at 'Akká and her esteem for Robert Turner."[13] She spoke to them all most ardently about the coming of Bahá'u'lláh. Tragic to relate, one or two unprincipled individuals who later left the Faith, took advantage of her great generosity and tried to extort money from Mrs. Hearst. As a result she became estranged from the Bahá'í community, but she never lost her love for the Master.

Although much saddened that the world had thrown dust in the eyes of his beloved mistress, Robert Turner never wavered in his faith. His recognition of the Station of Bahá'u'lláh when Lua Getsinger was teaching Mrs. Hearst, and the confirmation that came to him from his pilgrimage and most precious meeting with the Master, sustained him during this early period of the Faith when there were not only great bounties, but intense troubles.

A few years after the pilgrimage, he became seriously ill, and was cared for by those who were not Bahá'ís; "…. his attendants heard him often repeat, even when delirious, an expression strange and unknown."[14] On his death-bed, the last word that he spoke was the Greatest Name. Before his burial, the distinguished Mírzá Ali-Kuli Khan placed a Bahá'í ringstone upon his finger.

In 1900, after selling her mansion in Washington, Mrs. Hearst returned to California with her niece Ann Apperson to live in an attractive house of Spanish architecture, called Hacienda, which she had built at Pleasanton, not far from San Francisco. She began again and continued without ceasing her philanthropic work in California. She did more perhaps for the University of that State than for any other institution. In the summer of 1912 she helped to establish a permanent camp for the Young Women's Christian Association.

During the next October 'Abdu'l-Bahá visited California. Although still separated from the Bahá'í community, Mrs. Hearst invited Him and His attendants to visit her house in Pleasanton, and asked many of her friends to meet Him. "Because her invitation was sincere, 'Abdu'l-Bahá accepted it."[15] Arriving on October 13th He stayed there for three nights.

The first to bring up the Faith directly, she asked Him to

chant again a certain prayer in Arabic that had moved her deeply when she heard Him chant it during her pilgrimage fourteen years earlier. Without any hesitation He did so. Her guests seemed greatly affected by His chanting. The next day He said a prayer for them before lunch. On the night following, the last of His visit, He said one before dinner. One can well imagine that He and Mrs. Hearst spoke more than once about her devoted Robert. Before leaving, 'Abdu'l-Bahá asked to meet all of the servants in the house. He spoke to them like a father and gave each one a present of money. She drove the Master and His attendants back to San Francisco. During the trip He explained to her that those who tried to extort money from people and were anxious to get hold of possessions belonging to others could not be called Bahá'ís.

After she had strenuously served her country in humanitarian work during the First World War, she died on 13th April 1919. Her son's biographer has called her, "California's greatest lady and one of the nation's most remarkable women." [16]

In a Tablet to Mr. A. W. Randall in early 1920, referring to the 'San Francisco Examiner' founded by Senator George Hearst and at that time owned by his only son, 'Abdu'l-Bahá revealed, "The papers of Mr. Hearst are verily striving for the protection of the rights of the public. I am supplicating that they may become the first papers serving the good of the world of humanity, so that they may keep alive the blessed name of Mrs. Hearst and that this name (Hearst) may live permanently till eternity." [17]

The Master knew the inner secrets of all of us. It is obvious from this quotation that despite her tragic separation from the Bahá'í community her services to the Faith were of great importance. Undoubtedly the Master was keenly aware also of her unceasing efforts to help many worthy institutions and the poor. Does it not seem probable that Mrs. Hearst's devoted servant, Robert, who died many years before her, often prayed for her in the Kingdom and when he saw her again hurried to give her a spiritual welcome?

Helen Goodall and Ella Cooper

IN 1864 AN ATTRACTIVE, highly intelligent girl named Helen Mirrell moved from Maine, where she had been born, to San Francisco, where she became a teacher. Four years later she married Mr. Edwin Goodall and on 12th January 1870, their daughter Ella Frances was born.

Ella has written that her mother had an enquiring, unprejudiced mind and a deep interest in religion. Whenever she heard of a new school of thought, she carefully investigated it. During the summer of 1898, shortly after Lua Getsinger, 'the mother teacher of the West,' had attracted Mrs. Phoebe Hearst (q.v.) to the Bahá'í Faith, Mrs. Goodall and Ella heard of it for the first time from their friend, Miss Helen Hillyer.

At this time Lua Getsinger was holding a Bahá'í class. Before Mrs. Goodall had the opportunity of attending this class, Mrs. Getsinger, invited by Mrs. Hearst to join her party of pilgrims, had left for 'Akká in the Holy Land.

From what she had so far learned of the Faith, Mrs. Goodall felt that, without realizing the fact, she had always been seeking for knowledge of the Revelation of Bahá'u'lláh, and wanted to know more about it without delay. Ella, who had been able to attend some of Mrs. Getsinger's classes, became equally anxious to investigate the Faith further. Instead of waiting for their friends to return, mother and daughter decided to make a trip to New York and find another teacher. On 19th September 1898, they boarded the train for the East coast. They studied in New York with Antún Haddád, a Bahá'í of Syrian background. Unfortunately, Mrs. Goodall soon became ill and could not leave her room. Meanwhile Helen Hillyer, who was also in New York, received a letter from Mrs. Hearst asking her to come to Cairo at once and to bring Ella Goodall with her. By the time that Ella had received permission from the Master to visit Him, her mother was well enough to return home.

In February of 1899, after Mrs. Goodall had returned to California, the two young ladies sailed for Cairo to join Mrs. Hearst's party. Because of the serious dangers to which 'Abdu'l-Bahá and His family were constantly exposed, this party, which was finally composed of fifteen pilgrims, visited the prison city of 'Akká in three separate groups. The first one arrived there on 10th December 1898. The third one, to which Ella and her friend belonged, spent most of the following March in 'Akká.

More than one inspiring account has been written about this first pilgrimage of believers from the Christian West. Thirty-three years later Ella wrote: "Next to meeting the Beloved Master Himself was the privilege of meeting His glorious sister, Bahíyyih Khánum, known as the Greatest Holy Leaf .... Tall, slender and of noble bearing .... Her beautiful face was the feminine counterpart of 'Abdu'l-Bahá's—the lines of suffering and privation softened by the patient sweetness of the mouth; the dominating brow, bespeaking intellect and will, lighted by the wonderful understanding eyes, in. form like those of 'Abdu'l-Bahá, but deep blue rather than hazel. Watching their expressive changes—as one moment they darkened with sympathy or pain, the next moment sparkled with laughter and humor—only served to deepen the impression of her irresistible spiritual attraction." [1]

Ella has also vividly described a meeting between 'Abdu'l-Bahá and Shoghi Effendi, at that time a child of only just over two years old, when they were in the room of the Greatest Holy Leaf during early morning tea.

In part, Ella wrote, ".... Shoghi, that beautiful little boy, with his exquisite cameo face and his soulful appealing, dark eyes, walked slowly toward the divan, the Master drawing him as by an invisible thread, until he stood quite close in front of Him. As he paused there a moment 'Abdu'l-Bahá did not offer to embrace him but sat perfectly still, only nodding His head two or three times, slowly and impressively, as if to say—'You see? This tie connecting us is not just that of a physical grandfather but something far deeper and more significant.' While we breathlessly watched to see what he would do, the little boy reached down and picking up the hem of 'Abdu'l-Bahá's robe he touched it reverently to his forehead, and kissed it, then gently replaced it, while never taking his eyes from the adored Master's face." [2]

Deeply influenced by her pilgrimage, Ella now had one great aim: to serve the Cause of God.

On her return to Oakland, she found that her mother had already attracted a small group of people to the Faith. Ella has explained that no experienced teachers lived in the far west at that time, nor were any Bahá'í books available there. Only a few of the Holy Writings had so far been translated. Whenever a believer there received a translation of a Tablet from the Master, or a copy of one sent by Him to someone else, a special meeting of the friends took place. Realising the supreme importance of strict adherence to the Holy Writings, mother and daughter gently corrected anyone who offered his own interpretation of them. Travelling teachers and returning pilgrims, who often stayed at the Goodall house, helped gradually to increase the numbers of the group in Oakland and to bring members into this group from San Francisco and other places nearby.

The Master often revealed for Ella and her mother Tablets of advice, encouragement, and praise.

In a Tablet translated by Mírzá Ali-Kuli Khan on 16th April 1902, the Master warned Mrs. Goodall of a disaster that was soon to descend upon San Francisco. Among other statements He revealed: "Verily, I read thy latest letter, and My great love welled forth unto thee on account of its wonderful contents. Verily, it showed thy firmness in the Cause of God, and that thou wilt resist great tests in the future. *Still greater tests will appear in your great city.*" [3] As is well known, an earthquake and fire took place in San Francisco in April 1906, destroying a large part of the city.

In 1904, with the blessing of the Master, Ella married Dr. Charles Miner Cooper. A few years later they moved from Oakland to San Francisco.

Late in 1907, the Master granted Mrs. Goodall and Mrs. Cooper permission to visit Him in the Holy Land, the second visit for Mrs. Cooper but the first for her mother. After they had travelled from California to France, they left Paris for Alexandria on 19th December and arrived in 'Akká at noon on 4th January 1908.

In a short book which they called *Daily Lessons Received at Acca*, the two ladies wrote a stimulating account of their pilgrimage, which lasted two weeks. Mírzá Asadu'lláh-i-Iṣfahání and some other men met the two ladies at the gate of the prison house and escorted them through the inner court and up the long flight of stairs. A niece of 'Abdu'l-Bahá's showed them to their room. Even before they had seen Him, Mrs. Goodall and Mrs. Cooper heard the joyous ring of His voice as He gave them a warm welcome. The Master invited mother and daughter to sit down with Him. He asked them questions about the believers in America, in London and in Paris. When the two ladies named each believer who had sent Him a special greeting, "His beautiful face beamed with happiness." [4]

Every day the Master came to the door of the room that Mrs. Goodall and Mrs. Cooper shared and invited them to His table for lunch. He said to them more than once, "It makes me happy to sit at table with you, because you are the servants of Baha'o'llah. .... It makes me rejoice when I see you, for I love you very much." [5]

One day at lunch the Master spoke to them about the proposed building of the first House of Worship of the West on the shores of Lake Michigan. "To have it built is most important," He said. "Some material things have spiritual effect, and the Mashrak-el-Azkar is a material thing that will have great effect upon the spirits of the people. Not only does the building of the Mashrak-el-Askar have an effect upon those who build it, but upon the whole world." [6]

While speaking of sacrifice to those at His table the Master explained, "The great sacrifice is to forget one's self entirely .... Christ became a sacrifice that His qualities might appear in the people. If God forgave sins without the sacrifice, there would still be only the human qualities in the people.

The divine qualities would not appear." [7] He then turned to the two ladies and continued, "As the perfections of Christ appeared in His disciples, I hope, through the Sacrifice of Baha'o'llah, His perfections may appear in you." They replied that it would require much of God's mercy to make that possible. He answered: "If you follow His instructions, it is certain to be accomplished." [8]

On another occasion they told Him that Thornton Chase had said that "while he was at Acca he felt that the outside world was the real prison while Acca was the place of freedom." The Master smiled and said that it was the 'freedom' of the world outside that caused Him to be in prison. He explained, "This prison is free because of the presence of the Spirit." [9]

Sometimes the Master allowed Mrs. Goodall and Mrs. Cooper to walk on the house-top. Looking west they could see the blue Mediterranean, to the south the Bay of 'Akká, Haifa and Mt. Carmel, and to the north and east the rolling country where the shepherds still tended their sheep as shepherds had done in the past.

At table one day the Master asked the two ladies, "If the people here should not let you leave Acca, what would you do—how would you feel?" They answered: "We would stay here always and be perfectly happy." He smiled at this and said, "Suppose they should ask you why you came here? They might say, these prisoners are Persians. What have Americans and Persians to say to one another?" The two ladies answered, "We should like nothing better than to mount the house-top and shout to all the people the reason of our coming." He smiled again and said, "You are shouting although you are silent; but your words will be heard in the future. The words of Christ were not heard until three hundred years after His death." [10]

Mrs. Cooper's birthday was on January 12th. The Master congratulated her for being in the prison house for her anniversary. Someone asked Him to guess her age. He lightly guessed several years under the right one. After she had informed Him of this, He quickly rejoined, "I wish to make you as young as possible so that you will have many more years in which to live and spread this Truth." She said that since becoming a Bahá'í, nine years ago, she had been growing younger every day. He smiled and assented, "That is so, and, in reality, you are only nine years old." [11]

One day the two ladies remarked with some anxiety to the Master that to answer their many questions and to give them so much time must be a cause of trouble to Him. The Master said, "Whatever is done in love is never any trouble and—there is always time." [12]

On 19th January 1908 Mrs. Goodall and Mrs. Cooper left the Holy Land, their spiritual home, to go back to the world again. They have written: "Our hearts were full to over-flowing with the gracious gifts which had been bestowed—not only upon us, but upon all the friends to whom we were bearing 'Abdu'l-Bahá's loving messages." [13]

While the mother and daughter were away, Mrs. Emogene Hoagg, a close friend of theirs who was living in San Francisco, held weekly meetings in Oakland, so that the teaching there would not be interrupted. On her return from pilgrimage, Mrs. Goodall again opened her house to the Bahá'ís as before. In 1909, when Mr. Goodall died, Mrs. Goodall and her son Arthur moved to a house in San Francisco where Dr. and Mrs. Cooper were already living. For the next nine years, however, until obliged to sell her house in Oakland, she and Mrs. Cooper continued to hold regular meetings there and sometimes Feasts and Anniversaries.

As early as June 1903, in a Tablet addressed to the Bahá'ís of Chicago, the Master had first given His enthusiastic approval to their request for permission to build a House of Worship in the United States of America on the shores of Lake Michigan near Chicago. Mrs. Goodall and her daughter made strenuous efforts to support this tremendous project. Mrs. Goodall served on the Executive Board of the Bahá'í Temple Unity for a number of years. (See also the essay on Roy Wilhelm.)

In the spring of 1910, the Bahá'í group of San Francisco, to which Mrs. Goodall and Mrs. Cooper had belonged from its beginning, succeeded in establishing a spiritual assembly. The Master addressed to this new Assembly a Tablet which included these words: "O ye faithful friends! This Assembly was organized at the right time. It is my hope that it become a magnet of confirmation. If it remain firm and steadfast this Assembly will become so illumined that it will be a full, refulgent moon in the horizon of everlasting glory." [14]

A day or two after the Master had arrived in New York City, on the morning of 11th April 1912, to start His epoch-making journey of almost eight months throughout the United States, Mrs. Goodall and Mrs. Cooper took the train to Washington where they had learned that He was soon to be. From that city, accompanied by Miss Ella Bailey, they followed 'Abdu'l-Bahá to Chicago. On this, the first of His two visits there, which lasted a week, they stayed at the same hotel as He did. For this reason they were often able to see Him privately and to share with the Master "many quiet moments of His precious time." He spoke of His happiness at being with them. One day, He said, "Mrs. Goodall's value is not known now; it will be known in the future. She has no other thought than to serve the Cause. God has certain treasuries hidden in the world which He reveals when the time comes. She is like one of these treasures." [15]

The three ladies attended all of the great meetings addressed by the Master in Chicago. These meetings included the last public session of the Convention held by the Bahá'í Temple Unity and His dedication of the grounds chosen as a site for the future Mashriqu'l-Adhkár.

When on May 6th the Master moved on to Cleveland, Ohio, mother and daughter returned home. About a month later, they received a telegram from the Master which said that since He planned to leave America, He would like them to come to New York and see Him. Without hesitation, they and a close friend, Harriet Wise, travelled across the continent again. While these three ladies were in New York City, the Bahá'ís of California in daily letters to the Master expressed their painful disappointment that He was not going to visit them and entreated Him to change His mind. Deeply touched by their heartfelt desire to see Him, the Master decided to make this difficult journey to the West, some time after Mrs. Goodall, Mrs. Cooper and Miss Wise had returned home. Around midnight on 1st October 1912, the Master arrived in

San Francisco. At His own request only a few of the friends greeted Him at the terminus. With several Persian believers, who were travelling with Him, 'Abdu'l-Bahá drove immediately to a house at 1815 California Street which Mrs. Goodall had rented for them.

On the second evening of His visit on October 3rd He gave an address of "welcome" to California at the Goodall home in Oakland. After He had made some brief but beautiful statements about the Bahá'í teachings. He urged those who were present to study them thoroughly. He concluded: "Praise be to God! We have assembled here, and the cause of our gathering here is the love of God. Praise be to God! The hearts are kind toward each other and the heavenly radiance is resplendent. I am hopeful that the hearts may be moved, the souls may be attracted, and that all will act in accordance with the teachings of BAHA'O'LLAH." [16]

On Saturday morning, October 12th, at Temple Emmanuel at 450 Sutter Street, San Francisco, the Master gave an address of remarkable power to a congregation of about two thousand Jewish people. He encouraged them first to free themselves from the restrictions of dogma, tradition and human opinion, and then to investigate the Reality of religion.

When this meeting was over, the friends drove the Master directly to Mrs. Goodall's house in Oakland for the observance of Children's Day. A large group of children who were gathered there greeted the Master with the singing of a touching song, 'Softly His Voice Is Calling Now'. He gave candy and flowers to the children and to everyone there an envelope containing rose leaves. The children stayed close to Him. He took the small ones in His arms. On this joyful occasion an appealing photograph was taken of the Master as He stood on the top step of the entrance with the children and some of their parents around Him. [17]

On the evening of October 16th, after He had spoken that afternoon at the Century Club in San Francisco on the equality of men and women, He drove to the Goodall home in Oakland to join the friends there for the Feast of Knowledge. Vases filled with yellow chrysanthemums and bowls holding pyramids of fruit stood on tables in the handsomely furnished rooms of the house. Almost a hundred and twenty-five friends gathered quietly in these rooms and waited for the Master to appear. After everyone except the Master was seated, He walked among the friends at their tables, and asked them to continue eating. He referred to the Lord's Supper when His Holiness Christ had invited His disciples to His table and had given them both spiritual guidance and material food. 'Abdu'l-Bahá expressed His earnest hope that the results of the Lord's Supper would be realized at the present Feast and explained that "Every supper that is productive of love and unity, the cause of radiance throughout the world, of international peace and of the solidarity of man, is undoubtedly the Lord's Supper." [18]

On Friday morning, October 18th, Mrs. Goodall drove the Master to the train for Los Angeles. He particularly wanted to go there, so that He could visit the grave in nearby Inglewood of Thornton Chase, "the first American believer." Not expecting to join His party, which so far consisted of only a few believers, Mrs. Goodall had not brought even a comb or brush with her. When they reached the station, however, He insisted that she should come with Him just the same.

On the night of October 21st, the Master and His party returned to San Francisco. Two evenings later He made His last visit to the Goodall home in Oakland. Frances Orr Allen has reported that at this meeting, after He had spoken of the two years that Bahá'u'lláh had passed in solitude, "Abdul-Baha arose and, in no uncertain terms, declared Himself to be the CENTER OF THE COVENANT; and exhorted all believers to firmness, calling upon them to spread the message of the Kingdom both by deed and word." [19]

According to Mrs. Cooper, throughout His visit to California the Master showed every possible kindness to her mother. He asked her to come every morning to His house and to remain there all day if she could. Besides commending Mrs. Goodall many times for her services as a pioneer, He "addressed her as the spiritual mother of the Assembly, saying: 'I leave my sheep in your care.'" [20] During the next few years, Mrs. Goodall often visited the groups and new

Assemblies on the Pacific Coast and spoke to them on the meaning of the Covenant.

The city of San Francisco decided to hold what it called a Panama-Pacific International Exposition during 1915, in order to celebrate the completion of the Panama Canal. In 1914, the Spiritual Assembly of San Francisco appointed an Executive Committee composed of Mrs. Goodall, Ella, Dr. F. W. D'Evelyn and William and Georgia Ralston to organize an International Bahá'í Congress to take place during this Exposition. The Master not only gave His enthusiastic approval to the committee for its proposed plan, but also selected the speakers for the congress.

Mrs. Cooper has written: "Mrs. Goodall and her daughter travelled across the continent to meet the speakers and arrange the sessions. As Dr. D'Evelyn says, there were 'many long conferences with Mrs. Goodall as the directing voice. Never a moment of doubt or of shadow disturbed her.' Serene and gentle, but firm and certain, '"That is good; that is fine; we will leave the guidance to Abdul Baha," was ever the last word for all the complex problems that arose.'"[21]

Although conceived and planned by the Bahá'í Assembly of San Francisco, the Congress was held under the official auspices of the Exposition. Naming April 24th 'International Bahá'í Congress Day', the Directorate of the Exposition gave a reception at Festival Hall and presented a bronze medallion to the Bahá'ís in recognition of their efforts to bring universal peace. Every evening for a week, starting on Monday April 19th, well attended public meetings of the Bahá'í Congress took place in the auditorium at the Civic Center on Grove and Larkin Streets in San Francisco. At each of these meetings an experienced Bahá'í speaker gave a stimulating, informative address on the Faith and its concrete plan to achieve the unity of mankind.

On almost every day of this week the Bahá'ís met together to consult on problems concerning the Bahá'í community itself. On three of these days the Bahá'í Temple Unity held a convention to discuss the building of the first Mashriqu'l-Adhkár of the West, the purchase of the property for which had been completed a year before.

On April 21st, as part of the Congress, but with only Bahá'ís as guests, Mrs. Goodall gave the Feast of Riḍván in her house in Oakland. After all of the friends were comfortably seated, she briefly described to them the visit of the Master, two years and a half before. As He had walked through her rooms and up and down the broad stairway with His wonderful smile, He had repeated, "'This is *my* house, this is *my* house.'" [22] Later in the Feast Mrs. Cooper read some beautiful statements that the Master had made there. Harlan F. Ober has reported that the spirit of 'Abdu'l-Bahá permeated the Feast with increasing intensity as it continued. An interesting photograph published in 'Star of the West' shows all of the believers, around a hundred and fifty in number, at the Feast gathered on the terrace in front of the house.[23]

In 1916 and 1917, during the First World War, while He was living in the Holy Land under extremely difficult conditions, and for part of the time was cut off from any communication with the Bahá'í communities, the Master revealed the immortal 'Tablets of the Divine Plan,' in which He invested His American followers with a world teaching mission that would extend far into the future. In 1916, some months before the United States had declared war on Germany, the American Community received the first five of these fourteen Tablets. The Tablet to the Western States was actually addressed to Mrs. Goodall.

Mrs. Cooper has reported that her mother, realizing their enormous importance, immediately sent copies of them to the Assemblies, urged the editors of 'Star of the West' to publish them without delay and pledged her whole-hearted support to the Master's teaching plan which was gradually to spread the Cause throughout the planet. In a letter addressed to the President of the Bahá'í Temple Unity, published in 'Star of the West', in the issue following the one in which the five Tablets had appeared, Mrs. Cooper wrote: "The great Tablets have come. Abdul-Baha himself gives us the plan, and it is as clear as daylight—that we should instantly drop every other consideration and concentrate all our energies and resources upon this great work. This is a call to the whole body of believers. The friends here in the West are alive to the

31

supreme opportunity and we feel sure that their joyous enthusiasm is going to carry them through and make their work effective." [24]

On 12th December 1918, Shoghi Effendi translated the following priceless Tablet that the Master had revealed for Mrs. Cooper. [25]

To the maid-servant of God, Mrs. Ella Goodall Cooper, California—Upon her be greeting and praise!
He Is God!
O thou respected maid-servant of God!

Your letter, dated October 22nd, 1918, was received. Although for four years communication between us has been interrupted, yet the spiritual messenger was heartily and continually engaged. At all times I implored from the divine Kingdom, begging for the maid-servants of God and the friends of the Merciful divine assistance and confirmation.

At present, praise be to God, your detailed letter is at hand, and its news of the health and safety of the believers of God imparted a joy unlimited. From the unity of the friends of that land we have felt greatly happy and glad. I pray God that this union, firmness, steadfastness and spiritual consultation may become day by day more pronounced, and this rose-garden which has been planted in that continent may bestow perfume, through the scent of its flowers and blossoms, upon the nostrils of the people of the world.

How beautifully thou hast expressed the thought, namely: "We hope that the love and unity of the friends may soon become the magnet of attraction which will draw thee again to our shores." This is evident and sure—that if the light of love among the friends will be as resplendent as it ought to be and like unto a candle will illumine that gathering, it will surely exert the effect of a magnet.

Convey on my behalf the utmost longing and love to all the assemblies.

Upon thee be greeting and praise!

(Signed) Abdul-Baha Abbas.

In 1920, 'Abdu'l-Bahá again gave Mrs. Goodall and her daughter permission to visit Him in the Holy Land. Although by now Mrs. Goodall was very frail, the great happiness that she felt at the prospect of being there gave her the strength to make the strenuous journey. Accompanied by two dear friends, Mrs. Kathryn Frankland and Mrs. Georgia Ralston, mother and daughter reached Haifa on October 21st of that year.

During the first part of the month which they spent there, Mrs. Goodall recovered some of her former strength. In a photograph taken of her standing on the grass in front of the Master's house, her bright and beautiful face has a warm expression of spiritual understanding.[26] Although Mrs. Cooper declared that much could have been written about their visit, she made only a few remarks about it. One day the Master said to the pilgrims: "Never forget these days. Never forget these days. The more you remember them the more spiritual you will become."[27]

Like most of the friends in the United States of America, Mrs. Goodall heard of the Master's passing a day or two after it had taken place. According to Mrs. Cooper, although her mother accepted this heart-breaking news with outward calm, she felt an unbearable sense of loss. She had often said to her family and friends that as soon as the Master had left this world she hoped to do the same. After His passing she gradually became weaker. On the morning of 19th February 1922, less than three months later, "she soared like a freed bird to the Kingdom of Light, to live and serve forever in the glory of the presence of her Master."[28]

Both in *America and the Most Great Peace*, his masterful essay on the spiritual history of that country, and in *God Passes By*, his classic history of the first hundred years of the Bahá'í Faith, the Guardian has referred to the consecrated, imperishable services of Helen S. Goodall.

When in the middle of January 1922, the American Bahá'í Community first learned that 'Abdu'l-Bahá, in His Will and Testament, had appointed Shoghi Effendi Guardian of the Cause of God, Ella Cooper turned to him with deep love and entire confidence. From 1921 to 1934 she served on the Spiritual Assembly of San Francisco and for two years, starting in 1922, on the American National Spiritual Assembly. She worked hard to help organize the first 'Conference for World Unity'. This conference, which was held in San

Francisco for three days during March 1925, initiated a series of such conferences in other parts of the country.

In 1927, after John and Louise Bosch had given their property at Geyserville in the hills of northern California, for a proposed Bahá'í summer school, Mrs. Cooper took an active part in its establishment. She not only served on the committee for this school, but also taught there for many years. In 1939 she and the Hand of the Cause Leroy Ioas represented the Bahá'ís on a 'Committee of One Hundred', chosen from all Faiths, to plan the erection of a Temple of Religion for the Golden Gate International Exposition in San Francisco, and to guide all its religious activities. At the first United Nations Conference held in San Francisco in 1945, Mrs. Cooper served on a committee to promote the Bahá'í Plan for World Peace.

Whenever Bahá'í friends visited San Francisco, she always tried her best to make them happy. Towards the end of her life, when she could no longer be physically very active, Mrs. Cooper still followed the work of the Cause with undiminished interest. She carried on a large correspondence with Bahá'ís in many countries.

On 8th July 1951, her husband, Dr. Cooper died suddenly. She spent the next day in preparing the readings for his service. That night she fell into a coma from which she did not recover. She died a little less than four days afterwards on July 12th. Six days later Shoghi Effendi sent a heart-warming cable to the National Spiritual Assembly of the Bahá'ís of the United States of America. It reads:[29] "Deeply grieved sudden passing herald Covenant, Ella Cooper, dearly loved handmaid 'Abdu'l-Bahá, greatly trusted by Him. Her devoted services during concluding years Heroic Age and also Formative Age Faith unforgettable. Assure relatives, friends, deepest sympathy loss. Praying progress soul in Abhá Kingdom."

Howard MacNutt

IN JANUARY 1898 IBRÁHÍM KHAYRU'LLÁH, a Syrian doctor, first spoke of the Bahá'í Faith to Howard MacNutt. Soon afterwards Howard and his wife Mary recognized the station of Bahá'u'lláh. This meeting took place at the home of Arthur and Elizabeth Dodge, who had studied the Faith in Chicago and were now holding classes in their new home in New York.

Since February of 1894, Dr. Khayru'lláh had been teaching the Cause with astounding success in Chicago, in Kenosha nearby, and then in Kansas City, Ithaca, Philadelphia and New York. The Master honoured him for his extraordinary achievements with the titles of 'Bahá's Peter', 'The Second Columbus', and 'Conqueror of America'.[1]

Only a few months after his acceptance of the Faith, Mr. MacNutt was already giving Dr. Khayru'lláh assistance on a book that he was beginning to write called *Bahá'u'lláh*.

In the fall of 1898, Dr. Khayru'lláh and his wife left for Europe to visit 'Abdu'l-Bahá in the Holy Land, as guests of Mrs. Phoebe Hearst. On his return to the United States of America in December of 1899, it became tragically apparent that he had turned against 'Abdu'l-Bahá, the Centre of the Covenant, and was openly seeking leadership for himself. The MacNutts were naturally saddened by the defection of this teacher who had helped to lead them into the Faith. Instead of following him into the wilderness of error, however, they remained firm in the Covenant of God.

During their first four years in the Bahá'í community, the MacNutts lived in a house at 731 St. Nicholas Avenue in New York City. After that they moved to a much larger house at 935 Eastern Parkway in Brooklyn. They used both of their homes principally to serve the Faith. Early in his Bahá'í life,

35

Mr. MacNutt undertook the study of Persian and Arabic. As a result he was able to help in the first English translation of the priceless *Kitáb-i-Íqán* revealed by Bahá'u'lláh.

At this time Mr. MacNutt also became deeply interested in the development of the Green Acre Centre. During summer conferences at this delightful, historic spot on the sloping banks of the Piscataqua River, four miles from the ocean, he gave many inspiring lectures.

Early in 1905, the MacNutts and their friend, Julia M. Grundy, made a pilgrimage to the Holy Land. In her touching account of this unforgettable experience, which she called *Ten Days in the Light of Acca*, Mrs. Grundy made several vivid references to the MacNutts. The pilgrims stayed in the prison house. One day when the Master came to see them unexpectedly, He said:[2]

.... "Tonight there will be a Meeting of the believers here. At the table they will be gathered together from all parts of the world. This is the reason of my happiness, seeing the East and the West joined in the Kingdom of God. May all the believers in the world be so joined until the whole world shall come under one rule and all nations be as one family. This will surely come to pass." Then turning to Mr. MacNutt, he asked, "What do you say to this?" He answered, "What could I say that would add to an already perfect wisdom!" ABDU'L-BAHA responded: "May we all be perfected in the Wisdom and Light of the Blessed Perfection." Again to Mr. MacNutt, "Will you speak?" He answered, "It is a blessed privilege to listen. I am usually called upon to speak but I love to listen." Abdu'l-Baha said, "May you always listen, always hear, always speak with the power of the Spirit."

That evening at the Feast in the large hall of the prison house, while He was serving each guest, the Master said: "This is the blessed supper of the Lord for we have gathered under the shadow of the Blessed Perfection."[3]

A guest at this Feast, Mírzá Asadu'lláh-i-Iṣfahání, who in 1898, at the request of the Master, had safely taken the remains of the Báb from Írán to the Holy Land and who since 1900, in an extended visit to the United States of America, had helped the believers there to recover from the shock and confusion over the defection of Dr. Khayru'lláh,

A BAHÁ'Í GROUP AT THE HOME OF THE TRUE FAMILY IN CHICAGO, 1909

Front row, left to right: Carl Scheffler, Mr. Struven, Arthur Agnew, Mr. Woodruff, Mr. Fuller

Middle Row: Corinne True, Mrs. Ida Brush, Mr. Brush

Back row, left to right: Albert Windust, Charles Mason Remey, George Lesch, Albert Heath Hall, Thornton Chase, Mr. Jacobsen, Mr. Currier

THORNTON CHASE

PHOEBE HEARST

ROBERT TURNER

HELEN GOODALL

ELLA GOODALL COOPER

HOWARD MACNUTT
as a young man

introduced Mr. MacNutt with these words: "He is one of our eloquent American brothers who has great power. God has given him the power to attract souls to the Fountain of Life. His words are like a magnet." [4]

As he looked at those around him, Mr. MacNutt replied, "In these Bahai faces one can see the image of the Blessed Perfection. He is here. I will take this picture to the American believers. Their spirits are here with us at this table of love." [5]

The next morning when 'Abdu'l-Bahá joined the pilgrims for breakfast, Mrs. MacNutt stated to Him what she thought were "the three progressive spiritual steps—Obedience as Christ taught; Resignation as Mohammed taught; and Renunciation as revealed by BAHA'U'LLAH. ABDUL-BAHA said, 'I pray that you all may be assisted to attain these stations in the Cause of God.' He continued: 'The cause of my happiness is meeting you here and seeing your faces filled with the Light of God. I shall never forget the beautiful meeting last night. You must meet together in this way in America.'" [6]

On 7th May 1905 at Genealogical Hall in New York City, shortly after he and the rest of his party had returned from the Holy Land, Mr. MacNutt gave a moving talk, entitled 'Unity Through Love'. He first stated that his intention was to explain with as much force and simplicity as he could the essential principle of the Bahá'í Revelation which the Master had perfectly defined for him. As he had expected after His first greetings were over, the Master had asked him: "How are the beloved of God in the City of New York? Are they unified? Are they one in love and harmony? Are they enkindled by the fire of the Love of God?" Mr. MacNutt had answered, "There are more signs of unity and love among us in New York than there have ever been in the history of our organization; and this is owing more to the good work of our women than to any other one cause." "You should have seen the holy light of joy and happiness upon His face, as He heard this answer," Mr. MacNutt declared. [7]

He then told his audience that instead of encouraging the pilgrims to ask questions about science, metaphysics and philosophy, the Master tried to show them how to apply the divine principle of love to their lives, and that He was most anxious to know how the friends were behaving to each other and what efforts they were making to teach those who, because of ignorance and superstition, were veiled from the Glory of Bahá'u'lláh.

Mr. MacNutt also advised any Bahá'í who planned to visit the Master "not to make the pilgrimage from a mere motive of self satisfaction or spirit of enquiry, but to go to Acca for the people, to bring back from the Master that which will accomplish the work of God and assist in the development of humanity." [8] One day he had said to 'Abdu'l-Bahá, "I wish it were possible for me to take thy living face back to New York that the believers there might see as I see." He answered, "My love is my face; take it to them; tell them to see me in their love for each other." [9]

During the spring of 1911, in a Tablet which He revealed to the much-loved Juliet Thompson, the Master wrote: "Announce on my behalf to Mrs. MacNutt: 'I do not forget thee and my beloved friend, Mr. MacNutt, for one breath; nay, rather, I beg continually for your divine confirmations and supreme assistance.'" [10]

On that time-honoured morning of 11th April 1912, when the Master arrived on S.S. *Cedric* in the harbour of New York City, a large group of believers had gathered there to meet Him. He sent them a message of love, but in order to avoid a public scene, He asked the believers to leave and join Him at four o'clock that afternoon at the home of Mr. and Mrs. Edward Kinney. After everyone had obediently left the pier (except two believers and a deeply interested friend), Mr. MacNutt and Mr. Mills escorted the Master from the ship, and led Him a short distance down the pier to Mr. Mills's car.

The next day a large group of Bahá'ís assembled at the home of the MacNutts in Brooklyn to hear the Master's second formal talk in America. Mr. MacNutt took notes of it as he did of at least seventeen others that the Master gave in this country. He began this beautiful one by saying, "This is a most happy visit. I have crossed the sea from the land of the Orient for the joy of meeting the friends of God.

Although weary after my long journey, the light of the spirit shining in your faces brings me rest and reward .... This is a spiritual house; the home of the spirit. There is no discord here; all is love and unity." [11]

The Master then clearly explained that only through the intense sufferings and hardships that Jesus Christ, the Báb and Bahá'u'lláh had endured was it possible both to hold such a meeting and for all to proclaim the unity of the human family.

On April 14th, three days after the Master had arrived in New York City, the *Titanic*, the largest steamship that had ever been built, grazed an enormous iceberg on her maiden voyage from Southampton, England, and sank two and a half hours later. Since the number of life boats on board was not sufficient, fifteen hundred people were drowned. On the day the newspapers printed this tragic news, the Master was taking a drive through the streets of New York with Mr. MacNutt. "Shall any of these things you are now looking upon remain or endure?" He asked. "If you possessed all you could wish for,—these great buildings, wealth, luxury, the pleasures of life in this world, would any of these things increase your eternal happiness or insure you everlasting existence? I am summoning you to the world of the Kingdom .... For the world of the Kingdom is a world of Lights, a world of happiness, a world of accomplishment, the real and eternal world." [12]

Mr. MacNutt recorded that, in conclusion, after a long pause during which He looked thoughtfully out of the window, 'Abdu'l-Bahá said, "I was asked to sail upon the *Titanic*, but my heart did not prompt me to do so." [13]

During His first few days in New York City, while He was staying at the handsome Hotel Ansonia, 'Abdu'l-Bahá consented with much enthusiasm to appear in a short motion picture to be filmed in front of this hotel's imposing entrance. Mr. J. G. Grundy and Mr. MacNutt recounted that as 'Abdu'l-Bahá approached the camera He was "exhorting BAHA'O'LLAH to bless this means for the spreading of the Heavenly Cause throughout the world," [14] and that to watch Him do this was a most impressive sight.

Several weeks later the same two men arranged for the Master to take part in a much longer motion picture than the first one. On Sunday June 16th the Master had lunch at the home of the MacNutts. That afternoon He gave a most convincing address there in which He pleaded with the friends to "endeavor always, cry, supplicate and invoke the kingdom of God to grant us full capacity in order that the bestowals of God may become revealed and manifest in us."[15]

The next day, the weather being favourable, He returned to this house and appeared in His second motion picture. Dr. Zia Bagdadi has stated in 'Star of the West' that it consists of five scenes: first, the Master's arrival at the house, and the welcome that the friends gave Him; second, His conversation with His secretaries and interpreters as He walked with them on the lawn; third, His chants in Persian as He walked there alone; fourth, His blessings to the white and coloured children as He sat beside them, with the Persian believers standing in the background; and fifth, His farewell words to the friends.[16]

According to Mr. Grundy and Mr. MacNutt, "those who beheld his countenance in the final utterance of the 'Glad Tidings' will treasure the memory of it forever."[17]

Shortly after the making of this motion picture, the same two men made a record of the Master's voice on an Edison Talking Machine. They wrote, "The beloved friends one hundred years from now will be able to see the form, face, and actions of the Beloved Centre of the Covenant; and even more, listen to the actual tone of his voice speaking the words which the pictures so eloquently portray."[18]

During the Master's journey in the United States, and at frequent intervals for some years afterwards, His American addresses appeared in the Bahá'í Magazine 'Star of the West', often accompanied by fascinating stories about Him, and sometimes illustrated with excellent photographs. Thinking that a collection of these talks would make an impressive book, Mr. MacNutt compiled the ones that had already appeared with all the other American talks by the Master that he could find and prepared them for publication.

In two letters which he wrote to 'Abdu'l-Bahá on February 18th and 21st of 1919 respectively, he asked His approval for this plan. The Master concluded a Tablet in reply, translated by Shoghi Effendi on the following April 13th, with this most encouraging advice: "The addresses of Abdul-Baha which thou hast compiled and which thou intendest to print and publish is indeed very advisable. This service shall cause thee to acquire an effulgent face in the Abha Kingdom, and shall make thee the object of the praise and gratitude of the friends in the East as well as the West. But this is to be undertaken with the utmost carefulness, so that the exact text may be reproduced and will exclude all deviations and corruptions committed by previous interpreters." [19]

On 20th July 1919, in a Tablet revealed to Albert R. Windust, the Master gave this instruction .... "Name the book which Mr. MacNutt is compiling *The Promulgation of Universal Peace*. As to its Introduction, it should be written by Mr. MacNutt himself when in heart he is turning toward the Abha kingdom, so that he may leave a permanent trace behind him. Send a copy of it to the Holy Land." [20] Mr. MacNutt of course followed all His instructions. The Master gave the introduction His approval and asked him to include a Persian translation of it in the forthcoming book.

In this introduction, Mr. MacNutt wrote that 'Abdu'l-Bahá "proclaimed his message and teachings universally to every degree and capacity of humankind, with such pure and sincere motive that all heard him gladly and without prejudice or antagonism." [21]

After giving a brief but vivid outline of the Cause, he clearly explained the station of 'Abdu'l-Bahá, Whom Bahá'u'lláh had named the Centre of the Covenant. Mr. MacNutt described the Master like this: "He is the channel of purifying, unifying religious belief, the new impulse and dynamic, the creative spirit of regeneration, the power and healing direct from God, the irrigating current of life to the world of man, the answerer of questions, the explainer of the Book, the bestower of spiritual capacities, the uplifting impetus of civilization, the servant of all mankind, the point of agreement and reconciliation for all the divine religions, the standard-bearer of Universal Peace and messenger of the Glad-Tidings of the oneness of the world of humanity." [22]

Some months before the ascension of 'Abdu'l-Bahá, on 28th November 1921, the Executive Board of the Bahá'í Temple Unity published its first edition of *The Promulgation of Universal Peace*. Owing to Mr. MacNutt's foresight and painstaking work, believers and enquirers alike still have a precious opportunity to read and study all of the Master's available American addresses. They serve as models to many Bahá'í speakers. Distinguished historians of the Cause often quote from these gemlike talks.

'Abdu'l-Bahá once asked the MacNutts to try and keep their house in Brooklyn, where He had visited and where so many splendid meetings had taken place. Early in 1920, however, they decided to spend the rest of their lives in a concentrated effort to teach the Cause in other parts of the country. After Howard had retired from his profession, he and Mary sold the house and moved to Florida. They spent five of the next six winters serving the Faith in various cities of that state, and they stayed one winter in California.

Howard MacNutt was a close friend of Thornton Chase. There is a touching photograph of Mr. MacNutt, which he declared his favourite. It shows him standing close to Mr. Chase's grave in the cemetery of Inglewood, a suburb of Los Angeles. The photograph was taken in Howard's middle sixties and portrays a strong, handsome face and a sturdy body. His kind, gentle expression shows charm and humour. White hair covers his head. With deep love and much fervour, he seems to be praying for his departed friend.[23]

Howard and Mary both died in Miami, Florida, as a result of injuries received from accidents, he on 26th December 1926, and she one month before. The reason for this coincidence surely became apparent to them when they reached the Kingdom.

In *America and the Most Great Peace*, his magnificent essay on the spiritual history of that country, the beloved Guardian has numbered MacNutt among eight immortal names that "will for ever remain associated with the rise and establishment of His Faith in the American continent, and will continue to shed on its annals a lustre that time can never dim."[24]

Edward and Carrie Kinney

ON THE MORNING OF 16th DECEMBER 1950, during a trip to New York City, I telephoned Mr. and Mrs. Edward Kinney. When the clerk at the Hotel Woodward had promptly put me through to their apartment, Mrs. Kinney answered with calm and gentleness. I explained who I was. "May I see you?" I asked. "Yes, but not to-day. Ned died yesterday," she said. "I did not know. Please forgive me for telephoning you." "Oh no," she said warmly, "I am glad that you did. Maybe you can come to the service for him on Sunday evening at the Bahá'í Centre." "I will certainly be there," I replied. The clerk interrupted us to say that other people were waiting to talk to Mrs. Kinney.

At that time the Bahá'í Centre was situated in a somewhat dreary building of offices on West Fifty-seventh Street and was composed of two rooms—a small one where the Spiritual Assembly and committees met, and a large one where community gatherings, celebrations and public meetings took place.

As I entered the small room, a thickly-set fine-looking young man was standing in front of me. We shook hands. "I am Donald Kinney," he said. A young girl with an unhappy expression walked up to him. "I feel just terribly about your father," she said. "Why should you or any of us?" said Donald happily. "Have you read what Shoghi Effendi wrote in his cable about him?" Donald took a copy of it from his pocket and showed it to us both. The message said: "Grieve passing dearly loved, highly admired, greatly trusted staunch, indefatigable, self-sacrificing teacher, pillar Faith, Saffa Kinney. His leonine spirit, exemplary steadfastness, notable record services enriched annals closing period Heroic Age

43

opening phase Formative Age Bahai Dispensation. Bountiful reward assured Abhá Kingdom beneath shadow Master he loved so dearly, served so nobly, defended so heroically until last breath. Shoghi. (cablegram dated 16th December 1950)[1]

Mrs. Kinney was sitting among about two hundred believers gathered in the large room for the service. Her warm appealing face showed deep feeling, but self-control. She looked like a lady in the real sense of that often loosely used word. Despite the occasion, when she stood up to speak to someone, she became entirely erect. She showed no sign of defeat.

On the following Sunday evening I went to Mrs. Kinney's fireside meeting at her apartment. With love and understanding she mingled with her guests. After most of them had left she sat down beside me for a few minutes. She spoke to me about her husband as if I had always known them both. "He lay sick in this apartment for many months. Sometimes I was up most of the night taking care of him. I often prayed to the Master, asking Him to keep Ned with me for a little while longer." I felt close to the Kinneys, and wanted to know more about them.

Edward Beadle Kinney was born on 9th March 1863 in New York City. While still a child he showed talent for music and began to study both organ and composition. At the age of fourteen he secured his first professional job as organist at St. Luke's Church in New York City. A year before that he had become a protégé of the distinguished Dr. Leopold Damrosch and studied composition with him for eight years. He attended Richmond College in Virginia, and at the same time he served as choir-master and organist in the Monumental Episcopal Church there. On his return to New York he studied composition with Edward MacDowell at Columbia University, and in a competition sponsored by the American National Conservatory of Music, in which several thousand people took part, he and three others won scholarships to study composition with the great composer Anton Dvorak.

During his life Mr. Kinney held many positions as organist and choir-master in churches with high musical standards, wrote some fine religious music, developed his own method of voice production and became a remarkable teacher of singing.

Helene Morrette, the future Mrs. Carrie Kinney, was born in New York City in 1878. She wanted to become a doctor, but her socially-prominent family would not permit her to do so. She had the opportunity of marrying several men of worldly importance. They did not interest her. In 1893 she met Edward Kinney. Two years later against the wishes of her parents she married him.

Late one evening at her fireside, I asked Mrs. Kinney, "Who first spoke to you about the Bahá'í Faith?" Others there besides myself listened with great interest to her answer. The following remarks are my impression of what she said:

One morning during the winter of 1895 Howard MacNutt, an old friend of Ned's, sent word that he wanted us to come to his house in the Bronx that evening to hear some glorious news. A prophet like Jesus had been on this earth.

I said to Ned, "Your friend must be crazy to write you this. Why don't you go without me?" He said "No. I am sure that Howard wants to meet you." "My family never knew anyone from the Bronx," I said. "I have never been there in my life." "I am taking you there tonight," he said firmly.

We drove to the MacNutts' house in a horsecab that took us an hour and a half. Their house was attractive and fairly large, but few others had come to the meeting beside ourselves. Howard read us a few prayers by Bahá'u'lláh and then some Tablets that the Master had written to the Bahá'ís including Howard himself. I became very much frightened to hear that Bahá'u'lláh claimed to be the Spirit of Truth, whose coming Jesus had promised, and what the Master explained about His Father and Himself.

On the way home in the carriage I said to Ned, "The MacNutts are very nice, but I don't want to go back there to see them again." Ned replied, "I believe that what we heard to-night is true." I was very much disturbed and after the long drive home I went immediately to bed.

Ned stayed up very late. He wrote a letter to 'Abdu'l-Bahá asking for confirmation of His Father's station. I did not think that Ned would ever hear from Him Whom he now called the Master. Every day more than once Ned read aloud prayers by Bahá'u'lláh that Howard had written down on sheets of paper. In a month's time Ned received a Tablet from the Master written in red ink. It included the words, "You have been chosen."

The first time that the Bahá'ís came to the house they looked very strange to me. I tried to be polite, but I couldn't. They frightened me. Instead I ran upstairs to the bathroom and locked the door. They came back every week on Sunday nights. Gradually I was moved to come downstairs and meet them. Soon I started to listen. One night after everyone had left, Ned and I sat down in the living-room and talked together. He explained to me all over again who Bahá'u'lláh was. He had come to fulfil all that Jesus had brought. Suddenly I realized that I believed what Ned was saying.

From that moment she always shared with her husband a passionate desire to serve the Cause of God. They were both most anxious to visit the Holy Land and meet the Master, and in 1907 they received an invitation from Him to come there with their young sons, Sanford and Howard. At the end of that year, shortly before the Master's release from prison, they went to visit Him.

Donald, the youngest son of the Kinneys and not born at the time, has described in a letter to me some of the experiences that his parents had there. While in Haifa Mrs. Kinney became very ill, and the doctor told her husband that she was going to die. Mr. Kinney went to 'Abdu'l-Bahá for advice. The Master informed him that his wife would wake up shortly before midnight and ask for some soup, and that he should give it to her. Mr. Kinney followed the Master's directions on how to make this special soup. At just the hour that the Master had said, Mrs. Kinney woke up. Mr. Kinney gave her the soup for which she had asked, and shortly afterwards she began to recover.

The Kinneys were planning to go to India after their pilgrimage. But 'Abdu'l-Bahá warned them that if they went there she would die. Instead He asked Mrs. Kinney and Dr. Zia Bagdadi (Ḍíyá Baghdádí) to establish the first tuberculosis hospital in Alexandria in Egypt. Donald records: "At that time male doctors in that country were not allowed to examine female patients. They were left in a room and given food until they finally died. Dr. Bagdadi told mother what symptoms to look for. She went into their rooms, examined the patients, and called out the symptoms to Dr. Bagdadi, who called back the diagnosis." [2]

46

After they had spent a year in the Middle East, the Kinneys returned to New York City. He worked hard as a musician. She worked without salary in hospitals. Possessed of considerable wealth, they lived in a large house at 780 West End Avenue, which became more and more a meeting place for the Bahá'ís. 'Abdu'l-Bahá arranged to have many of His Tablets to the American believers sent there, and Mrs. Kinney had them translated into English.

In the summer of 1909 the Kinney family, accompanied by Juliet Thompson and Alice Beede, again visited the Holy Land. According to Juliet, the Master described to Edward the hardship that Bahá'u'lláh experienced after He had lost His wealth. He ended with the words: "May God give you the treasure of the Kingdom, the breath of the Holy Spirit. If, perchance, you are overtaken by poverty, let it not make you sad. At best, you will then become companions of Christ." [3]

On the morning of 11th April 1912, the Master arrived in New York City. Although a large group of Bahá'ís had gathered at the dock to meet Him, the Master sent word from the ship that He wanted them to leave and join Him that afternoon at the home of the Kinneys.

In her precious diary, *Abdul Baha in America*, Juliet Thompson has movingly described this occasion: "When I arrived Abdul-Baha was sitting in the center of the dining-room, near the flower-strewn table .... At His knees stood Sanford and Howard Kinney and His arms were around them .... No words could describe the ineffable peace of Him. The people stood around Him in rows and circles—several hundred in the rooms; many were sitting on the floor in the dining-room. We made a dark background for His effulgence." [4]

In the talk He gave on that afternoon, His first in America, the Master said that He had longed to meet the friends and that the spiritual happiness that He felt at doing so had made Him forget His weariness from travel. Greatly pleased with New York as a city, and its material progress, He said: " .... I hope that it may also advance spiritually in the kingdom and covenant of God so that the friends here may become the cause of the illumination of America; that this city may become the city of love and that the fragrances of God may be spread from this place to all parts of the world." [5]

The Master spent many weeks of His journey in New York. He would sometimes leave there to visit other cities and then return. On June 19th, to a gathering of Bahá'ís in that city, after a believer had read the recently-translated 'Tablet of the Branch' revealed by Bahá'u'lláh, 'Abdu'l-Bahá forcefully explained the meaning of the Covenant and His own station, 'The Centre of the Covenant'. From that time New York has been rightly called 'The City of the Covenant'.

During one of His visits the Master stayed with the Kinneys. Asking them to be His guests, He paid all the expenses of the household including the wages of the servants. At His invitation Mrs. Kinney arranged to have a photograph taken of her family with Him. The believers gathered there night and day whenever it was possible to see Him.

Many years later Mírzá Valí'u'lláh Khán-i-Varqá, who served as one of the Master's secretaries while He was in America, said to Donald Kinney: "While 'Abdu'l-Bahá stayed in your family's home, He would go up to His room around three or four in the afternoon to rest. During this time of rest He would dictate to His secretaries .... simultaneously." [6]

In his fascinating, richly informative spiritual auto-biography, *Portals to Freedom*, Howard Colby Ives has described the Kinneys and their home, where he had his second meeting with the Master, in terms that surely showed the feelings of many others besides himself. "It was in the beautiful home of Mr. and Mrs. Kinney, a family of the friends who seemed to feel that the gift of all which they possessed was too little to express their adoring love. Entering their home the roar of the city, the elegance and luxury of Riverside Drive, the poverty and wealth of our modern civilization all seemed to merge into a unity of nothingness and one entered an atmosphere of Reality. Those heavenly souls who thus demonstrated beyond any words their self-dedication had a direct influence upon my hesitating feet of which they could have had no suspicion. My heart throughout all worlds shall be filled with thankfulness to them." [7]

The Master gave Edward Kinney the name of Saffa

(serenity); He likened him to Peter, saying, "This time you will not deny your Lord."[8] He named Carrie Kinney, Vaffa, which means certitude and fidelity, Sanford for one of the martyrs, 'Abdu'l-'Alí, and Howard, 'Abdu'l-Bahá after Himself. Juliet Thompson records: "One day in the autumn He took Saffa for a long walk in the strip of park along Riverside Drive, New York City. Suddenly 'Abdu'l-Bahá stood still on the path and looking deep into Saffa's eyes asked in heart-piercing tones: Do you love me? Do you love me?—words very much like those Jesus spoke to Peter."[9] Saffa never felt that he could love the Master enough.

On December 2nd, in one of the last recorded talks that He gave at the Kinneys, the Master stressed again His appointment by Bahá'u'lláh as Centre of the Covenant, to protect the Faith from any individual interpretation, and eventually to ensure unity and agreement among all the peoples of the world.

A few years after the Master had left America, the Kinneys, who up until that time had lived in absolute comfort and free from financial worries, began to lose their money. "At one time Ned and I had a great deal of money, all invested in New York property," Mrs. Kinney explained to me. "It went steadily down in value. We could not sell the property because it was entailed." Forced by their situation to practise strict economy they first moved from their large house in New York City to a small cabin in Eliot, Maine, near Green Acre, the Bahá'í Summer School.

In 1919, while they were living in a modest house in Wollaston, a suburb of Boston, their son, Sanford, became seriously ill. Although his parents, two nurses and the Bahá'ís did all that they could for him he grew steadily worse. Fully realizing that his condition was critical, the sick boy only wished that the will of God should be accomplished. On the third day after Sanford's passing, his parents held a service for him in their home to which many Bahá'ís came. Nineteen years before, a short bit of candle brought by a believer from the Most Holy Tomb of Bahá'u'lláh had burned in the room where Sanford was born. His parents now lit the candle again. "At the close of the prayers, when the burial ring had been placed upon the boy's finger, the candle burned up high, then flickered and went out,"[10] one close friend wrote.

On 23rd November 1919 in Haifa, 'Abdu'l-Bahá revealed a Tablet for Sanford which Mrs. William H. Randall brought to the Kinneys.

For Abdul-Ali Sanford Kinney—
Upon him be Baha-el-Abha!
He is God!
O Thou divine Providence!

Sanford was a child of the Kingdom and, like unto a tender shrub, was in the utmost freshness and grace in the Abha paradise. He has ascended to the world of the Kingdom, that in the everlasting rose-garden he may grow and thrive on the banks of the river of Everlasting Life and may blossom and attain fruition.

O Thou divine Providence! Rear him by the outpouring of the cloud of mercy and nourish him through the heat of the sun of pardon and of forgiveness. Stir him by the breeze of bounty and bestow patience and forbearance upon his kind father and mother, that they may not deplore his separation, and may rest assured in meeting their son in the everlasting Kingdom. Thou art the Forgiver and the Compassionate!

(Signed) Abdul-Baha Abbas.[11]

After the Kinneys had lived for several years in Wollaston, they moved back to New York City and settled down in the apartment at the Woodward Hotel that I have already mentioned. Saffa continued to work hard at his profession, and in this most difficult, uncertain field, he successfully managed to support his family.

Although the passing of the Master on 28th November 1921 caused Saffa and Vaffa intense grief, they did not relax in their constant efforts to serve the Faith. With good cause had He designated them 'Pillars of the Faith in the City of the Covenant', in one of His many letters of encouragement.

In 1938 their son Howard died at the age of thirty-three. Only their fine youngest son Donald whom 'Abdu'l-Bahá had named Vahíd, for one of the martyrs, was left to them.

* * *

On Christmas eve, nine days after her husband's passing, I went to a fireside at Mrs. Kinney's. Only a small group, all of them Bahá'ís, were there. Someone asked, "Can we sing Christmas carols?" Mrs. Kinney said, "Of course. Bahá'ís recognize the station of Jesus. We can certainly sing carols in honour of Him." Everyone in the room sang them with the joyful realization that the Spirit of Jesus had returned in the Station of the Father.

At Mrs. Kinney's apartment I met Mrs. Maud Gaudreaux. Trained by Mr. Kinney, she had become a leading member of the Chicago Opera Company. She was now in retirement and, since the beginning of Mr. Kinney's illness, she had been teaching his pupils. The money from these lessons had provided the main support for the three of them, and now was doing the same for the two ladies.

Brought up in a severely restricted social circle, Vaffa Kinney had long ago learned to mingle with people of all classes, religions and nationalities. No matter what motives had brought people to her apartment, she still tried to help them. She became like a mother to a great many people who turned to her in their hour of need. One evening at her fireside, referring to a thickset man seated in the back row, she said to me, "He is a communist. We must try to teach him the Faith."

Another time, after a Bahá'í speaker talked clearly about the Revelation of Bahá'u'lláh, a gentleman of Jewish background said, "When I was in the Holy Land, I had a revelation too." Instead of speaking to him with impatience, Mrs. Kinney said, "Before you decide that is true, why don't you listen a little more to what Bahá'u'lláh has revealed?" With apparent sincerity the gentleman replied, "I will come here again."

Once she was teaching two young sisters the Faith. The girls admitted their true motive for attending firesides: "What we are really trying to do is to find husbands." With a smile of understanding Mrs. Kinney said, "We must pray that you will find them." The sisters asked her, "Why should we study the Bahá'í Faith?" She firmly answered, "So that you will recognize your Lord."

When the Guardian inaugurated the World Crusade in April 1953, Mrs. Kinney wrote to him, "I will go anywhere that you ask me to go." He wrote back, "Stay in the City of the Covenant."

At the Feast of Unity in West Englewood on 29th June 1953, she stood on the same spot where the Master had stood at the first Feast of Unity in 1912, and read to a large group of people the beautiful talk that He had given on that moving, historic occasion. After she had finished reading it, she said to those of us still gathered around her, "When Ned and I first came into the Faith there were only a few believers in 'the City of the Covenant' and in the surrounding towns and villages, but look now at the wonderful change that has taken place."

During the first year of the Crusade, in obedience to the Guardian, Vaffa stayed in New York City. Sincere young Bahá'ís in difficulties boarded with her. If they became discouraged she tried to convince them that their situation was not hopeless. She advised them to deepen in the Faith. Surely they knew that if they turned their hearts wholly to Bahá'u'lláh, He would help them.

After the Feast of Riḍván in 1954, Vaffa and her household asked for and received the Guardian's permission to pioneer to River Edge, a small town in New Jersey, not far from New York City. Although by this time not physically strong, she and her household moved into a small house there a few months later. In her new home she taught the Faith as before, and with the firm assistance of her dear friend, Maude Gaudreaux, held regular weekly meetings.

During my pilgrimage in January 1955, I was privileged to speak of her to Shoghi Effendi. He said with much enthusiasm: "She is bringing a long and distinguished Bahá'í career to a climax by pioneering from the City of the Covenant to a neighbouring town."

In 1956 she had a serious operation from which she did not entirely recover. Because of her illness she left River Edge, and moved to her son Donald's house in West Englewood, New Jersey. News of the Guardian's passing on 4th November 1957 was a great shock to her. She had never expected to outlive him.

Donald has written to me that although his mother was ill

during much of the last three years of her life, she still taught the Cause as forcefully as before. "A few days before her death she went into a coma. At times she would appear to be having detailed conversations with the old believers who had already passed on. It seemed as if she was making the transition from this Kingdom to the next."

On the morning of 16th August 1959, Donald came into her room to see how she was, and found that her passing had quietly taken place. Her warm, gentle, loving, and distinguished personality remains with me always, and I feel sure it remains with countless others. She spoke the language of the heart.

Ethel Rosenberg

ETHEL JENNER ROSENBERG, the first English woman to embrace the Bahá'í Faith in her native land, was born in Bath on 6th August 1858. She came from a family of artists. Her grandfather, Thomas Eliot Rosenberg, was a well-known painter of miniature portraits and landscapes. His youngest son, her father, worked mostly on still life at first, but later turned to landscapes. In July of 1856 he married Hanner Fuller Jenner. They had three children, two daughters and a son. Ethel, the eldest of the three, spent her childhood in Bath. When she was a young girl her mother counselled her, "Watch for a great teacher sent from God."

Ethel became a deep student of the Old and New Testaments. She also gained a thorough knowledge of French. During her early teens she moved to London, where she studied art under LeGros, a fine teacher at the Slade School. Although at the start of her career she painted both landscapes and full sized portraits, she gradually became accomplished in the field of miniature portraits. A large number of colourful personalities sat for Ethel, and her work has often been exhibited in the Royal Academy.

Early in 1898 her close friend Miriam Thornburgh-Cropper, an American living in England, received from Mrs. Phoebe Hearst in California a letter which contained some impressive statements about the Bahá'í Faith. Soon convinced that Bahá'u'lláh was the Promised One, Mrs. Cropper accepted Mrs. Hearst's invitation to join her party of fifteen on a pilgrimage to 'Akká late in the same year. Deeply affected by "the spirit and words of the Master," and by her whole imperishable experience in the Holy Land, on her return to

England Mrs. Cropper began, as she has described, "to spread the teaching, to mention the Name of Bahá'u'lláh, and acquaint the world with the Message."[1]

During the summer of 1899 she, the first believer in the British Isles, helped to lead Ethel into the Faith. Starting to serve it without delay, this gifted woman, in company with her friend, was soon speaking of the Faith to many people in London. At the end of January in 1901 she enjoyed the priceless experience of visiting 'Abdu'l-Bahá in the Holy Land. Not yet confined to the city limits of 'Akká, He was living in Haifa.

In that portion of her valuable notes on this pilgrimage available to the general reader she has recorded moving stories, now historic, that the Master and members of His family told her of their life with Bahá'u'lláh in the Most Great Prison in 'Akká, explanations that the Master gave her of many difficult passages in the Gospels, and advice that He offered to the Bahá'í community.

He informed her, "It is said of Mary Magdalen that out of her went seven devils. This means seven evil qualities which Jesus cast out of her by teaching her the Truth. She was not such a bad woman as some suppose before her conversion but the wonder is that such a saint and miracle of purity and goodness could have been created by the New Birth. She was greater than all the disciples of Jesus because she alone stood firm after His death and never wavered."[2]

The Master also said to Ethel, " .... In these early days of the Faith it is of the first importance that all the believers should have the right qualities and show forth the right attributes. One unconquered fault could cast one down in a single moment from the highest station to the lowest. We must strive to change our bad qualities into good ones, quick temper must be changed into calmness, pride into humility, falsehood into truth, deceit into frankness, laziness into activity .... "[3]

Ethel left Haifa in April. About four months later on 20th August 1901 the Governor of 'Akká informed 'Abdu'l-Bahá that He and His brothers, by the decree of Sulṭán 'Abdu'l-Hamíd, would now be strictly confined within the city limits.

On her return to London Ethel often read from her pilgrim notes at Bahá'í meetings. She gave excellent public talks before large audiences. She also spent some time in the study of Persian and thus she was able to assist in some early translations of the Holy Writings.

Late in 1901, when in accordance with the request of 'Abdu'l-Bahá the greatly revered Mírzá Abu'l-Faḍl visited the United States of America in order to strengthen the newly born community there in its understanding of the Covenant and to protect this community from those who had broken the Covenant, Ethel accompanied him to help in the teaching.

Early in April 1904 Ethel made a second pilgrimage to the Holy Land. Laura Clifford Barney, a brilliant young American Bahá'í who was living in Paris, went with her. Still confined to the city of 'Akká, the Master and His family were living in the prison house. For eight months Ethel stayed there as His guest. She has written: "To sit at Abdul Baha's table, in his simple home, with Christians, Mohammedans, Jews, and those of other faiths, all of them breathing forth the spirit of living brotherhood is a privilege not readily forgotten." [4]

During her visit enemies of the Cause became particularly vicious in their attacks against 'Abdu'l-Bahá and caused Him and His loyal followers enormous problems and indescribable grief. Deeply distressed by this fact, she asked the Master why He, a perfect man, had to go through such sufferings. He answered her: "How could they (God's teachers) teach and guide others in the way if they themselves did not undergo every species of suffering to which other human beings are subjected?" [5]

The Master often instructed her in the Holy Writings. In His words of assurance on the power of intercession He explained "that by the mercy of God, not through His justice, the condition of those who have died in sin and unbelief can be changed .... As we have the power to pray for those souls here, so we shall have the same power in the after-life in the Kingdom. The power of this prayer of intercession is a special teaching of this religion." [6]

What she had learned directly from the Master gave her,

of course, an invaluable source of accurate knowledge and information. She made a second and then a third teaching trip to the United States of America. She also served the Cause for long periods of time in France. During 1907 in Paris, Ethel and the distinguished first French believer, Hippolyte Dreyfus, explained in detail the Mission of Bahá'u'lláh to the saintly Sara Louisa, Lady Blomfield, and her daughter Mary.

In 1908 the Young Turks made their successful revolt. On July 23rd of that year their Central Committee issued a decree that forced Sulṭán 'Abdu'l-Hamíd to restore within twenty-four hours the constitution which he had suspended, and to release all political and religious prisoners. In spite of these events, the hostile officials in 'Akká refused to release 'Abdu'l-Bahá until in answer to their telegram instructions came from Constantinople to do so.

In January 1909 Ethel made another pilgrimage to the Holy Land. Although He was free, the Master had not yet left 'Akká to live in Haifa. Ethel asked Him what the friends could do to increase their numbers and to make their work more effective. He answered that "the members of the little groups should love each other very much and be devoted friends. The more they loved each other, the more the meetings would attract and draw others, and the more they loved, the more their influence would be felt .... I say also in English, that you may understand how much I mean it, that love is the foundation of everything .... " [7]

During her visit Ethel painted a fine miniature portrait of the Master's beloved sister, Bahá'íyyih Khánum, the Greatest Holy Leaf. This portrait is now in the Bahá'í archives of the United Kingdom.

Ethel often corresponded with the Master. He revealed to her precious Tablets, some on the Holy Writings, and others consisting of personal advice. In one which she received in London on 17th August 1909, according to her own translation, He wrote:

To the attracted maid servant of God, Miss Rosenberg. Upon her be Baha'u'llah Abha!

Oh you who are attracted to the Kingdom of Abha!

Your letter has arrived and informed us that you had some nerve trouble. I hope it is removed by this time. Do not be sad and be sure of the blessings of God, for you are accepted in the Kingdom and are mentioned in this heavenly gathering.

Give my respectful greetings to Mrs. Cropper and say to her that she is becoming like a shining candle in that country and giving light to all and that you both are causing the divine enlightenment to dispel the darkness of doubt in that region, so that the morn of reality may illumine with great splendour that horizon.

Upon you be Baha'u'llah Abha.[8]

Elsewhere the Master stressed to Ethel that it was important for her to work on her painting so that she would have sufficient means of support.

In 1910, when there was still a scarcity of literature about the Faith in English, Ethel wrote a brilliant, informative essay entitled, *A Brief Account of the Baha'i Movement*. Published during the following year by two commercial firms for the Bahá'í Society of London and sold for one penny a copy, this stimulating work is composed of a brief, but varied, history of the Faith from its beginning until the time that she wrote it, a convincing explanation of the Stations of the Báb, Bahá'u'lláh, and 'Abdu'l-Bahá, pertinent comments about the Holy Writings, with quotations from them to show the logic of her remarks, and forceful statements about the aims of the Faith.

She defined the Bahá'í belief that Revelation is progressive in these words: "Just as the rising of the sun chases away darkness and floods the earth with light, so does the rising of the heavenly sun of the prophet above the horizon of humanity flood the world with light. As long as His teachings in their purity shine upon humankind, the world is illuminated; but as through the lapse of time the teachings become forgotten, misunderstood, and obscured, the night once more returns, until at its darkest period we may again expect the coming of the dawn, and once more the sun of truth arises in a special manifestation of the Holy Spirit." [9]

In a concluding passage she affirmed: "Bahais declare that in this revelation all the expectations of various faiths are fulfilled, and that the way is open to a great mutual recognition that we are, indeed, all children of the Supreme, and that the world is entering upon an inheritance that has been foretold by the prophets since the beginning of time. A world-consciousness is arising, that will cause all nations to think and to act like one man." [10]

Shortly after her essay was published, the Master arrived in England on 4th September 1911, to make His proclamation of the Revelation of His Father for the first time in person to the Christian West. Except for three days when He stayed in Bristol, 'Abdu'l-Bahá spent this visit, which lasted a little over four weeks, at Lady Blomfield's home at 97 Cadogan Gardens in London. On the day of His arrival Ethel, among some other believers, waited there to give Him a joyful welcome. His hostess has written, "It was especially touching to see Mrs. Thornburgh-Cropper and Miss Ethel Rosenberg, who had visited Him in the prison fortress of 'Akká, and who had been the first to bring the Message to London, coming day after day, as though transported with gratitude that He was now free to give His Message to those who were hungering and thirsting after righteousness .... " [11]

Not content just to attend these daily meetings and to delight in the presence of the Master for as long as possible, Ethel, and also Mrs. Thornburgh-Cropper, Miss Elizabeth Herrick, and Miss Marion Jack, arranged for Him to speak at other places. On 8th September 1911, the Master gave an address at Ethel's house. He opened by saying, "Praise be to God, that such a meeting of purity and steadfastness is being held in London. The hearts of those present are pure, and are turned towards the Kingdom of God. I hope that all that is contained and established in the Holy Books of God may be realized in you. The messengers of God are the principal and the first teachers. Whenever this world becomes dark, and divided in its opinions and indifferent, God will send one of His Holy Messengers." [12]

On October 3rd 'Abdu'l-Bahá left London to visit Paris, Egypt and the United States and Canada. On 16th December 1912 He returned to London. From the time that Ethel, one among a large group of believers, met Him at the station, until He had left for Paris on January 21st of the following year, she did all that she could to serve Him.

Owing to these two visits of the Master to England, the Bahá'ís in London became more closely united than ever before. According to His instructions they intensified their efforts to teach the Cause. During the First World War exacting wartime duties often kept the friends from teaching and from attendance at meetings. Throughout this conflict, however, despite her frail health, serious financial difficulties, and the lack of public interest, Ethel continued her Bahá'í classes without an intermission.

In January 1915, as Secretary of the Bahá'í Society in London, Ethel wrote a touching letter to Miss Buikema, Editor of 'The Star of the West', to inform her of the tragic passing of a young English believer, much loved by the Master. This was Daniel Jenkyn, of St. Ives in Cornwall, who had died the preceding December 31st. She referred to his association with the Christian Commonwealth Fellowship, which gave him excellent opportunities to speak of the Cause to many seekers of Truth, his recent teaching trip to Holland and the vast correspondence in which he had engaged in order to help spread the Glad Tidings.

She wrote, "I have asked Mirza Lotfullah Hakim who was his close personal friend, to enclose a copy of the last letter he received from Mr. Daniel Jenkyn, for it breathes a most ardent and uplifting spirit of devotion which will prove an inspiration to us all." [13]

In this letter he had declared, "Oh! if the Bahais were more in number and more powerful in spirit so that they could have prevented this carnage! We are not yet a great influence in the world, as the beloved Abdul-Baha wants to see, and yet he says: 'A weak man can, through assistance, become a strong man, a drop can become a sea .... through the assistance of God any of us can perform wonders.'" [14]

Accepting her suggestion, Dr. Luṭfu'lláh Ḥakím, who many years later was to be one of the first members of the Universal House of Justice, also enclosed his own warm letter about their friend, a charming photograph of the two men standing together, and most importantly, of course, two moving Tablets revealed to Daniel Jenkyn by the Master, in one of which He strongly commends him for his proclamation of the Cause in Holland. All the enclosures were promptly published in 'Star of the West.'

In the fascinating diary which Dr. John Esslemont kept of his first visit to Haifa in 1919, he has recorded that on the day of his departure the Master spoke to him with much concern about Miss Rosenberg's difficult financial situation, her delicate health, and her brother's illness. The Master gave Dr. Esslemont fifty pounds in Turkish gold to take to her and said that the friends must try to help and take care of her.[15]

In the autumn of 1921 she made another pilgrimage to the Holy Land. Some minutes after one o'clock in the morning of 28th November 1921, the Master ascended to the Abhá Kingdom. Deeply thankful to be near Him at that time, on December 8th Ethel wrote a beautiful letter to the beloved friends of England in which she vividly described that heart-breaking event. Among other matters she related this unforgettable incident. "About ten days before the end, he left His little bedroom in the garden and came into the house. He told his family that he had dreamed in the night that Baha'u'llah had come to him and had said, 'Destroy this room immediately,' and therefore he did not like to sleep outside any more, but would come into the house. The family were thankful, as they felt he would be nearer to them if he needed any service during the night. They now understand the symbolism of the saying—the 'room' being the Beloved One's body."[16]

In conclusion she wrote, "I am sure we all feel that now is the time for us all to be united with the utmost love and firmness—to increase our activities tenfold in teaching and spreading the good news of the Kingdom."[17]

When during March 1922 Shoghi Effendi, the newly appointed Guardian, called together a small group of Bahá'ís from America, England, France, Germany and Persia, well-known for their devoted services, to consult with him on vital matters concerning the development of the Cause, he asked Ethel to join this group.

In April she returned to England. Shortly afterwards, in an effort to obey the Guardian's instructions, the communities of London, Manchester, and Bournemouth, elected nine from their membership to what was called the Bahá'í Spiritual Assembly for England. This body met at the home of Mrs. Thornburgh-Cropper in Westminster, in London. In 1923 the first National Spiritual Assembly of the British Isles was established. A member of both, Ethel also served as Secretary of the Spiritual Assembly of London.

On 19th October 1923, in this latter capacity, she wrote a happy informative letter to 'Star of the West', which it published soon afterwards. She reported that the friends in Switzerland had told her that the Guardian, now in that country, was in excellent health and that at the end of October or early in November he would return to the Holy Land; that Mrs. Thornburgh-Cropper, whose attendance at meetings was always inspiring, would soon be back in London after an absence of several months; that Lady Blomfield was now giving talks on the Faith in the Bahá'í Centre which she had successfully established in Geneva, and that she was also preparing a book about the early events of the Faith.

Ethel further remarked that the National Spiritual Assembly of the British Isles had just published, with the Guardian's permission, a new edition of *The Hidden Words*, translated by him, with Bahá'í prayers placed at the end of the book; that Dr. Esslemont's recently published introduction to the Bahá'í Faith, *Bahá'u'lláh and the New Era*, "is considered to be the best, most complete account of the Cause in English;"[18] that *Unity Triumphant*, a book by Elizabeth Herrick, a believer from London, also just published, contained precious talks by the Master and important information about the Faith; and that the Bahá'í Library in London run by Mrs. Florence George was composed of over a hundred books on the Cause.

She concluded her letter with a simple greeting from the Bahá'í friends in England to the Bahá'í friends in the world and wished them "every success in their work for the help of mankind and for Eternal Love."[19]

In two photographs of Ethel, one taken when she was

middle-aged and the other some years later, her face has a warm, sensitive expression and a homely charm.[20, 21] She died in London on 17th November 1930, at the age of seventy-two.

Mrs. Annie B. Romer, at that time Secretary of the London Assembly, an American who had worked for the Faith in the British Isles for many years, wrote, "The end was peaceful for this devoted servant of 'Abdu'l-Bahá, whom He knew and loved so well and to whose devotion and untiring labours He often paid priceless tribute by voice and pen." [22]

As soon as Shoghi Effendi had been informed of her passing, he sent by cable this message to the friends in London:[23] "Deeply grieved passing Rosenberg, England's outstanding Bahá'í pioneer worker. Memory of her glorious service will never die. 'Abdu'l-Bahá's family join me in expressing heartfelt condolences to her brother and relatives. Urge friends hold befitting memorial service."

Thomas Breakwell

DURING THE LATTER PART OF 1898, when Mrs. Phoebe Hearst, the famous American philanthropist, passed through Paris with her party of pilgrims on the way to visit 'Abdu'l-Bahá in the Holy Land, May Ellis Bolles, a young American, was living in Paris with her mother. Mrs. Hearst generously asked May to join the party.

This historic journey was the first by a group of believers from the West to the Holy Land. May's vivid, deeply moving impression of it, entitled *An Early Pilgrimage*, published in April 1917, has already been a source of joyful enlightenment to many readers.

Among other things the Master said to her: "You are like the rain which is poured upon the earth making it bud and blossom and become fruitful; so shall the Spirit of God descend upon you, filling you with fruitfulness and you shall go forth and water His vineyard." [1]

At the end of her visit, the Master asked May to return to Paris and establish a Bahá'í centre in that city. Obedient to His instructions she was able to accomplish this task within a few months. May has described an unforgettable event that she experienced during the summer of 1901. Not yet understanding the Bahá'í Cause, her mother disapproved of May's constant service to it, particularly since her journey to 'Akká. Early in the spring of that year, her mother wrote to the Master asking His permission to take May to Brittany for the summer together with her brother. The Master answered that under no account was May to leave Paris. Learning that 'Abdu'l-Bahá's refusal had made Mrs. Bolles most unhappy, the great teacher Mírzá Abu'l-Faḍl wrote to the Master to explain her feelings. But He still did not change His decision.

When her mother and brother left the city, May moved to a small apartment in a charming house belonging to a friend, Edith Jackson. During the first month that May spent there, she held wonderful meetings which led to the conversion of many precious souls. Early in the summer, Mrs. Milner, whom May had got to know some months earlier, met a young Englishman on a ship sailing from the United States to France. Although Mrs. Milner had never shown any apparent interest in the Bahá'í Faith, she still felt moved to invite him to come with her to see "a special friend" in Paris. The day after Mrs. Milner and he had arrived in that city, May found them standing at her door.

She has described her first sight of this young man. "It was like looking at a veiled light. I saw at once his pure heart, his thirsty soul, and over all was cast the veil which is over every soul until it is rent asunder by the power of God in this day." [2] She has described him as "of medium height, slender, erect, and graceful with intense eyes, and an indescribable charm." [3]

May soon learned that although he was English he held an important post in a cotton mill in a southern state of America, where he had been living for some time, and that he usually spent long summer vacations in Europe.

They discussed his work and the trip that he was planning. He spoke of his great interest in theosophy and seemed to think that she shared it. She did not mention the Bahá'í Faith. Even so, she felt that he was studying her carefully. As he was leaving he asked May if he might come to see her again and hear about some teachings that Mrs. Milner had referred to on the steamer, without mentioning what they were. Since he only planned to stay in Paris for a few days she asked him to return on the following morning.

He arrived with "his eyes shining, his face illumined, his voice vibrating under the stress of great emotion." He looked at her very intently and then said: "I have come to you to help me. Yesterday after I left you, I walked alone down the boulevard and suddenly some great force nearly swept me off my feet. I stood still as though awaiting something, and a voice announced to me distinctly, 'Christ has come!'" Then he asked, "What do you think this means?"[4]

In answer she immediately gave him the Bahá'í Message. For the next three days, during many hours which they spent together, she spoke to him about the exalted Mission of His Holiness the Báb, His early martyrdom, the martyrdom of many more who believed in Him, and about "Bahá'u'lláh, the Blessed Beauty Who shone upon the world as the Sun of eternity, Who had given to mankind the law of God for this age—the consummation of all past ages and cycles."[5] She gave him the small amount of Bahá'í literature in her possession. She described to him her visit to the Prison of 'Akká, and the unforgettable days that she had spent there in the presence of the Master. As she taught him, the veil that she had first seen over him disappeared. "He was like a blazing light."[6]

On the third day of their conversation he became entirely transformed. No former ambition remained. He now had only a single passionate longing—to meet the Master. On this same day Thomas Breakwell wrote this supplication to Him: "My Lord! I believe; forgive me, Thy servant, Thos. Breakwell."[7]

Although deeply moved by the depth and simplicity of his words, May did not yet fully understand why he had so urgently asked the Master for forgiveness. Without delay she wrote a letter to Him asking His permission for her young friend to make the pilgrimage and enclosing his supplication. That evening when May went to the concierge of her apartment to get her mail, she found a little blue cablegram from 'Abdu'l-Bahá that had just arrived. It said, "You may leave Paris at any time."[8] May realized that, thanks to her unquestioning obedience to the Master, she had served as "the link in the chain of His mighty purpose."[9]

In an informal talk that He gave in England on 16th January 1913, the Master said, "I have a lamp in my hand searching through the lands and seas to find souls who can become heralds of the Cause."[10] And in a Tablet to one of

May's spiritual children, He wrote of her, "her company uplifts and develops the soul." [11]

The next day, with her heart filled with gratitude to Him, May most happily joined her mother and brother at the seaside. After she had told her mother all that had taken place and had read her His cablegram, "she burst into tears and exclaimed, 'You have, indeed, a wonderful Master.'" [12]

Breakwell soon left for the prison city of 'Akká. He was the first Englishman to go there as a pilgrim, and went in company with Herbert Hopper, a young American Bahá'í whom May had also taught.

On their arrival at the prison house (of 'Abdu'lláh Páshá), the two young men were ushered into a large room where they expected to meet the Master. At one end of this room stood a group of men from the East. Not impressed with any of them, Breakwell became deeply troubled and was afraid that he had failed to recognize His Lord. "Sorrow and despair filled his heart, when suddenly a door opened, and in that opening he beheld what seemed to him the rising Sun. So brilliant was this orb, so intense the light that he sprang to his feet and saw approaching him out of this dazzling splendor the form of 'Abdu'l-Bahá." [13] Breakwell's mood instantly changed from complete despair to indescribable joy.

In a conversation with the Master he described his position in the cotton mills of the South. Now clearly realizing that such a condition was wrong, he said, "'These mills are run on child labor.' The Master looked at him gravely and sadly for a while, and then said 'Cable your resignation.'" [14] With great relief Breakwell hastened to obey Him.

Memories of Nine Years in 'Akká by Dr. Yúnis Khán Afrúkhtih contains some inspiring passages about Breakwell's visit of two days in the prison city. His visit was unfortunately short because of restrictions reimposed by the authorities, but the intense love and great enthusiasm that he showed touched the hearts of all those who met him. "The fervour and the faith of this young man were so sublime in character that his blessed name shall ring throughout centuries, and shall be remembered with deep affection in many chronicles." [15]

On the day that he left, the Master asked him to stay in

Paris on his return. He also requested Yúnis Khán to accompany Breakwell back to Haifa, to the ship on which he was to sail. While they were resting at a believer's house on the way, Breakwell turned more than once towards 'Akká and prayed so fervently that everyone in the room was deeply moved.

Breakwell asked Yúnis Khán to correspond with him, so that he might also enjoy the divine fragrances of the Holy Places.

On his return to Paris, Breakwell, wonderfully influenced by his precious communion with the Master and by the overwhelming experience of his short visit to 'Akká, taught the Faith with increased spiritual power. "He had become the guiding star of our group .... In the meetings he spoke with a simplicity and eloquence which won the hearts and quickened the souls .... " [16] Knowing that money was always urgently needed to assist in the progress of the Cause, he lived in an inexpensive apartment far from where the other friends lived and always walked to the meetings.

Intensely sympathetic, he had a genuine love for people. Despite any inconvenience to himself he always tried to help them. May has told this touching story about him: "Well I remember the day we were crossing a bridge over the Seine on the top of a bus, when he spied an old woman laboriously pushing an apple-cart up an incline; excusing himself with a smile, he climbed down off the bus, joined the old woman, and in the most natural way put his hands on the bar and helped her over the bridge." [17]

Although May and he were devoted friends and, as Bahá'ís, had no lack of important matters to discuss, whenever he visited her family he gave most of his attention to her mother, who had not recognized the station of 'Abdu'l-Bahá and was in need of love and kindness. As May has remarked, "He knew well the secret of imparting happiness and was the very embodiment of the Master's words, 'The star of happiness is in every heart. We must remove the veils, so that it may shine forth radiantly.'" [18]

Every fortnight, Breakwell corresponded with Dr. Yúnis Khán, who showed all the letters of his friend to the Master. According to the memoirs mentioned above, Breakwell wanted to know whether or not the Master would allow him to visit England for two or three days if one of his parents became ill or died. But in the same letter, he added: "It is not necessary to trouble Him with the above question, because Jesus has already answered this enquiry—Let the dead bury the dead."[19] When the doctor read a translation of this letter to the Master, He "smilingly answered: 'Write to him, today the living ones must bury the dead.'"[20]

Breakwell's parents came to see him in Paris, with the intention of taking him back to London. He explained to them that he could not leave Paris, because the Master had asked him to stay there. Nonetheless, Breakwell's parents were kind to him during their visit, and he led his father into the Cause of God. Breakwell enclosed his father's letter of supplication to the Master with his own next letter to Dr. Yúnis Khán. The Master read translations of both these letters, and although He made no remark at the time, after some days He gave a Tablet to Dr. Yúnis Khán which He had revealed for Breakwell's father.

Physically frail, Breakwell was stricken with an illness that developed into serious consumption. Although often in great pain, he in no way relaxed in his passionate efforts to serve the Cause throughout the dark city of Paris. In his last letter to Dr. Yúnis Khán, Breakwell wrote: "Suffering is a heady wine; I am prepared to receive that bounty which is the greatest of all; torments of the flesh have enabled me to draw much nearer to my Lord. All agony notwithstanding, I wish life to endure longer, so that I may taste more of pain. That which I desire is the good-pleasure of my Lord; mention me in His presence."[21]

A few days after the doctor had received this letter Breakwell died, a fact which the Master seemed to know without receiving any message. Deeply grieved, He wrote a prayer of visitation for Breakwell and asked Yúnis Khán to "translate it well, so that whoever reads it will weep."[22]

Yúnis Khán first translated it into French and then with the help of Lua Getsinger into English. This eulogy is heart-breaking and yet joyful in the infallible assurance that the Master has given of the exalted spiritual station that Breakwell had attained.[23]

O Breakwell, my beloved! Where is thy beautiful countenance and where is thy eloquent tongue? Where is thy radiant brow and where is thy brilliant face?

O Breakwell, my beloved! Where is thy enkindlement with the fire of the love of God and where is thy attraction to the fragrances of God? Where is thy utterance for the glorification of God and where is thy rising in the service of God?

O my dear, O Breakwell! Where are thy bright eyes and where are thy smiling lips? Where are thy gentle cheeks and where is thy graceful stature?

O my dear, O Breakwell! Verily thou hast abandoned this transitory world and soared upward to the Kingdom, hast attained to the grace of the Invisible Realm and sacrificed thyself to the Threshold of the Lord of Might!

O my adored one, O Breakwell! Verily thou hast left behind this physical lamp, this human glass, these earthly elements and this worldly enjoyment!

O my adored one, O Breakwell! Then thou has ignited a light in the glass of the Supreme Concourse, hast entered the Paradise of Abhá, art protected under the shade of the Blessed Tree and hast attained to the meeting (of the True One) in the Abode of Paradise!

O my dearly beloved, O Breakwell! Thou hast been a divine bird and forsaking thy earthly nest, thou hast soared towards the holy rose-garden of the Divine Kingdom and obtained a luminous station there!

O my dearly beloved, O Breakwell! Verily thou art like unto the birds, chanting the verses of thy Lord, the Forgiving, for thou wert a thankful servant; therefore thou hast entered (into the realm beyond) with joy and happiness!

O my beloved, O Breakwell! Verily, thy Lord hath chosen thee for His Love, guided thee to the court of His Holiness, caused thee to enter into the Riḍván of His Association and granted thee to behold His Beauty!

O my beloved, O Breakwell! Verily thou hast attained to the eternal life, never-ending bounty, beatific bliss and immeasurable providence!

O my beloved, O Breakwell! Verily, thy Lord hath chosen most exalted horizon, a lamp among the angels of heaven, a living spirit in the Supreme World and art established upon the throne of immortality!

O my adored one, O Breakwell! I supplicate God to increase thy nearness and communication, to make thee enjoy thy prosperity and union (with Him), to add to thy light and beauty and to bestow upon thee glory and majesty!

O my adored one, O Breakwell! I mention thy name continually, I never forget thee, I pray for thee day and night and I see thee clearly and manifestly, O my adored one, O Breakwell!

Breakwell had died within a few months of returning from his pilgrimage, probably in the early days of 1902. A year passed before the Master heard any news from his parents. Then one day, as He was examining certain envelopes which He had received from different places, "He, all of a sudden, picked out one and said [to Dr. Yúnis Khán]: 'How pleasing is the fragrance that emanates from this envelope. Make haste, open it and see where it comes from. Make haste'". The envelope contained a letter and a beautifully coloured postcard with a violet attached to it. On the card was written in gold ink: "He is not dead. He lives on in the Kingdom of God," and at the bottom, "This flower was picked from Breakwell's grave." [24] The enclosed letter said: "Praise be to the Lord that my son left this world for the next with the recognition and love of Abdul-Baha." [25]

As soon as the doctor had translated this letter for the Master, "He at once rose up from His seat, took the card, put it on His blessed brow, and tears flowed down His cheeks." [26]

With his unerring knowledge the Guardian called Thomas Breakwell the first English believer [27] and a luminary in the Cause of God. [28]

Juliet Thompson

WHILE I WAS VISITING NEW YORK in December 1950, I went
to a fireside meeting at Juliet Thompson's home at 48 West
Tenth Street. She had shared the apartment for many years
with her friend Marguerite Smyth, and their devoted servant
Helen James.

Mirza Ali-Kuli Khan, his daughter Hamiden, and Marjorie
Morten, joined us before Juliet. I liked their faces. I wanted
to get to know them. Then Juliet walked modestly into the
room as if she did not expect anyone to notice her. She had
wonderful, warm eyes and a delightful smile. She sat down on
a comfortable chair near the fireplace. In a hoarse attractive
voice, she said to two or three of those present in turn, "Speak
to us a little."

She drew them out easily. Mirza Ali-Kuli Khan gave a
brilliant, fascinating analysis of a talk by the Master.
Marjorie Morten told a touching, humorous, and dramatic
story of her first meeting with Him. Then someone asked
Juliet to describe His visit to the Museum of Natural History
in New York. Without hesitation she began her story:

One Saturday afternoon in July 1912, when the Master was in
New York, Mother and I decided to visit Him. As we approached
the house where He was staying we saw Him coming down the
steps with some of the Persian friends. He greeted us warmly and
said to Mother and me, "Come with us to the Museum of Natural
History."

Neither Mother nor I could understand why the Master had
decided to visit this museum on such a hot July afternoon. Mother
and I just happily followed Him and the Persian friends across the
street to Central Park and into the park itself.

73

With weary steps the Master walked ahead of the rest of us. Perspiration streamed down His neck. When we were close to the museum I saw the many steps that led up to the entrance. I could not bear to see the Master climb them. I looked for another way of getting into the museum and I found a little door to the right hand side of the steps. Between us and the door was a grass plot with a sign in the middle that said 'Keep Off.' In spite of this I started to walk across the plot. Before I had reached the door it opened. An old guard appeared from inside. He had grey hair and rather Semitic features. I stood where I was, but he walked up to me, and said, not unkindly, "Don't you see the sign?"

I said, "Yes, but couldn't you make an exception just for this afternoon? We have with us a most distinguished guest who has come to this city with a message of world peace."

The old guard looked at 'Abdu'l-Bahá with much interest and said, "He reminds me of the Prophets of Israel, of Isaiah and Daniel." I said to him, "His name is 'Abdu'l-Bahá, the Servant of God. We sometimes call Him the Master." The guard continued to look at 'Abdu'l-Bahá. Finally he said, "I feel sure that it would be all right for him to come through this door."

The Master came towards us with my mother and the Persian friends following Him. The guard led us through the door up into the main hall of the museum. The Master looked up at the huge whale suspended from the ceiling. He said with much amusement, "Fifty Jonahs could have gotten into that whale." Then the guard showed us an exhibition of old Mexican Art. The Master said, "A great similarity between the art of Mexico and Egypt exists because at one time what is now Egypt and Mexico were joined together. A holocaust separated them."

The Master stayed only for a short time in the museum. He walked in front of us down the steps, through the side door and onto the grass, where He sat down with His back against a tree.

The old guard came up to me and said, "Do you think that your friend would mind if I went over and spoke to him?" I told him that I was sure that He would be very glad if he did. The old guard walked over and stood beside 'Abdu'l-Bahá. "Is it all right for me to sit here?" the Master asked. "I am sure that it is," said the guard. "Don't you want to sit down here with me?" said the Master. "Oh! no, that would never do," said the guard, "but after you have rested for a while, would you like to come into the museum again and see some of the other exhibitions?"

The Master replied, "No, I have seen enough for to-day. Often

I get tired of this world and yearn to explore the other worlds of God. May I ask you this? If you could choose either to be in this world or in the next, which one would you take?"

After a moment of thought the old guard answered, "I think that I would stay in this world because I am sure of it." "Would you?" said the Master, "I'd take the next world. When one goes there it will be like going to the second floor of a house. One will still know of this world, and yet be in the next." The old guard remarked, "I had never thought of that before."

The Master said good-bye to the old guard warmly, but to my surprise He did not ask him to a meeting where he might meet the friends. Two or three days later I went to see the old guard. He wasn't there any more. A young guard had taken his place and had never heard of the old guard before.

Much moved by this story, I asked Juliet to tell us another one. She looked at me and smiled with understanding, and began again. She said:

Some of the Bahá'ís, including myself, decided to give the Master a birthday party, and a few of them baked a cake. We took several taxis to the Bronx, with the Master riding in the first one. As soon as His taxi had arrived there, the Master got out and walked into the park ahead of the rest of us.

A group of young boys gathered around Him and started to laugh. Two or three of them threw stones at Him. With natural concern many of the friends hurried towards the Master, but he told them to stay away. The boys came closer to the Master, jeered at Him and pulled at His clothes. The Master did not become cross. He merely smiled at them radiantly, but the boys continued to behave as before. Then the Master turned towards the friends. "Bring me the cake," he said. No one had mentioned to Him that we had brought a cake.

Some of us said, "But 'Abdu'l-Bahá, the cake is for your birthday." He repeated, "Bring me the cake." A friend uncovered a large sponge cake, with white icing, and gave it to the Master. As soon as the boys had seen the cake they began to calm down, and stared at the cake hungrily.

The Master took it in His hands and looked at the cake with pleasure. The boys were now standing quietly around Him. "Bring me a knife," said the Master. A friend brought Him a knife. The Master counted the number of boys who were standing around Him and then cut the cake into the same number of pieces. Each boy eagerly took a piece, ate it with relish, and then ran away happily.

Juliet was born in Washington D.C. in 1873, and from childhood she showed talent for painting. Her parents sent her to the Corcoran Art School in Washington, but when she was almost twelve her father died. He left his family little money. Fortunately Juliet was already able to sell her portraits in pastel. By the time that she was sixteen, although she had not yet completed her training, she had gained a fine reputation for her work.

One afternoon when I was alone with Juliet, I asked her how she had heard about the Bahá'í Faith. "When I was a young girl living in New York I became seriously sick with diphtheria," she said. "One evening, while I was lying in bed, I heard the doctor say to mother from the next room, 'Juliet is dying.' When I went to sleep that night I did not expect to wake up again. I had a dream and in it I saw a most wonderful-looking man. He said to me with complete assurance, 'You will get well.' By the next morning my fever had gone away. In two or three days I had almost recovered. I did not know who this man was nor did I know how to find out. Several years after this experience I went to study art at the Sorbonne in Paris. While I was there I saw a photograph that I knew was of Him. Someone told me, 'He is 'Abdu'l-Bahá, The Servant of God.' I became a believer in 1901."

Juliet did not say more to me about her conversion. But others have recorded that in 1901 Alice Barney, the mother of Laura Clifford Barney, generously invited Juliet to come to Paris with her mother and brother and study art there. In that city Juliet became close to May Bolles, the first Bahá'í who lived in Europe, Lua Getsinger, 'the mother teacher of the west,' Thomas Breakwell, the first English believer, Hippolyte Dreyfus-Barney, the first French believer, who adopted the surname of his wife Laura, and the great teacher Mírzá Abu'l-Faḍl, from Persia, whom the Master had sent to France. Deep study with Mírzá Abu'l-Faḍl and May Bolles greatly helped to confirm Juliet in the Faith and she became one of the distinguished group of Bahá'ís just mentioned.

After she had finished her studies at the Sorbonne, Juliet

returned to New York with her mother and brother. Service to the Cause of God now became the major aim of her life. Possessed of rare spiritual attraction, she taught the Faith with much love to all those who seemed to her 'seekers of truth.' Many have recorded that the regular meetings at her studio brought great happiness to countless people who attended them.

Ever since recognizing the station of Bahá'u'lláh, Juliet had longed to make a pilgrimage to the Holy Land and meet the Master. In 1909 her precious opportunity came to do this with two close friends, Edward and Carrie Kinney, their two sons, Howard and Sanford, and Alice Beede. From 2nd July 1909, two days after Juliet first met the Master in 'Akká, until 5th December 1912, the day of His sailing from New York City and the last time that she met Him in this physical world, she wrote a vivid and thrilling diary of her personal encounters with Him and what she saw Him do.

During her visit at the House of 'Abbúd in 'Akká she wrote:

Our Lord called Carrie, Alice, and me separately to His room and gave us the priceless privilege of seeing Him dictate Tablets. I sat on the divan, my eyes upon His white-robed figure—I could scarcely raise them to His Face—as He paced up and down that small room with His strong tread. Never had the room seemed so small—never had He appeared so mighty! A lion in a cage? Ah no! That room contain Him? Why!—as I felt that great dominant Force, that *Energy of God*, I knew that the earth itself could not contain Him. Nor yet the universe. No! While the body, charged with a Power I have seen in no *human* being, restless with the Force that so animated it, strode up and down, up and down in that tiny room, pausing sometimes before the window below which the sea beat against the double seawall, I knew that the Spirit was free as the Essence Itself, brooding over regions far distant, looking deep into hearts at the uttermost ends of the earth, consoling their secret sorrows, answering the whispers of far-off minds.

Often in that walk back and forth He would give me a long, grave glance. Once He smiled at me.[1]

During a visit with Him a little over two years later in August 1911, at the Hotel du Parc, Thonon, on Lake Geneva, she wrote, ".... I said to myself as I looked on that Celestial radiance, if He never gave me so much as a word, if He never glanced my way, just to see that sweetness shining before me, I would follow Him on my knees, crawling behind Him in the dust forever!" [2]

On Fifth Avenue and Tenth Street in New York, just half a block from the house where Juliet and her mother lived, stands the Church of the Ascension, so called because of the beautiful and famous painting of the Ascension of Jesus Christ that hangs on the wall above the altar. Before she became a Bahá'í, and for many years afterwards, Juliet often attended this church. Juliet once said to me, "I was very much in love with the Rector, Dr. Percy Grant, and wanted to marry him." Of course, she earnestly hoped and often prayed that he would become a Bahá'í.

On 11th April 1912 the Master arrived in New York. Thanks to Juliet's suggestion, Dr. Grant asked Him to address the congregation on the following Sunday morning. According to notes in *The Promulgation of Universal Peace*, he started His talk by saying, "In his scriptural lesson this morning the revered Doctor read a verse from the Epistle of St. Paul to the Corinthians, 'For now we see through a glass darkly, but then face to face!'" [3] With clarity and force the Master explained what Bahá'u'lláh had come to do and His relationship to Jesus Christ.

Juliet continued, "At the end of the Master's talk Percy asked the choir to sing, 'Jesus Christ is risen to-day.' I hurried into the vestry and waited impatiently for Percy to appear. When he did the suspense became unbearable. 'Juliet,' he said, 'I did it all for you.' My heart sank. I was almost sure that I could never marry him. He did not come into the Faith."

The Bowery Mission in New York was a place of refuge for poor derelicts who often slept on park benches or doorsteps. Her mother had forbidden Juliet to give the message there. In February 1912 for the first time in her life she deceived her mother. Accompanied by a close friend, Silvia Gannett, Juliet went there and gave a talk. When she had finished speaking Dr. Hallimond said, "We have heard from Miss Juliet

Thompson that 'Abdu'l-Bahá will be here in April. How many of you would like to invite Him to speak at the Mission?"[4] The whole three hundred rose to their feet.

On His acceptance of this invitation, the Master gave Juliet a thousand franc note to change into American quarters and asked her to meet Him on the following evening at the Mission with these quarters in a bag. She and Edward Getsinger, both carrying a huge bag of quarters, arrived there promptly and sat down with the other believers on the platform behind Him.

Although Juliet felt unworthy to introduce the Master, she obeyed Dr. Hallimond and did so. In a most moving and compassionate address, the Master assured these broken men that the mercies and bounties of God were always with them. At the end of the service the Master and those who had come with Him walked down the aisle together to the main door. When they had reached it, the Master turned to Juliet and Edward and asked them to hold open their bags of silver and stand on either side of him. Juliet recorded, "Then down the aisle streamed a sodden and grimy procession—three hundred men in single file .... Broken forms. Blurred faces .... Into each palm, as the Master clasped it, He pressed His little gift of silver—just a symbol and the price of a bed. Not a man was shelterless that night. And many, many, I could see, found a shelter in His Heart."[5]

When Juliet was ten years old, she began to dream and pray that someday she would be able to paint the Christ and make Him look not just sweet and ineffectual like some artists had done, but like 'The King of Men'. As soon as she had met the Master, she gave up all hope of doing this. She felt that it would be impossible. In the city of Washington one evening late in April, the Master invited Juliet to paint Him. He promised to give her three half hours. On June 1st, at His apartment in New York City, He posed for her for the first time. Juliet has described this occasion:[6]

The Master was seated in a dark corner, His black 'abá melting into the background—and again I saw Him as the *Face of God*— and *quailed*. How could *I* paint the Face of God? "I want you," He said, "to paint My *Servitude* to God."

"Oh! my Lord," I cried, "only the Holy Spirit could paint *Your* Servitude to God. No human hand could do it. Pray for me, or I am *lost*. I implore You, inspire me."

"I will pray," He answered, "and as you are doing this only for the sake of God, you will be inspired."

And then something amazing happened. All fear fell away from me, and it was as though Someone Else saw through my eyes, worked through my hand.

All the points, all the planes in that matchless Face were so clear to me that my hand couldn't put them down quickly enough— couldn't keep pace with the clarity of my vision. I painted in ecstasy—free as I had never been before.

Although the Master gave Juliet twice the sittings that He had promised her, she actually finished His portrait in three.

Juliet was always with the Master whenever it was possible for Him to see her. On 15th November 1912, less than a month before His departure from the United States, He gave a most powerful and comprehensive talk in her house. He said that He would speak on "the distinctive characteristics of the manifestation of BAHA'U'LLAH .... and prove that from every standpoint His cause is distinguished from all others."[7]

The great pain that Juliet felt on the morning of His departure from New York only became intensified when He could not assure her that she would again attain His physical presence. In June 1916, the Master revealed a Tablet for Juliet:[8]

To the maid-servant of God, Miss Juliet Thompson—Upon her be greeting and praise!

He is God!

O thou beloved daughter of the Kingdom!

Thy letter was received. It contained the most great glad tidings—that is, praise be to God, in New York the divine believers are united and agreed. For my heart there is no greater happiness than the unity and concord of the friends. The progress of the world of humanity and the illumination of the hearts and lives of the people are realized through unity and agreement and the promotion of the Word of God. Difference destroys the foundation of the divine edifice, causing coldness amongst the souls and the lethargy of all the active members. I hope that, day by day, this bounty may become more revealed in New York. Truly, I say, if the believers of God become united together with heart and soul, in a short while they will shine forth like unto the sun; they will obtain a joy and happiness the splendor of which will be cast upon all the regions of America.

Like all deeply spiritual people Juliet found even the thought of war abhorrent. When the First World War dragged on in Europe and she realized that the United States was gradually coming closer to a direct involvement, she spoke out against it. Only the absence of the Master's permission kept her from appealing to President Wilson personally. In a Tablet revealed after the war on 30th December 1918 the Master advised her, "Do ye not refer regarding any matter in these days to the President of the Republic." [9]

Juliet once said to me, "I was anxious to teach the Faith in prisons. The Master did not encourage me to do this. He said that I should work hard in my profession, and give my free time to the Cause." A Tablet from the Master, which Shoghi Effendi translated on 4th April 1919, included the following council: "O thou Juliet! Endeavor in thy profession that thou mayest secure comfort for thy respected mother." [10]

Although Juliet often wrote to the Master and received from Him Tablets that clearly showed His deep love for her and His appreciation of her services, she was not able to visit Him again. In 1926, about five years after His passing, she next made the pilgrimage and shared with her attractive young companion, Mary Maxwell (Amatu'l-Bahá Rúḥíyyih Khánum), the priceless privilege of meeting the Guardian, Shoghi Effendi.

During her first pilgrimage to the Holy Land, Juliet had been drawn to walk down a little known path that led to a small dome-shaped house. She was thrilled to learn that Mary of Magdala was said to have lived where this house stood. The Master told Juliet the true story of this Mary, and in the late nineteen-thirties Juliet wrote a most moving book about her entitled *I, Mary Magdalen*.

While Mary was living happily with her only lover, the Gentile, Novatus, "general of the Roman legions in Judea, half-brother to Rome's philosopher, Seneca,"[11] John of Capernaum brought her word that he had seen the Messiah and urged her to come and see Him.

Although at her first meeting with Jesus she was not sure if He "were indeed Messiah, or some false prophet to be forgot,"[12] she became impatient to see Him again. On her second visit to Jesus she found His teachings gloomy and felt that they could only offer her trouble. What He said also implied that her relationship with Novatus was adulterous. She could not accept this judgment as correct. With no intention of going to see Jesus again, she returned to her lover, to enjoy for a while unclouded human happiness. She shut out thoughts of Jesus when they came. Soon, however, vivid dreams of Him greatly troubled her. Again she was filled with a passionate desire to see Him. During a third visit she passed from doubt into certainty and, without knowing why, she recognized her Lord. Immediately afterwards she met with Him alone.

Juliet recounted this beautiful scene much as she did one of her own first meetings with 'Abdu'l-Bahá in her journal. In a concluding passage she wrote: "I looked up to behold Him— His hands raised in blessing above my head, His face uplifted in prayer, His eyes closed, His lips apart. Then He held my head against His heart .... and I, Mary of Magdala, heard the heart of Jesus beat."[13]

Juliet has vividly described the great suffering of Jesus in the Garden of Gethsemane, Mary's appeal to Claudia, the wife of Pilate, to save Jesus from crucifixion, the walk with Him to Golgotha, the crucifixion itself, the meeting of Mary with her Lord in His heavenly body near the threshold of His tomb, her meeting with John directly afterwards, to whom the Lord had also just spoken, and their efforts, at first unsuccessful, to convince the ten other disciples that Jesus would be with them forever.

This fascinating book is bound to attract more and more readers. Written with a fine understanding of the eternal relationship between Mary Magdalen and her Lord, its beautiful account of her transformation from the gentle, appealing mistress of Novatus to the saintly disciple of Jesus

Christ will certainly encourage countless people to investigate the Word of God for this day.

In 1939 Juliet wrote a stimulating essay on 'The Valley of Love', the second valley of seven that the soul must pass through on its journey from self to God, as revealed by Bahá'u'lláh in *The Seven Valleys*. In her penetrating analysis of the seeker's state in that valley, Juliet wrote: "He has found the Messenger, has seen for the first time, powerfully reflected, the unclouded Beauty of God. And he has become like a new-born babe in a strange and glorious world." [14]

Besides the precious portrait that Juliet gave of the Master in her diaries she wrote a remarkable essay about Him, entitled 'Abdu'l-Bahá, The Center of the Covenant.' It is composed of a touching account of His life, and a clear and forceful explanation of His station. "When 'Abdu'l-Bahá ascended in 1921 to His 'original abode,' plunging the Bahá'í world into such grief as is only felt once in an age, when disciples mourn their Lord, His last Will and Testament came as a complete surprise, an inestimable bounty to His confused and desolate believers. For in it He appointed His own grandson, the beloved Shoghi Effendi, as the Guardian of the Bahá'í Faith and His successor as sole Interpreter of the sacred Books. So we found our Faith still safeguarded from schisms and dissensions—still led through a Focal Point of 'unerring guidance.'" [15]

With rare compassion Juliet tried to help everyone whom she met, irrespective of their present character or past life. She gave much attention to the maladjusted and to moral failures. She did not judge people. When she heard that two people who had apparently betrayed their country were about to be executed she said, "I feel sorry for them. I am praying for them." She once told a sincere believer who had a serious psychological problem that he was trying to overcome, "When I reach the kingdom I will speak to the Master about you."

In obedience to the Master's words, she had grown to love all people. In spite of this she did not naively think that even the believers always behave well, and also realized that they sometimes hurt each other. One afternoon when I was sitting with Juliet, a young pianist who was an agnostic joined us and attacked the Faith violently. I became angry and could not understand why Juliet put up with him. She just smiled and looked at her friend with fondness unmixed with irritation. After he had left, I asked her, "Doesn't he disturb you?" She said strongly, "He doesn't affect me in the least."

Juliet firmly believed that, in the future, all of humanity would come into the Bahá'í community. She realized, however, that the world had so far veiled most people and that it might take them a long time to cast off these veils. Once I said to her, "Since I last saw you I have found several young people who show interest in the Faith." She firmly corrected me. "You mean that the Master brought them to you."

During part of the Second World War Juliet and Daisy Smyth went as pioneer Bahá'í teachers to Mexico. After the war was over they spent some time teaching in New Orleans, Louisiana. On my return to New York City from Los Angeles in June 1953, a few weeks after the start of the Guardian's Ten Year Crusade, I went to see them. They now lived in an apartment next to the graveyard of St. Mark's in the Bowery. Situated on the first floor, this long and narrow apartment had high ceilings and big windows. Their bedrooms were on opposite sides of the living room. Comfortably seated in Juliet's bedroom, they greeted me warmly. Juliet said, "We wrote to Shoghi Effendi and asked him if we should pioneer. He answered that we should as soon as I am well enough to go." In the meantime the two ladies planned to hold fireside meetings in their new apartment. Much to their disappointment, Juliet's doctor advised them to wait until her health had improved. When I left for my pilgrimage in early January 1955 the two ladies still hoped that they would be able to pioneer. On the last night of my pilgrimage at dinner, I said, "Shoghi Effendi, Juliet Thompson and Daisy Smyth are most anxious to leave the City of the Covenant according to your instructions, but Juliet's frail health keeps her in bed most of the time." With his perfect understanding he said, "Tell them to get the best medical aid possible for Juliet and not to worry. Say that I thank her for her past services." Soon

A GROUP OF BAHÁ'ÍS IN LONDON, C. 1912

Front row, left to right: Miss Phillips, unknown, Mary Basil Hall

Middle row, left to right: Mrs. Ginman, Mrs. C. Morris, Ethel Rosenberg,
Lady Blomfield, Miss Elizabeth Herrick

Back row, left to right: Yu'hanná Dávúd, Miss Beatrice Platt, unknown,
Arthur Cuthbert, Lutfu'lláh Hakim, Mr. Jenner, M. S. Hakim

ETHEL ROSENBERG

THOMAS BREAKWELL
from a photograph of the first Bahá'í group in Europe, Paris, *circa* 1902

JULIET THOMPSON
in her studio

ROY WILHELM
at the time of his last illness

LADY BLOMFIELD

FRED MORTENSEN

ALBERT HEATH HALL

after my return to New York I went to see them, and told them what the Guardian had advised.

On the evening of 2nd December 1956, during a meeting of the Spiritual Assembly of New York, a telephone call came from Daisy informing us that Juliet was dead. The funeral took place on the following Saturday morning. About a hundred and fifty Bahá'ís, and a few people not in the Faith, attended the service. Borrah Kavelin, at that time Treasurer of the National Spiritual Assembly of the United States, and I were privileged to conduct it.

Mr. Kavelin read the Guardian's most moving message, mixed with grief and joy:[16] "Deplore loss much-loved, greatly admired Juliet Thompson, outstanding, exemplary handmaid 'Abdu'l-Bahá. Over half-century record manifold, meritorious services, embracing concluding years Heroic, opening decades Formative Age Bahá'í Dispensation, won her enviable position glorious company triumphant disciples beloved Master Abhá Kingdom. Advise hold memorial gathering Mashriqu'l-Adhkár pay befitting tribute imperishable memory one so wholly consecrated Faith Bahá'u'lláh, fired such consuming devotion Center His Covenant. (Signed) Shoghi."

When the burial service in the afternoon began, the sky was dark. It was raining a little. The branches of the pine trees shook in the wind. As I started to read the following passage from a prayer for the departed, the sky brightened and the sun came out. It shone on Juliet's coffin and her grave. "O Thou who art the Lord of all men! Grant then, O my God, that Thy servant may consort with Thy chosen ones, Thy saints and Thy Messengers in heavenly places that the pen cannot tell nor the tongue recount."

Juliet once described to me the death of a believer in these words: "He has taken a little trip to the Kingdom." In the Abhá Kingdom could she not be helping many of us? Maybe the Master has asked her to wander spiritually through this earthly planet in search of all those who are looking for the Spirit of Truth.

Roy Wilhelm

ROY WILHELM WAS BORN IN ZANESVILLE, Ohio, on 17th
September 1875. Although he did not remember that she ever
attended church, his maternal grandmother always showed a
deep interest in religion. When Roy was still a child, she
spoke to him of Bible prophecies which she felt were in the
process of fulfilment. Convinced that the 'Promised Age' was
near, she advised him and all those to whom she felt close
to watch carefully so that they would "recognize the Great
Day when it came." [1] Like his grandmother, Roy's parents
had unorthodox opinions. They belonged to a church, however, and naturally took him to its services. About 1890,
because of her growing dissatisfaction with all Christian
doctrine, Roy's mother, Laurie, began a thorough investigation of other religious teachings and philosophies. She soon
agreed whole-heartedly with what her mother had said.

According to Doris Holley, who knew the Wilhelms well,
when Roy was sixteen he jumped from the window of a barn
on to a wagon that he thought only contained hay. But he
landed on a pitchfork. After this tragic accident he always had
a weak back and was often in severe pain. In order to ease
this pain, he would sometimes work standing up.

The Wilhelms lived near a Miss Laura Jones. Thinking
much the same on spiritual matters, she and Mrs. Wilhelm
became close friends. The two ladies often discussed what was
to them a strong possibility, that "the Spirit might be upon
the earth at this time," [2] and asked each other how they
could find Him. About 1895, Miss Jones moved to Chicago. A
few years later she sent her friend several Bahá'í pamphlets,
one of which consisted of some selections from *The Hidden*

Words, and a letter informing her that Bahá'u'lláh was the Promised One for Whom they had been seeking. As soon as she had read these pamphlets and the letter, Mrs. Wilhelm became convinced that her friend was right.

About 1898 or 1899, while Roy was working as a travelling salesman for his father's coffee company, he received from his mother a photograph of 'Abdu'l-Bahá and a short, vaguely written article about Him, from the page of a newspaper. Accustomed to her "various explorations", he was not much impressed with either the photograph or the article. He merely wrote upon the margin of the page, "Strange if true" [3] and returned the clipping to her.

In 1900, Roy moved to New York. During the next two years, on numerous occasions when his mother and father were visiting him, the Wilhelms went to Bahá'í meetings in that city.

During September 1901, the illustrious Arthur Pillsbury Dodge and his wife, Elizabeth Ann, recently returned from 'Akká where they had spent nine days with the Master, rented a large house at 261 West 139th Street. This house, which was open to all of the friends, became famous as a Bahá'í home. Roy and his parents were often guests there. Although most of the believers who gathered at the Dodges' house had only a limited knowledge of the teachings, they still taught the seekers with great fervour and intelligence. Roy has written, "I was conscious of a strong heart attraction before much understanding came." [4]

As her devotion to the Cause increased, Mrs. Wilhelm spent more and more of her free hours in teaching. She was soon carrying on a steady correspondence with believers and enquirers in various parts of the world.

In April 1907, Roy and his mother made the pilgrimage and stayed with 'Abdu'l-Bahá in the prison house. A year later, Roy wrote an impression of this pilgrimage which he entitled "Knock and it shall be opened unto you". (Matt. 7 : 7) On the front cover of this short booklet he placed a reproduction of a photograph which he had taken of 'Abdu'l-Bahá's doorway. He recorded: "At the right of 'Abdu'l-Bahá's room was a small room in which he often dictated to

His secretaries. His room adjoined ours on the second floor with dining-room between. I was not well in those days, often wakeful, and I would hear 'Abdu'l-Bahá about working much through the nights as well as days." [5]

On one occasion the Master came to see them in their room. With a warm welcome He led His new guests to the divan and asked them to sit on it beside Him. With Mrs. Wilhelm's hand in His own and with His arm around Roy, He spoke to them in Persian through an interpreter. His first question was this: "How are the believers?" They answered: "They are well and are becoming more united." The Master then said: "This news is the cause of my happiness, for the more they are united the more they will receive God's confirmation." [6]

At this same meeting the Master said to them: "In you I see all the American believers. Your faces are shining.... Thank God that you came." They replied: "We do thank God and hope to become worthy." He answered: "You will become more worthy." [7]

Every day of the six that Laurie and Roy remained in the prison house other pilgrims came to their room, who often recounted stories of their priceless experiences with Bahá'u'-lláh, and other stories too of the early days of His Revelation.

At the evening meal, which began at nine, 'Abdu'l-Bahá always spoke to His guests and the members of His household. One evening when He was describing the spiritual authority of Jesus Christ the Master concluded, according to Roy: "When Christ passed away, He had eleven disciples. The greatest among them was Peter and he denied Christ three times, but when Bahá'u'lláh departed He had a hundred thousand believers who were calling out Yá-Bahá'u'l-Abhá while they were under swords and daggers, and in these late years many men and women in Yazd were killed by inches without uttering a single cry or complaint, but rather called out the Greatest Name. From these incidents we may judge the future of this Revelation." [8]

Roy has written, "During our last meal 'Abdu'l-Bahá broke a quantity of bread into His bowl; then asking for the plates of the pilgrims He gave to each of us a portion. When the meal was finished, He said: I have given you to eat from My bowl—now distribute My Bread among the people." [9]

In 1908 Roy and his father transferred the main office of their successful coffee company from the Middle West to Wall Street in New York City. Early in the winter of that year, the Wilhelms moved to a charming house in West Englewood, New Jersey. Father and son commuted each day to the city. During the following summer the Wilhelms gave a picnic in the lovely evergreen grove beside their house to which more than a hundred Bahá'ís came from neighbouring towns.

As Roy has remarked, "In those days it was very difficult to awaken interest." [10] His and one or two other families held regular meetings in their homes. Only after several years of teaching did the believers succeed in establishing a permanent group there.

During 'Abdu'l-Bahá's third visit to New York, on 20th June 1912, He said to the friends who had gathered to see Him: "I am about to leave the city for a few days' rest at Montclair. When I return it is my wish to give a large feast of unity. A place for it has not yet been found. It must be outdoors under the trees, in some location away from city noise; like a Persian garden. The food will be Persian food. When the place is arranged all will be informed and we will have a general meeting in which hearts will be bound together, spirits blended and a new foundation for unity established. All the friends will come. They will be my guests." [11]

The Master decided to hold this Feast in the grounds of the Wilhelms' house. Leaving on the train from Montclair early in the morning of 29th June, 'Abdu'l-Bahá arrived at their house around noon. Tired from His journey, which had taken several hours on four different trains, He rested for a while in the room where He was going to spend the night.

On that same morning the much-loved Juliet Thompson and her dear friend, Silvia Gannett, travelled by train from New York to West Englewood. Juliet has written in her precious diary: "We walked up from the little station, through the sweet, wild country, past the grove where the tables were set for the feast, a great circle cleared of underbrush, shady and fragrant with tall pine-trees, in the midst of tangled woods; then on up to the house where he was, he whose presence filled our eyes with light and without whom our days had been very dim and lifeless! Ah, there he was again!—sitting in a corner of the porch! I sped across the lawn forgetting Silvia, forgetting everything. He looked down at me with grave eyes—and I saw a fathomless welcome in them ...." [12]

A few moments later the Master walked down to the grove. He sat under a large tree, with a poor, old, humble, spiritually beautiful woman on one side of Him, and a rich, charming devoted young woman on the other. Well over two hundred Bahá'ís gathered in circles around Him. He gave them a simple, direct, uplifting talk that has now become immortal. In part He said: "This is a new Day and this hour is a new Hour in which we have come together. .... This assembly has a name and significance which will last forever. Hundreds of thousands of meetings shall be held to commemorate this occasion and the very words I speak to you today shall be repeated in them for ages to come .... Be happy and joyous because the bestowals of God are intended for you and the life of the Holy Spirit is breathing upon you .... May you become as the waves of one sea, stars of the same heaven, fruits adorning the same tree, roses of one garden; in order that through you the oneness of humanity may establish its temple in the world of mankind, for you are the ones who are called to uplift the cause of unity among the nations of the earth." [13]

By the time He had finished His address, supper was ready. Just as it was announced, however, a sudden storm erupted. According to Juliet, the Master, followed by the Persian friends, walked away from the group and down the road to a crossroads where someone had left a chair. As the Persians gathered around Him, He took the chair and sat down on it, and raised His face to the sky. The ominous signs of a storm soon disappeared.

The Master Himself served the friends supper. Afterwards as He mingled with the guests, He anointed each one with attar of rose. Early in the evening He left the friends and took a long walk by Himself. When He returned to the house it was already dark. Almost sixty friends were waiting to see Him, either on the porch or on the front lawn. Seated in a chair on the top step of the porch He spoke to them again. The Master spent that night and the next one at the Wilhelms' house.

On a second visit there, the Master, accompanied by Roy and his parents, went to dinner at the neighbouring home of Louis Bourgeois, the distinguished French-Canadian architect and future designer of the Mother Temple of the West.

On June 29th of the next year the Bahá'ís of New York City and its surrounding communities gave a Feast at the Wilhelms' house to celebrate the one just described.

In a Tablet which He revealed to Roy from Ramleh in Egypt in answer to his letter of 13th July 1913, the Master expressed His happiness that this divine Feast had taken place. He wrote: "That annual memorial meeting will be the souvenir of Abdul-Baha, especially when it is passed with infinite delight and gladness." [14]

During the early years of this century the believers of the West could only obtain a small amount of Bahá'í literature. They usually had to rely for their reading and private study upon certain prayers and tablets which were typed, copied, and then distributed. Intensely aware of the great need that both Bahá'ís and seekers had for more of the Holy Writings, Roy made many compilations of them, had these writings printed in pamphlets, and arranged for them to be easily available to all those who wanted them.

At the first Bahá'í Convention of America, which was held during March of 1909 in Chicago, the delegates established a permanent national organization called the Bahá'í Temple Unity, and an Executive Board was elected at this same Convention. Roy served on this board of nine members from that time on for the whole of its existence, except for one year when he was prevented by illness. When, in 1922, the Bahá'í Temple Unity was replaced by the National Spiritual Assembly, he was elected to that body also, and served on it in every succeeding year until in 1946, at the age of seventy-one, he retired from administrative work.

The revered Hand of the Cause Horace Holley has referred in these words to Roy's service as Treasurer of these two bodies: ".... the integrity of his character and the simple, direct humaneness of his exposition of financial matters brought about a rapid development of the Bahá'í fund as an organic institution of the community."[15]

Roy often spoke at the Annual Convention. According to the minutes of the eighth one, which took place from 29th April to 2nd May 1916 at the Auditorium Hotel in Chicago, he remarked to the assembled delegates and friends: "Abdul-Baha said to me in New York, that if from the beginning we had lived up to the Bahai principles in New York and had actively delivered this message to others—yes, if we had lived and proclaimed one of the Bahai principles, it would have made such a spiritual impression that by this time one half of New York City would have been Bahai. So I sharpened my pencil and figured out that if I had done my part 7183 would have caught the Bahai spirit."[16]

In the following portion of a Tablet which the Master revealed for Roy on 27th December 1916, from Haifa, He certainly expressed satisfaction with his efforts: "O thou My heavenly son! Several letters and cards have been received from thee, and each one indicated thy firmness and steadfastness in the love of God. Praise be to God, that that illumined youth is like unto an enkindled candle and hast dedicated thy life in the service of the Kingdom of God, and day by day thou art adding to thy illumination and spirituality."[17]

The beloved Martha Root has reported that one of the bright features of the Feast of Riḍván at the next year's Convention was the first display of Roy's attractive Bahá'í booklets, in large and small sizes, which he called respectively by the amusing titles of 'Big Ben' and 'Little Ben'. She mentioned that thousands of these reasonably priced booklets had already been sold. She explained: "The plan is for every Bahai in the United States to keep these at hand and daily put some into circulation."[18]

Soon after the First World War, Roy sent a letter to 'Abdu'l-Bahá. The Master revealed a beautiful Tablet in reply,

which was translated by Shoghi Effendi on 12th December
1918. In the postscript referring to 'Big Bens' and 'Little
Bens' the Master wrote: "The enclosed booklets have been
perused. Send for us one hundred copies of each for they are
exceedingly praiseworthy." He concluded: "Verily, you are
engaged in serving the Cause and thus His Holiness
BAHA'O'LLAH is well pleased with you and I am also satisfied
and content." [19]

As head of his family's coffee company, Roy always used
some carefully selected quotations from the Holy Writings
whenever he put advertisements in trade journals. He also
made frequent business trips for the company. The bulletin of
the Teaching Committee of the United States and Canada
commented in its issue of 19th July 1920: "He left New York
City on June 27th for an extensive trip to the Pacific Coast.
It is supposed to be a business trip, but the greater part of
Roy's thinking and serving is in the greatest business in life—
the Bahai Cause—and as all friends know this, a wave of
rejoicing is set in motion when the friends hear that Roy is
to make a Western business trip, for this means that in every
city where he abides for a time, the glad-tidings will be shared,
and his sisters and brothers in the Cause refreshed and
encouraged." [20]

Roy spoke of the Cause to everyone who would listen to
him. If he was in a restaurant, not content just to teach the
person who was serving him, he would often leave his table
for a while, enter the kitchen and give the message to those
who worked there. He constantly gave booklets and pamphlets
to people. According to A. K. Kalantar, Roy would say, "I'd
like to add this to your library. Read Page .... You'll find
something very interesting in it." [21]

He had a delightful sense of humour. During his talks
to the community, or in public, he often made serious
remarks in an amusing manner that made his audience laugh.
As the esteemed Doris Holley once said to me: "Roy was
pure-hearted. He never seemed to have an evil thought.
He inspired affection and confidence in all those who knew
him."

The ascension of Bahá'u'lláh took place at the hour of

dawn on 29th May 1892. Nine days afterwards, when His Will and Testament was read, it became known that He had appointed His eldest son, 'Abdu'l-Bahá, the Centre of His Covenant. From then until the end of the Master's Ministry ruthless enemies, such as certain members of His own family jealous of His station, tyrannical rulers of Persia and Turkey, and teachers of unusual capacity ambitious for leadership, viciously attacked 'Abdu'l-Bahá with the hope of destroying Him. Encouraged by these powerful enemies of the Cause, some disloyal and malicious persons made strenuous attempts to create a division in the American Community. They only succeeded, however, in misguiding a group of weak, vacillating individuals who had never truly understood the station of the Master.

'Abdu'l-Bahá often strongly advised Roy and others in whom He had great confidence to try to protect the community from the insidious tricks of the Covenant-breakers. During the summer of 1920, He revealed for Roy in a Tablet that ".... thou and all the friends should encourage the souls (people) to become firm in attachment to the Testament and Covenant, for the power of the Covenant brings together and makes them united and harmonious; otherwise every ambitious soul arises to bring about their separation, in order to draw a few souls around himself .... " [22]

The Master expressed His great joy on hearing from Roy that owing to the splendid confirmation which the 'House of Spirituality of New York' had received, the number of the friends there was increasing. In part He wrote, "My hope is that New York may become the center of this great Cause." [23] He also remarked that, while on His journey in America, He had made five visits to New York, and had spent a long time there because of His attachment to that city.

Along with the many urgent matters that the Master often brought to Roy's attention, He sometimes wrote of His love and respect for Roy's mother and father and His concern for their health and welfare. For some years the Master used to send Tablets intended for groups and individuals to Roy, with directions to forward these Tablets to those for whom they were intended.

During those periods of the First World War when 'Abdu'l-Bahá was unable to communicate with the friends in the United States of America because of His isolation in the Holy Land, some Covenant-breakers, who had settled there, renewed their efforts to destroy the American Bahá'í Community. Two weeks before His passing the Master revealed a most persuasive Tablet for the American friends, in which He warned them about those who had risen against the Centre of the Covenant, and pleaded with the friends to be vigilant and awake.

In her invaluable study of the Guardian, *The Priceless Pearl*, the Hand of the Cause Amatu'l-Bahá Rúḥíyyih Khánum records that on 8th November 1921 'Abdu'l-Bahá "cabled Roy Wilhelm, His trusted correspondent, 'How is situation and health friends?' to which Mr. Wilhelm, the next day, was obliged to reply: 'Chicago, Washington, Philadelphia agitating violation centering Fernald, Dyer, Watson. New York, Boston refused join, standing solidly constructive policy.'"[24]

On November 12th, the Master cabled Roy to inform the friends, three of them telegraphically, to stay away from the violators. Later on that same day He sent to Roy what was to be His last message to the American community: "I implore health from divine bounty."[25] As the Hand of the Cause Hasan Balyuzi has simply stated: "The American Bahá'í community remained firm and undivided."[26]

'Abdu'l-Bahá died in the early hours of the morning on 28th November 1921. On this same day Roy received in New York this cable from 'Abdu'l-Bahá's beloved sister, Bahá'íyyih Khánum: "Wilhelmite N.Y. His Holiness Abdul-Baha ascended to Abha Kingdom. Inform friends, Greatest Holy Leaf."[27]

In March 1922 Shoghi Effendi, the newly-appointed Guardian, called together a small group of Bahá'ís from various countries to consult with him in the Holy Land on important matters vital to the future of the Cause. After the Guardian had held long conferences with them for many days, he gave some of the believers definite instructions. He asked Roy Wilhelm and Mountfort Mills, two of the four American believers who were present, to inform the American community at the Fourteenth Annual Convention in Chicago during Riḍván, which was only a few weeks away, "that the Executive Board—the national body of the North American Bahá'ís—was to become a legislative one in function, guiding all national affairs rather than merely implementing decisions and recommendations arrived at in the Annual Convention by delegates in consultation." [28]

When these two American believers had fulfilled the Guardian's instructions, the delegates to this convention elected the first American National Spiritual Assembly.

At the Feast of Riḍván held during this convention, these two recently-returned pilgrims spoke about Shoghi Effendi. As reported by the Hand of the Cause Louis Gregory, Roy stated in part:

"Abdul-Baha says: 'God created the world; man worked out the boundaries.' No one in the world today, except the Bahai who has the universal, selfless mind, can see without prejudice. He has no interest save the happiness of all. When one reaches Haifa and meets Shoghi Effendi and sees the workings of his mind and heart, his wonderful spirit and grasp of things, it is truly marvelous. Our world boundaries must fade!" [29]

Ever since the first issue of 'Star of the West' had appeared in 1910, the Master had greatly encouraged its publication, not only as a source of information about events in the Faith, but also for its inspiring articles. Anxious for 'Star of the West' to become a major contribution to the Faith, in his letter of 5th March 1922 to the American believers, the Guardian asked them to transfer its direction from a group of friends to "a special board, elected by the National Body" always to be under this body's "constant and general supervision." [30] According to his direction, the newly-established National Spiritual Assembly elected Roy and four others to a committee for this purpose. On the following December 23rd, after more members had been added to this committee, the Guardian wrote to the National Spiritual Assembly: "Regarding the Star of the West, I wish to congratulate in particular the members of the Publishing

Committee on the quality of their work. I have perused with particular interest the last numbers of the Magazine and am glad to note an encouraging improvement in its management, its style, its general presentation and the nature and number of its articles." [31]

On this same day, in a letter to the English friends, he made reference to Dr. John Esslemont's immortal work, then in progress, *Bahá'u'lláh and the New Era*. The Guardian wrote: "I am enclosing various suggestions of Mr. Dreyfus-Barney and Mr. Roy Wilhelm, made by them at my request, during their last sojourn in the Holy Land. I submit them to Dr. Esslemont's consideration as well as to that of the Spiritual Assembly." [32]

Roy was a close friend of Martha Root's. He often gave this "Star-Servant of the Cause of Bahá'u'lláh" generous help in her extensive travels to other continents. At the end of her second teaching tour of Europe, which started in January of 1932 and lasted until the middle of 1936, the Guardian sent her back to the United States, so that she might take a much-needed rest. She stayed with the Wilhelms for two months at their home in West Englewood.

Laurie Wilhelm died in 1937. According to Roy, soon after she had recognized the station of Bahá'u'lláh until the end of her life, even during the last two years and a half, when she was physically helpless, and the final weeks when she could speak only with much difficulty, "her mind was centered upon means for the advancement of the Faith." He concluded: "It is indeed comforting to now have the assurance of the Guardian that Mother is making a near approach to the Beloved." [33]

A portrait of Roy (between pp. 36 & 37) shows a face of enormous charm. His expression certainly indicates deep spirituality, a warm, lovable nature, and a subtle, infectious sense of humour. [34] I think that many people who had only seen this portrait, even without knowing who he was, would say, "There is someone whom I would like to have known." The Master once wrote to Roy, "The sight of your portrait brought joy to My heart, because it is luminous and celestial ...." [35]

Four days after Roy's death on 24th December 1951, the Guardian cabled the following message to the American Bahá'í Community:[36] "Heart filled sorrow loss greatly prized, much loved, highly admired herald Bahá'u'lláh's Covenant, Roy Wilhelm. Distinguished career enriched annals concluding years Heroic opening years Formative Age Faith. Sterling qualities endeared him to his beloved Master, 'Abdu'l-Bahá. His saintliness, indomitable faith, outstanding services local, national, international, exemplary devotion qualify him join ranks Hands Cause, insure him everlasting reward Abhá Kingdom. Advise hold memorial gathering Temple befitting his unforgettable services lofty rank."

Lady Blomfield

IN HER INSPIRING, RICHLY informative book about certain phases of Bahá'í history, *The Chosen Highway*, Sara Louisa, Lady Blomfield, named Sitárih Khánum by 'Abdu'l-Bahá, has given an account of the first time that she and her daughter Mary, called Parvine by Him, heard the Bahá'í Faith mentioned. At a reception given by Madame Lucien Monod at her house in Paris in 1907, an attractive young guest, Miss Bertha Herbert, after seating herself between them, said to the Blomfields, "We have been taught to believe that a great Messenger would again be sent to the world: He would set forth to gather together all the peoples of good will in every race, nation, and religion on the earth. Now is the appointed time! He has come! He has come!" [1]

Lady Blomfield wrote, "These amazing words struck a chord to which my inner consciousness instantly responded, and I felt convinced that the portentous announcement they conveyed was indeed the truth. Great awe and intense exaltation possessed me with an overpowering force as I listened." [2]

Assured by Lady Blomfield that she and Mary were deeply interested in her remarks, Miss Herbert soon made an appointment for them to meet a gifted miniature painter, Miss Ethel Rosenberg, the second woman in the British Isles to enter the Faith, and a distinguished scholar, Hippolyte Dreyfus, the first French believer. These two remarkable people gave the Blomfields much information about the Faith.

On their return to London, they became acquainted with Mrs. Thornburgh-Cropper, the first Bahá'í in the British Isles. She and Ethel Rosenberg held meetings with the Blomfields

101

to make plans for spreading the message. After hearing about the Revelation of Bahá'u'lláh, Lady Blomfield's foremost aim became to serve His Cause.

Mary has described her mother: "At this time she had the beauty of a mature soul. The moulding of her face was lovely .... Her facial expressions, ever changing, reflected the spiritual harmony within .... She wore garments with long flowing lines which made her seem taller than her natural height ...." [3]

Early in August 1911, when 'Abdu'l-Bahá was still in Egypt, but preparing to leave for Europe, she sent Him an invitation to stay at her house at 97 Cadogan Gardens in London. A few days later, she received the following telegram in reply: "'Abdu'l-Bahá arriving in London 8th September. Can Lady Blomfield receive Him?" [4]

Lady Blomfield has written that when 'Abdu'l-Bahá entered her house, "A silence as of love and awe overcame us, as we looked at Him .... One saw, as in a clear vision, that He had so wrought all good and mercy that the inner grace of Him had grown greater than all outer sign, and the radiance of this inner glory shone in every glance, and word, and movement as He came with hands outstretched." [5]

Every day the famous, the obscure, the talented, the ordinary, the rich and the poor came there to meet the Master. With much charm and consideration Hippolyte Dreyfus-Barney and his wife, Laura, both of whom knew Persian, translated what the Master said into English for everyone to hear. His hostess has told touching stories of His deeply compassionate treatment of individuals in great distress, other stories that showed His delightful sense of humour, and described occasions in which He answered pertinent questions like the following: "Will this misery-laden world ever attain happiness?" a visitor asked one day. The Master replied: "It is nearly two thousand years since His Holiness the Lord Christ taught this prayer to His people: 'Thy Kingdom come, Thy will be done *on earth* as it is in Heaven.' Thinkest thou that He would have commanded thee to pray for that which would never come? That prayer is also a prophecy." [6]

After 'Abdu'l-Bahá had been in London for almost four weeks, He left for Paris on 3rd October, and stayed in an attractive apartment that the Dreyfus-Barneys had found for Him at 4 Avenue de Camoens near the Quai de Passy and the Trocadéro Gardens. Every morning in His sitting-room, 'Abdu'l-Bahá explained the Bahá'í Teachings to the many people of all types and conditions who came to see Him. He gave special attention to workers in humanitarian societies who were trying to relieve the suffering of the poor. The Dreyfus-Barneys now translated what He said into French.

Lady Blomfield, Mary, her sister Ellinor named Nuri by the Master, and their friend Miss Beatrice Platt called Verdiyeh by Him, who had all followed the Master to Paris, took notes in English on His addresses. After the ladies had carefully assembled their notes, they sent them to the Master for His consideration. Well pleased with their work, He asked for its immediate publication. As a result, during May of 1912 this collection of superlative lectures came out in England under the title of *Paris Talks*, and somewhat later in the United States as *The Wisdom of 'Abdu'l-Bahá*. Thanks to the devotion and efficiency of the four ladies just mentioned, who had the foresight to record the Master's words in English, this book will always serve as a priceless introduction to the Faith and as a source of illumination to the believers of the West.

The Master gave lectures not only in His own apartment, but in many other places. On October 22nd He concluded a most powerful address with these reassuring words:

God leaves not His children comfortless, but, when the darkness of winter overshadows them, then again He sends His Messengers, the Prophets, with a renewal of the blessed spring. The Sun of Truth appears again on the horizon of the world shining into the eyes of those who sleep, awaking them to behold the glory of a new dawn. Then again will the tree of humanity blossom and bring forth the fruit of righteousness for the healing of the nations. Because man has stopped his ears to the Voice of Truth and shut his eyes to the Sacred Light, neglecting the Law of God, for this reason has the darkness of war and tumult, unrest and misery, desolated the earth. I pray that you will all strive to bring each child of God into the radiance of the Sun of Truth, that the darkness may be dissipated by the penetrating rays of its glory, and the winter's hardness and cold may be melted away by the merciful warmth of its shining.[7]

On December 2nd, 'Abdu'l-Bahá left Paris for Egypt. After He had spent the winter there, He sailed from Alexandria to New York City, where He arrived on 11th April 1912. At the end of His historic journey throughout the United States of America, lasting almost eight months, He sailed for England to arrive at Liverpool on December 13th, and in London three days later.

Staying with Lady Blomfield as before, 'Abdu'l-Bahá again received a constant stream of visitors at her house.

The Hand of the Cause Hasan Balyuzi has reported this delightful incident that took place there: "When 'Abdu'l-Bahá sat down to dinner on Christmas Eve, He said, playfully, that He was not hungry, but He had to come to the dinner table because Lady Blomfield was very insistent; two despotic monarchs of the East had not been able to command Him and bend His will, but the ladies of America and Europe, because they were free, gave Him orders." [8]

One evening, in the drawing-room of her house, the Master asked Mrs. Gabrielle Enthoven, "What is your great interest in life?" She replied, "The Drama." 'Abdu'l-Bahá said, "I will give you a play. It shall be called *The Drama of the Kingdom*." [9] Without notes and only pausing for the translator to speak, the Master gave her the outline of a moving, elaborate pageant about the coming of the Promised One. Some years later, Mary Blomfield, by then married to Captain Basil Hall, R.N., wrote a play based on the Master's outline. It was published by the Weardale Press in London in 1933.

Lady Blomfield's father-in-law, Dr. Charles James Blomfield, Bishop of London for twenty-eight years, had once been a tutor to Queen Victoria. Through him Lady Blomfield knew people at Court. On 16th January 1913 she gave the Master a statement which she had written about the Faith and the purpose of His visit to London. She asked His permission to send this statement to George V hoping in this way to arrange a meeting between 'Abdu'l-Bahá and the King.

Although the Master liked her statement, He advised her not to send it to the King for fear that her action might result in misunderstanding.

On that same day at her house, the Master gave an enormously instructive talk. He said that the believers needed to have wisdom, divine insight and steadfastness and that they should give their undivided attention to the Cause in order to achieve its advancement. On 21st January 1913 He left London to visit Paris for the second time.

When the First World War began, Lady Blomfield, Mary and Ellinor were living in Geneva. Soon afterwards they moved to the Hotel d'Jena in Paris and began to work for the French Red Cross in the Haden Guest Unit at the Hospital Hotel Majestic. Mary has written: "Any kind of suffering touched my mother profoundly, but the sight of young men maimed for life, and the new and horrible experiences she had to endure during the dressing of their wounds, tortured her beyond words." [10]

Despite the heart-breaking experiences to which they were constantly exposed, the Blomfields continued to help with the wounded in Paris, until in March 1915 their hospital unit was sent to another city. For the remaining three years of the war, Lady Blomfield served on committees in London, gave regular assistance in various hospitals and kept open house for wounded soldiers. Despite her vigorous pursuit of these tasks directly concerned with the war, she never failed to support Bahá'í meetings whenever it was possible to hold them and irrespective of how many were able to attend.

In the spring of 1918 she received a deeply disturbing telephone message from a source of authority. "'Abdu'l-Bahá in serious danger. Take immediate action." [11] Without delay she went to Lord Lamington, a prominent member of Parliament who much admired 'Abdu'l-Bahá, and told him what she had just heard. Lord Lamington promptly wrote a letter to the Foreign Office in which he stressed the noble services that 'Abdu'l-Bahá was rendering, not only to the people of Palestine, but to all humanity, and he gave this letter to Arthur Balfour, at that time Secretary of State for Foreign Affairs. On the same day Balfour sent a cable to

General Allenby. It said: "Extend every protection and consideration to 'Abdu'l-Bahá, His family and His friends, when the British march on Haifa."[12] As soon as General Allenby had taken Haifa, several days before he was expected to do so, he sent a cablegram to London the news of which brought joy to the heart of every Bahá'í: "Have to-day taken Palestine. Notify the world that 'Abdu'l-Bahá is safe."[13]

Lady Blomfield learned afterwards that her old friend, Major Wellesley Tudor-Pole, had sent the terrifying message which she had heard on the telephone. On learning that the Turkish High Command had threatened to crucify 'Abdu'l-Bahá on Mount Carmel if their army should have to evacuate Haifa, Major Tudor-Pole had made every effort to insure His safety. Although the influential men whom he first approached knew nothing about 'Abdu'l-Bahá and saw no urgent reason to assist Him, Tudor-Pole found one officer with important connections who showed some interest in the matter. With his help, Tudor-Pole was able to send a message to the British Foreign Office.

At the end of the war, domestic affairs at home kept the Blomfields from making their intended pilgrimage. Around 1920 Lady Blomfield decided to spend part of each year in Switzerland, in Geneva. While in that country she became a close friend of Eglantyne Jebb, founder of the 'Save the Children Fund'. After Miss Jebb had seen at first hand the tragic situation of great numbers of children in Central and Eastern Europe at the end of the war, she, with her sister's help, had set up this fund to save starving and refugee children from all over the world. Deeply interested in this noble work, Lady Blomfield established a special 'Blomfield Fund' at 4 rue Massot in Geneva, under the sponsorship of Lord Weardale in London. She explained in a pamphlet called *The First Obligation* that the purpose of this fund was to finance "workrooms for children or for other relief work of a constructive character, which will increasingly constitute a more and more important part of the activities of the Save the Children Fund movement."[14]

A Tablet which Lady Bloomfield received from 'Abdu'l-Bahá dated 23rd July 1921 served as a perfect foreword to her pamphlet. He revealed: "To contribute towards the cause of these pitiful children, and to protect and care for them is the highest expression of altruism and worship, and is well-pleasing to the Most High the Almighty, the Divine Provider."[15]

During the long periods of time that she lived in Geneva, Lady Blomfield struggled hard to attract people to the Faith who were working for the League of Nations. She gave weekly meetings at her hotel and as many as a hundred people often gathered there to hear speakers of noble intention and pioneers in philanthropic work. Every speaker illustrated a Bahá'í principle. At the end of each talk, Lady Blomfield, acting as Chairman, always gave a further explanation of this principle. In quiet conversations that she had with them after the meetings, individuals often asked her, "Who is this Persian Prophet you quote so much?" "She would tell them and thus the seed was sown."[16] She also spent many hours in writing to people about the Faith.

Early in July 1920 Shoghi Effendi arrived in England from Haifa in order to attend Balliol College, Oxford. He brought with him Tablets from the Master to Lady Blomfield, Lord Lamington and Major Tudor-Pole. These three arranged for Shoghi Effendi to meet distinguished professors and oriental scholars, both from Oxford and London University. During his sixteen months' stay in England the future Guardian became close to Lady Blomfield and several others.

On 29th November 1921 at midday, in the office of Major Tudor-Pole in London, Shoghi Effendi read in an open telegram the heart-breaking news that 'Abdu'l-Bahá had ascended to the Abhá Kingdom. When the Major entered the room a moment later, he found Shoghi Effendi in a state of collapse. Miss Grand, a believer, took him to her home nearby and put him to bed for several days. Lady Blomfield, Miss Grand, Shoghi Effendi's sister Rúhangíz, and some others, did what they could to comfort him.

Delayed for some days by passport difficulties, Shoghi Effendi, Rúhangíz and Lady Blomfield sailed from England to Egypt on December 16th, and taking a train from there they arrived in Haifa on December 29th. Mary, who had now become Mrs. Basil Hall, felt sure that her mother's companionship on this trip was of great help to the grief-stricken Shoghi Effendi.

During her first weeks in the Holy Land, Lady Blomfield had the great privilege of collaborating with Shoghi Effendi, now the Guardian of course, on a pamphlet entitled *The Passing of 'Abdu'l-Bahá*. It is composed of authentic accounts that they collected, and moving reflections by themselves about this agonizing event. In one most eloquent passage they have written:

The eyes that had always looked out with loving-kindness upon humanity, whether friends or foes, were now closed. The hands that had ever been stretched forth to give alms to the poor and the needy, the halt and the maimed, the blind, the orphan and the widow, had now finished their labour. The feet that, with untiring zeal, had gone upon the ceaseless errands of the Lord of compassion, were now at rest. The lips that had so eloquently championed the cause of the suffering sons of men, were now hushed in silence. The heart that had so powerfully throbbed with wondrous love for the children of God was now stilled. His glorious spirit had passed from the life of earth, from the persecutions of the enemies of righteousness, from the storm and stress of well nigh eighty years of indefatigable toil for the good of others.[17]

In March 1922 Shoghi Effendi called together a group of Bahá'ís from various countries, including Lady Blomfield. For as long as the Guardian remained in the Holy Land during her visit, he often consulted her and other Bahá'ís of experience on vital matters concerning the development of the Faith, but mainly about the possibility of his establishing the Universal House of Justice at that time. The Guardian decided that he could not possibly do this until the Local and National Assemblies were functioning in those countries where Bahá'í communities existed.

While he was experiencing almost unbearable grief over the passing of the Master, and added strain and acute suffering caused by the enemies of the Faith, Shoghi Effendi, for the first few months of his ministry, carried out with no interruption his manifold and overwhelming tasks. At the end of this period on 5th April 1922, however, he left the Holy

Land to make an extended trip to various countries in Europe and to remain there until he had regained sufficient physical strength and spiritual energy to resume his work of service. Before his departure, he appointed Bahá'íyyih Khánum, the daughter of Bahá'u'lláh, the Greatest Holy Leaf, to "administer, in consultation with the family of 'Abdu'l-Bahá, and a chosen Assembly, all Bahá'í affairs during his absence." [18]

Lady Blomfield stayed in the Holy Land for several months after the Guardian had left. She listened to thrilling stories about the Heroic Age of the Faith from Bahá'íyyih Khánum, Munírih Khánum, the widow of 'Abdu'l-Bahá, Túbá Khánum, His daughter, and several others who had lived through those early years. Lady Blomfield took comprehensive notes on these stories and kept her notes for some future time when she hoped to include them in a book.

Munírih Khánum wrote to Basil Hall: "We are all very glad to have the honourable Lady, Sitárih Khánum, Lady Blomfield in our midst. Her presence gives us much joy. We look upon her, not only as a friend, but as one of our own dear family." [19]

In 1930 Lady Blomfield made a second journey to the Holy Land. While there, she gathered more material for the book that she now definitely planned to write. At the end of her visit, she returned to England and for the rest of her life shared a house in Hampstead, a part of London, with the Basil Halls. Happy meetings with Bahá'í travellers from many parts of the world often took place there. For several years Lady Blomfield worked constantly on her book. After overcoming great difficulties in so doing, she finished it a few weeks before her passing, after a brief illness, on the last day of 1939.

The Hand of the Cause Hasan Balyuzi, who at her request wrote the preface, but not in time for her to read, has declared: "*The Chosen Highway* will forever remain the greatest monument to the achievements of its author .... And to generations unborn it will hand a message rich in enlightenment." [20]

Although Mary had visited her mother in the nursing home twice on the day of her passing, she was not there at the

actual moment that it took place. The nurses said that her
mother had a peaceful, beautiful death.

While going through her papers, Mary was much surprised
to find how much her mother had written. With no apparent
thought of publication, she had described in diaries and in
engagement books some of her dreams and visions. Mary
felt that a prayer[21] which she had discovered written faintly
in pencil on an old piece of paper well expressed the theme
of her beloved mother's beautiful and saintly life:

O God! My Beloved!
All my affairs are in Thy hands.
Be Thou the Mover of my actions,
The Lode Star of my soul,
The Voice that crieth in my inmost being,
The object of my heart's adoration!
I praise Thee that Thou hast enabled me
To turn my face unto Thee,
That Thou hast set my soul ablaze
With remembrance of Thee!

Fred Mortensen and
Albert Heath Hall

IN A BRIEF BUT DEEPLY moving autobiographical sketch
entitled 'When a Soul Meets the Master', Fred Mortensen
has described with refreshing simplicity his conversion to the
Bahá'í Faith and his thrilling, dramatic and now historic
meeting with 'Abdu'l-Bahá. He also stressed the major part
that Albert Heath Hall played in changing him from an
irresponsible criminal into a devoted, much loved Bahá'í. It
is interesting to learn what brought these two men of different backgrounds together, and to try and understand how
Mr. Hall was able so greatly to influence his young friend.

Albert Heath Hall was born on 11th July 1858, in
Alexandria, Licking County, Ohio, the son of the Reverend
Levi and Lucinda Mitchell Hall. At the age of fifteen he
moved with his parents to Austin, Minnesota, and in 1875
he entered the University of that state. After he had worked
his way through university both in a sawmill and for the
first telephone company established in Minneapolis, he
studied law in the office of Judge Frederick Hooker. Sometime later, while he was employed at the Treasury Department
in Washington, D.C., he again studied law at what was then
called Columbia University (later George Washington
University). After his graduation in 1884, he returned to
Minneapolis and began a lifelong practice of law. He made
the same effort for his clients whether they were rich or poor;
"if he believed that his client's cause was just, that cause
became the paramount matter with him and it took precedence
over his self-interest, his family and his friends."[1]

Already well-known for his services to the Bahá'í Faith in the United States of America, in Riḍván of 1910 he was elected Chairman of the Convention of the Bahá'í Temple Unity, and in 1911 also President of its Executive Board, posts which he held until 1914. This Unity had been established at the Convention of the preceding year, and its Executive Board of nine members decided to make plans and to find means for the construction of the first Temple of the West in Wilmette, Illinois, on the shore of Lake Michigan.

In his opening address as Chairman of the Convention he said: "God chooses the weak things to confound the mighty. You have made the choice of a weak instrument. I feel very weak and lowly, as nothing, and I would not bear the responsibility of this place were I not possessed with the sense of my own emptiness, seeking only the inpouring of His Spirit, strength, and wisdom."[2]

During the remarkable journey of 'Abdu'l-Bahá throughout America, from 11th April to 5th December 1912, the Master spent four days in Minneapolis. Late in the evening of September 16th, He arrived there from Chicago and went directly to the Plaza Hotel. Early the next morning, Mr. Hall, along with Dr. Clement Woolson and several other Bahá'ís, called to see Him.

On the afternoon of 20th September, 'Abdu'l-Bahá gave an illuminating talk at Mr. Hall's house. As reported by Ellen T. Pursell, He said in part:

Man must spiritually perceive that religion has been intended by God to be the means of grace, the source of life and cause of agreement. If it becomes the cause of discord, enmity and hatred, it is better that man should be without it. For in its teachings we seek the spirit of charity and love to bind the hearts of men together. If on the contrary we find it alienates and embitters human hearts we are justified in casting it aside. Therefore when man through sincere investigation discovers the fundamental reality of religion, his former prejudices disappear and his new condition of enlightenment is conducive to the development of the world of humanity.[3]

On Monday afternoon, 28th April 1913, at the fifth Annual Convention of the Bahá'í Temple Unity, held for the first time in New York City, Mr. Hall, as President of the Executive Board and Chairman of the Convention, stressed the great importance of building "a Temple Beautiful, not because it is in Chicago," he said, "but because it is the first Mashrak-el-Azkar [Mashriqu'l-Adhkar] in the West .... [a] Temple of prayer, with its nine open doors of welcome to all the people of the earth ...." In the same address he declared, ".... we want this Temple to be raised as the result of the gifts of men and women who give what they have and give intelligently and who give to the point where the giving becomes a blessing ...."[4]

In a Tablet revealed for Mr. Albert Vail on 27th December 1916, but not received by him until almost two years later, 'Abdu'l-Bahá wrote, "Day and night I remember Mr. Hall and do not forget the days that I spent with him. This personage has rendered many services to this Cause. The value of his services must be appreciated."[5]

At the ninth National Convention held in Boston, Massachusetts, from 29th April to 2nd May 1917, Mr. Hall moved that the Bahá'í Temple Unity, guided by its Executive Board, should do all in its power to further the Divine Plan of Teaching as revealed by 'Abdu'l-Bahá ·in the five Tablets recently received by the American Community and just read to those assembled (see also p. 136).

Later on in the Convention, after he had recommended that most of the Bahá'í Literature thus far available in English should soon be published in a uniform translation, and that a special committee composed by Mr. Roy Wilhelm and Miss Mary Lesch be appointed to help the Unity and the Publishing Society in this work, Mr. Hall said with enthusiasm, "In our meetings there is nothing so good"[6] as the 'Star of the West.' 'Abdu'l-Bahá had already confirmed the importance of this magazine and commended its editors. The Guardian was later to do the same.

Against the advice of his doctor who had warned him that to do so might shorten his life, he insisted on travelling from Minneapolis to New York City in the spring of 1920, in order to attend the National Convention. Someone wrote in 'Star of the West': "Everyone present at the Feast of

El-Rizwan will remember the ring of his voice, though feeble, when he cried out to the assembled delegates and friends: 'Arise, shine, for thy light has come and the glory of God has risen upon thee!'" [7] On the train home, sitting up with difficulty because of his frail condition, he gave an old friend, Mr. Ole Hansen, at one time mayor of Seattle, "the glorious Message of the coming of The Kingdom ...."[8]

Critically ill by the time that he had reached home, he died less than two weeks afterwards on May 25th. On hearing of his death, and that of the noble Charles Herman Greenleaf, one of the first Bahá'ís in America, 'Abdu'l-Bahá sent this cable about them: "Supplicating Lord of the Kingdom to submerge these two blessed souls in the ocean of His Mercy,—Abbas." [9]

* * *

Fred Mortensen was born on 7th February 1887 at Fort Dodge, Iowa. He has written how, despite his dear mother's noble efforts to lead him in the right direction, he became involved with boys of hard character and spent much time in the saloon. These influences made him rebel against a certain feeling inside of him that he was doing wrong. He fought, stole, and destroyed other people's property. Arrested and confined to jail before his trial, he escaped and remained a fugitive for four years.

While he was trying to prevent a policeman from arresting a friend, two detectives approached him, and as Fred has described ".... in my haste to get away from them I leaped over a thirty-five foot wall, breaking my leg, to escape the bullets whizzing around about—and wound up in the 'garden at the feet of the Beloved' as Bahá'u'lláh has so beautifully written it in the *Seven Valleys*." [10]

Besides handling the case for Fred's defence, Mr. Hall told him ".... hour after hour, about the great love of 'Abdu'l-Bahá for all his children and that he was here to help us show that love for our fellowmen."[11] With much patience and love Mr. Hall led Fred into the Ark of the Covenant. Certain that only the Word of God for this day could have freed him from the prison of self and made him into a new person, he declared, "I have been resurrected and made alive in the Kingdom of El Abhá." [12]

Early in August 1912, when 'Abdu'l-Bahá was visiting New England, Fred heard that the Master might return home without coming west. Determined not to miss seeing Him, Fred decided to make a trip to Green Acre in Eliot, Maine, where He was staying. On the night before leaving Cleveland, where he had been attending a convention of printers, Fred dreamt that he was 'Abdu'l-Bahá's guest with many others at a long table. Using His hand for emphasis the Master walked up and down alongside the table and told them stories.

Not having sufficient money to buy a ticket, Fred rode on the bumpers between the baggage cars of the train, first to Buffalo, New York, and then from around midnight until nine the next morning to Boston, Massachusetts. From there he rode on top of a passenger carriage to Portsmouth, New Hampshire. By then only about four miles from Green Acre, he first took a boat and then a street-car for the rest of the way.

Situated on the sloping banks of the Piscataqua River, called by the Indians 'The River of Light', because the sunset turned it to gold, this spot once served as a Council ground for the Penacock Indians, where they settled their tribal differences with a pipe of peace.

Late in the evening of August 20th, "tired, dirty, and wondering, but happy," [13] Fred arrived at that centre. Mr. Hall had given him a letter of introduction to the esteemed Bahá'í and distinguished attorney from Boston, Alfred E. Lunt. Although Fred could not find him, Mrs. Edward Kinney, with her wonderful consideration for other people, came to Fred's rescue and offered him a bed.

Early the next morning in the main hall of Green Acre Fred first saw 'Abdu'l-Bahá and found He looked as He had in his dream. When 'Abdu'l-Bahá was introduced to Fred, He did not shake hands with him and said only a few short words. Very much embarrassed, Fred did not know what was the matter. Only a few moments after He had gone to His room, however, the Master asked to see Fred, who felt strange and uncomfortable as he went upstairs to His room. After the Master had given Fred a warm welcome, He asked Fred three times, "Are you happy?" Fred thought, "Why do you ask me that so many times? Of course I am happy; didn't I tell you so the first time?"

On hearing from Fred that he came from Minneapolis, 'Abdu'l-Bahá asked him if he knew Mr. Hall. Fred answered "Yes. He told me about the Cause." 'Abdu'l-Bahá asked him, "Did you have a pleasant journey?" Fred wrote, "Of all the questions I wished to avoid this was the one! I dropped my gaze to the floor—and again he put the question. I lifted my eyes to his and his were as two black, sparkling jewels, which seemed to look into my very depths." As Fred began to describe his trip to Green Acre, he again looked into the eyes of 'Abdu'l-Bahá and saw that they had changed, "a wondrous light seemed to pour out. It was the light of love ...."

When 'Abdu'l-Bahá was ready to leave Green Acre, Fred walked up near to Him in order to say good-bye. Much to his astonishment, 'Abdu'l-Bahá asked Fred to get into the automobile with Him. He took Fred to Malden, Massachusetts, and kept him there as a guest for a week. At the end of that time He gave Fred a sufficient present of money so that he could return home in comfort. Within a few weeks Fred was again privileged to be near Him for several minutes.

A little over a year later, Fred received this inspiring Tablet from 'Abdu'l-Bahá:[14]

To Mr. Fred Mortensen, Minneapolis, Minn.—Upon him be Baha'o'llah-el-Abha

O thou illumined youth!

Thy letter was received. Its perusal produced the utmost joy; for its contents indicated faith and its significances were proofs of firmness in the Covenant. That trip of thine from Minneapolis to Green Acre will never be forgotten. Its mention will be recorded eternally and in books and works of history. Therefore, be thou happy that, praise be to God, thou hast an illumined heart, a living spirit and art vivified with a merciful breath. Convey my greeting, longing and respect to the Editor of *Labor Review* and say: "This paper of yours in the future ages will become superior to all the newspapers of the world, because you have·published in its columns the proclamation of the kingdom of Abha. I hope thou wilt become assisted to promote the teachings of Baha'o'llah. Then thou wilt observe that this paper has become a luminous star and the cause of the illumination of the hearts of humanity.

Upon thee be greetings and praise!

Abdul-Baha Abbas.

From this period on Fred served the Faith in many different ways. In 1916, at the request of the Bahá'í Temple Unity, he helped to plan humanitarian relief in Haifa, Syria and Turkey.

For many years he made teaching trips throughout the United States. While he was pioneering in Montana, he achieved valuable publicity for the Cause there, particularly in the cities of Helena and Butte. In its issue of Saturday 15th February 1919, the 'Montana Record-Herald' published an article that gave credit for the conception of the League of Nations to an unspecified King of France, and also stated that the idea of a League "peacefully reposed under the dust of ages until after the great war broke out ...."[15]

Three days later a forceful letter, which Fred had written with the encouragement of the friends in Helena, appeared in the People's Forum of this newspaper. In this letter he clearly stated that the Founder of the Bahá'í Faith had revealed the basic principles of the League at least fifty years before its establishment, that His eldest Son, 'Abdu'l-Bahá, had explained these same principles in a book entitled *The Mysterious Forces of Civilization* (later entitled *The Secret of Divine Civilization*), which He had written in 1875, and that the Master had travelled throughout America in 1912 to proclaim His Father's Divine Plan for World Peace.

Some years later, Fred wrote an essay entitled 'The Three Great Lights' for 'The Bahá'í Magazine' of March 1925. It is a most convincing explanation of the Bahá'í belief in progressive revelation. With the same appealing sincerity with which he described his conversion and subsequent meeting with the Master, he wrote: "It is about thirty-five hundred years since the advent of Moses, and all this time the Jews have been praying, beseeching God to send their Messiah unto them. It is nearly two thousand years since the Sun of Jesus arose in the heaven of Christianity, and we, too, have been praying and watching for the return of that Sun. The Sun of Muhammad appeared on the horizon thirteen hundred and fifty years ago and they, too, are ever praying night and day for the return of their Sun of Truth. So it is with all peoples of every religion, each praying and each expecting the reappearance of their Sun of Truth." [16]

In a concluding passage of this moving, informative essay, which quotes from both the Revelation of St. John and an Epistle of St. Paul to the Corinthians, Fred has written:

"And I saw a new heaven and a new earth, for the first heaven and the first earth were passed away." That is, the rays (teachings) of this Sun will cause to blossom forth in the world of humanity a new feeling, a divine brotherhood, the love and Fatherhood of God, of peace. Therefore, a new earth will come into being, the old thoughts and ideals having passed away. "And there was no more sea." That is, no more the causes separating mankind, such as various religious beliefs causing peoples to be submerged in a sea of names—as I am a Christian, I am a Jew. But the heat of the Sun of Bahá'u'lláh will dry up all those seas of differences and man will stand firmly upon the earth and he shall "see not as through a glass darkly, but face to face." [17]

As a resident of Chicago, Fred served the Faith in that city for twenty-one years. Early in 1946, shortly after the end of the Second World War, he was preparing to go and teach the Cause in Austria, with the approval of the Guardian. But a serious illness, which caused his death a few months later, prevented him from leaving Chicago.

Although his daughter, Kathryn Penoyer, has written about her father with much love, by her own admission she could not find words strong enough to express his devotion to the Faith of Bahá'u'lláh. According to her, shortly before his passing he wrote to Shoghi Effendi, "I am happy that you chose to include the story of my visit to 'Abdu'l-Bahá at Green Acre in *God Passes By*." [18] She has also reported that "on the very eve before his death he spent his last time teaching the Faith of Bahá'u'lláh." [19]

Fred died on 13th June 1946 at the Chicago Hospital, of a cerebral haemorrhage. The Guardian sent the following cable to Fred's family: "Grieve passing beloved Fred. Welcome assured Abhá Kingdom by Master. Praying progress his soul. His name forever inscribed Bahá'í history." [20]

It is hard for some of us to understand how Fred, at one time a convicted and self-admitted criminal, was able to recognize the station of Bahá'u'lláh, while countless others with undeniably fine qualities have not shown even the smallest interest in Him. During my pilgrimage to the Holy Land in January 1955, one evening at dinner I asked Shoghi Effendi, "Why do many people of strong character, apparent goodness, and belief in Jesus, criticize the Cause and fail to come into it, while others of comparatively weak character and lack of belief often do?" He answered, "Recognition of Bahá'u'lláh comes from a quality of the soul."

The story of Fred certainly shows that no matter what serious mistakes a person may have made, instead of becoming discouraged, he should turn with all his heart to Bahá'u'lláh, with absolute confidence that He will lead him in the right direction. As Bahá'u'lláh has revealed in "that marvellous collection of gem-like utterances," *The Hidden Words*:

O SON OF MAN! Transgress not thy limits, nor claim that which beseemeth thee not. Prostrate thyself before the countenance of thy God, the Lord of might and power.

Alfred E. Lunt

SEVERAL GENERATIONS BEFORE he was born, the ancestors of Alfred E. Lunt left Europe to live in New England. Strong, able and highly principled, they became pioneers in education. As a student at Harvard University, Mr. Lunt successfully managed its Illustrated Magazine. While still an under-graduate he showed unusual ability in politics. He was elected both President of Harvard's Republican Club and President of the National Republican College League. Those who were aware of his early accomplishments felt that he had a brilliant future before him.

In 1901 'Abdu'l-Bahá sent Dr. Ali-Kuli Khan, the dis-tinguished Bahá'í teacher and translator, from Persia to the United States of America, so that he might help the Faith there. During the winter of 1905, he gave an address at Harvard. By now a student of law, Mr. Lunt attended this address. Convinced that what he had heard was true, he soon realized that political means could never adequately solve the vast problems of world government and that human wisdom could not give sufficient guidance for the spiritual development of mankind. Shortly after he had made a thorough study of the Cause, he declared his belief in Bahá'u'lláh.

In 1906, after he had graduated from Law School, Mr. Lunt joined a well-known law firm in Boston. During the same year, he became a member of the first Spiritual Assembly of that city.

On 22nd and 23rd March 1909, the first general Bahá'í Convention of America was held at the Masonic Temple in

Chicago. As one of thirty-nine delegates from thirty-six cities, Mr. Lunt was present at this Convention. Often, either as President or as Secretary, he served on the board of the Bahá'í Temple Unity for almost every year of its existence.

From the start of his Bahá'í life, he took an enthusiastic part in the work at Green Acre. On 4th July 1894, Miss Sarah J. Farmer had formally opened the Center of Green Acre at Eliot, Maine, "for the purpose of bringing together all who were looking earnestly towards the New Day, which seemed to be breaking over the entire world." In 1896 Miss Farmer heard of the Bahá'í Faith and found that the ideals of love and unity that she was trying to foster, with help from such men as Ralph Waldo Emerson and John Greenleaf Whittier, were perfectly expressed in the Bahá'í Holy Writings. Already a member of the Bahá'í community, in 1900 she made a pilgrimage to 'Akká and asked 'Abdu'l-Bahá to accept from her the facilities of Green Acre. On her return home she invited the Bahá'ís to use these facilities. In 1907, not yet recovered from a long illness, Miss Farmer had a serious fall, which made her an invalid. No longer able to serve as the head of Green Acre, she wisely put it into the hands of a Fellowship. As the Hand of the Cause Hasan Balyuzi has written, 'Abdu'l-Bahá advised the Bahá'ís not to intervene in the affairs of this Fellowship. Nevertheless Miss Farmer found it necessary to engage Mr. Lunt as her lawyer, so that he might help her "to safeguard the future of the precious gift which she had made to the people of America".[1]

Those who were opposed to the establishment of this Fellowship engaged able lawyers to attack it. Through their stimulation of adverse criticism in the newspapers they were able to influence much public opinion against the Fellowship. After Mr. Lunt had undergone a long and hard struggle, the Supreme Court of Maine, where the lawsuit finally reached, made a decision in favour of the Bahá'ís, Miss Farmer, and their loyal friends. The Master called Mr. Lunt's work in this lawsuit "lion hearted".[2] As a result of this victory, the centre of Green Acre came under the administration of the Bahá'í community, and some years later in 1929 the National

Spiritual Assembly of the United States was able to establish the second Bahá'í Summer School of America there.

Although much impressed by the unusual ability that Mr. Lunt had shown in his handling of the case, the head of his firm was deeply disturbed that Mr. Lunt had aroused unfavourable publicity because of his close association with the Bahá'í Faith. Told that he could no longer stay in the firm unless he resigned from the Bahá'í community, he chose without hesitation to leave the firm and to open his own office.

Clients from all strata of society came to Mr. Lunt. Whether these clients were rich or poor, he gave them the same careful consideration and always tried to deepen their spiritual understanding.

For many years he served as legal adviser to the Massachusetts Committee of Manufacturers and Merchants. Because of the excellent work that he did for it, he became closely involved with prominent business men. He tried to show them that only Bahá'u'lláh could teach mankind the perfect way to bring about industrial peace. The wide experience he had gained in his legal practice assisted him greatly in his painstaking efforts to help in the development of the Bahá'í administrative order in the United States and Canada.

During His historic journey to the United States and Canada in 1912 the Master made two short visits to Boston and one to some of its neighbouring cities.

On the evening of July 23rd He gave an eloquent talk at the Victoria Hotel in Boston to Bahá'ís, seekers, and members of the press, on the perfect solution for man's economic plight, as revealed by Bahá'u'lláh. Among his statements were these: "The fundamentals of the whole economic condition are divine in nature and are associated with the world of the heart and spirit .... Hearts must be so cemented together, love must become so dominant that the rich shall most willingly extend assistance to the poor and take steps to establish these economic adjustments permanently .... Strive therefore to create love in the hearts in order that they may become glowing and radiant .... When the love of God is established, everything else will be realized. This is the true foundation of all economics." [3]

In his address to the sixth Annual Convention of the Bahá'í Temple Unity in April 1914, Mr. Lunt said: "From Boston I would bring you the greetings of the hearts .... The work there began in 1906, but I think only within the last few years, has the Assembly been really founded in stead-fastness. When Abdul-Baha came to Boston in the spring of 1912 he brought with him that wonderful cup of love and severance, that pure blessing which has quickened every Assembly in this country and from that moment Boston began to flourish as a rose in the desert." [4]

On 19th January 1916, while Mr. Lunt was its President, the Executive Board of the Bahá'í Temple Unity issued a special Mashriqu'l-Adhkár edition of 'Star of the West' with the heart-felt desire of helping the friends to understand the great importance of building the first House of Worship not only of America but of the Western world.

The foreword of this issue clearly describes the progress already made on the plans for this tremendous undertaking. It stated that on 30th May 1903, in answer to a letter from the Bahá'ís of Chicago asking His permission to erect the proposed Temple, the Master had revealed for them the first of many inspiring Tablets in which He had encouraged them to achieve this great service.

In the last Tablet from the Master quoted in this issue, revealed in June 1913, He wrote, "Verily, I pray God to confirm thee with the All-Power so that the means may be prepared for the establishment of the Masrak-el-Azkar." [5]

The eighth Convention of the Bahá'í Temple Unity took place in May 1916 in Chicago. A few moments after he had been elected President of this convention, Mr. Lunt spoke briefly to an audience of about two hundred and fifty delegates and friends. One of his remarks was this: "There is a burning issue and one only which this convention must solve before it adjourns. We must answer the call of Abdul-Baha and provide the material means which will build this temple." [6]

Mr. Lunt explained that, in 1909, some American believers had come together and provided a bond to buy the temple land on mortgages; that by the end of four years, Bahá'ís from the east and the west had given sufficient money to the building fund to enable the Executive Board to pay off these mortgages; that, although in 1914 and 1915 contributions had fallen off considerably, on February 4th of the next year a letter, sent to the believers by the Executive Board with the intention of expressing the Bahá'í ideal of unity, had resulted in an unprecedented increase in the fund.

In a Tablet for Mr. Lunt of 12th October 1916, the Master revealed:[7]

.... O thou my friend of the Kingdom!
Praise be to God, that the city of Boston is stirred into cheerfulness and the believers of God and the maid-servants of the Merciful in the utmost firmness and steadfastness in the Covenant and Testament are engaged in the diffusion of the fragrances of God, that the divine favors and bestowals are continually descending upon the assembly of that city, for they have attained to capacity, and capacity like unto a magnet attracts the heavenly graces unto men .... According to what is heard the convention of Masrak-el-Azkar was going to be held in Boston. The believers of Boston must consider this as one of the greatest divine bounties and strive with all their strength so that all the delegates coming to the convention from the different cities of America may become attracted, thankful and grateful and spend a few days with the utmost joy and happiness ....

The Convention to which 'Abdu'l-Bahá alluded opened on Monday morning, 30th April 1917, at the Hotel Brunswick in that city. As Miss Martha Root reported: "The chairman, Mr. Alfred E. Lunt, concisely stated its purpose: 'We are here to do Abdul-Baha's will. We are here with illumined vision, we pray, with ears listening for the divine guidance, to catch the desire of the Center of the Covenant for this gathering, and to do it; for he has in a Tablet indicated, as he always indicates, that there is a great purpose in each one of these gatherings.'"[8]

The first five of the fourteen immortal Tablets of the Divine Plan, revealed by the Master to entrust the American community with a world-wide teaching mission, had already been received by this community. Referring to them, Martha further reported: "The vision of the 1917 Convention was glimpsed when the teaching tablets of Abdul-Baha were read, and action was taken to translate that vision into enduring form in firm and permanent action." [9]

Believers now much revered in the Bahá'í world took an enthusiastic part in the consultation, mostly on plans to spread the Cause of God throughout the United States of America. A few of them gave impressive formal talks. Beautiful music was often played between sessions. This convention must have moved many persons to serve the Faith with increased fervour.

During that summer the Executive Board of the Bahá'í Temple Unity held a meeting at Green Acre. Now that the United States was at war, the Board asked Mr. Lunt to compose a letter to the Department of State that would plainly state the attitude and duty of Bahá'ís towards existing governments, and more particularly the government of the United States at such a time.

Using as his text some well-chosen passages revealed by Bahá'u'lláh and 'Abdu'l-Bahá, pertinent to the tragic situation which now faced his own and other countries, Mr. Lunt declared that, although like all lovers of humanity the Bahá'ís abhorred war, they could be relied upon during the present emergency, as always, loyally to obey their government and its laws.

On 29th April 1919, at the Bahá'í Congress held in New York City, Mr. Lunt gave a moving and forceful address, in which he explained that only by rejecting the savage law called "the survival of the fittest", and by adhering to the divine laws revealed by Bahá'u'lláh, will mankind find it possible first to avoid self-destruction and then to bring in a world civilization.

On 22nd July 1919 Shoghi Effendi translated a fascinating Tablet of advice and encouragement revealed by the Master for Mr. Lunt. It contained these remarks: "Rest thou assured in the bounty of the Merciful, and be hopeful for the blessings of the Abha Kingdom, for thou doth exert the utmost effort in service for Truth and this magnet attracts assistance and confirmation. The addresses thou hast delivered with reference to economic problems are highly suitable. The essence of the Bahai economic teachings is this, that immense riches far beyond what is necessary should not be accumulated."[10]

The Master concluded this Tablet by asking him to embrace his son and daughter for Him, and gave both of them a Persian name.

A photograph of Mr. Lunt taken about this time shows a strong, noble face, a penetrating expression, and exceptional charm. In 1925 the institution of the Bahá'í Temple Unity came to an end. The first National Spiritual Assembly of the United States and Canada was immediately established to replace it. Mr. Lunt served on this Assembly for most of the remaining twelve years of his life, often as an officer.

Starting with the issue of July 1925, the 'Bahá'í Magazine' published a series of absorbing, informative, and scholarly essays by Mr. Lunt on various aspects of the Bahá'í Faith.

In 'Truth—and Its Counterfeit Aspect', the first essay to appear, he pointed out that the real progress of humanity has never taken place through the influence of brilliant philosophers and man-made ethical systems, but only through the coming of the Prophets of God. He persuasively wrote: "Through these focal centers of Oneness flows the healing of the Nations, the potentiality of converting humanity into its true image and likeness, of demonstrating the falsity of the counterfeit, banishing superstitions and instilling into human nature that mysterious elixir of divinity that transfers imagination into knowledge."[11]

In 'World Peace and the World Court', which was published a few months later, Mr. Lunt has stated: "The Bahá'í teachings affirm with the most profound emphasis that the edifice of humanity is destroyed and subjected to the greatest humiliation and degradation by no less than five outstanding prejudices. These are religious, racial, political, economic and patriotic."[12]

He forcefully explained that only after these prejudices have been cleansed from the heart of humanity, and an International Tribunal as revealed by Bahá'u'lláh has been established, will world peace and the universal brotherhood of man be brought into being.

In a comprehensive essay, 'The Supreme Affliction—A Study in Bahá'í Economics & Socialization', to which a special number of the 'Bahá'í Magazine' in July 1932 was entirely devoted, Mr. Lunt strongly reaffirmed what he had expressed somewhat differently before—that in the future, mankind, freed from its supreme affliction, which means attachment to its animal nature, will turn to the laws and ordinances of Bahá'u'lláh and create a just society.

In 'The True Sovereign,' which was published during the next year in five instalments, Mr. Lunt remarked that the masses have turned in worship to a false sovereign which "is none other than the usurping power of Nature". After explaining with compelling logic that only Bahá'u'lláh is the 'True Sovereign' for this day, he declared: "For Nature's selfish isolation and discord, the True Sovereign grants union and brotherhood. For her cruelty and unreason He establishes love and knowledge. For her dark and treacherous suggestions, her hypocrisies, her sanguinary wars, and her economic injustice, He bestows guidance, truth, order, and that happiness that the exile feels when he has entered his real home." [13]

In 'True Enthusiasms', which appeared in 'World Order Magazine' of February 1937, then published to replace the 'Bahá'í Magazine', Mr. Lunt again pointed out the dangers to which mankind is exposed when it turns for perfect guidance to a mere human personality instead of to the Manifestation of God.

Mr. Lunt's inspiring last essay, 'Mankind the Prodigal', was published in May 1937, a few months before his passing. It includes this powerful passage about the coming of Bahá'u'lláh: "While the prodigal son returned to his father, which is a necessary and inescapable journey for all who would attain their divine destiny, today the Father Himself has sought out the prodigal, entered the world of man, dwelt in the very midst of the confusion and corruption of the husks of human wreckage, and even suffered His Holy Manifestation to submit to the chains and cruelties of a prison worthy only of the dregs of the most abandoned among men." [14]

During the early 1930s Mr. Lunt like many others was faced with serious financial difficulties, with a wife and five children to support. At this time of world depression a wealthy friend offered him an excellent position in a law firm with a guaranteed salary of ten thousand dollars a year. Although he was only asked to do his work, fearful that his association with this firm might be harmful to the Faith, he turned down the offer and stayed in his own office.

During the last few months of his life Mr. Lunt suffered from a painful illness. Despite this fact, he continued to serve the Faith without interruption. The Hand of the Cause Louis G. Gregory and the eminent Harlan Ober wrote, "Just two days before his passing, he wrote a most cheerful and hopeful letter to one of his friends, telling of his plans for future activities." [15]

Mr. Lunt died on 12th August 1937 at his home in Beverly, Massachusetts. Attended by Bahá'ís from his own and other communities, by relations, and by friends of various beliefs who loved him, his simple funeral service brought many people closer to the Faith.

The Guardian sent this cable to the National Spiritual Assembly of the United States and Canada: "Shocked distressed premature passing esteemed well-beloved Lunt. Future generations will appraise his manifold outstanding contributions to rise and establishment Faith Bahá'u'lláh American continent. Community his bereaved co-workers could ill afford lose such critical period so fearless champion their Cause. Request entire body their National representatives assemble his grave pay tribute my behalf to him who so long and since inception acted as pillar institution they represent. Convey Boston community assurance prayers, deepest brotherly sympathy their cruel irreparable loss." [16]

Isabella Brittingham

BORN ON 21ST FEBRUARY 1852, Mrs. Isabella D. Brittingham had a distinguished ancestor. Her great-grandfather, Mr. John Morton, was a signer of the American Declaration of Independence. Her father was an Episcopal clergyman. At the age of thirty-four she married James D. Brittingham, and twelve years later in 1898 she attended the first Bahá'í class held in New York City. Always an enthusiastic student of the Bible, the meaning of the prophecies in the Old and New Testaments soon ceased to be a matter to her of unending speculation. She realized that Jesus Christ and the Messengers before Him had often described in symbolic terms the coming of Bahá'u'lláh.

Not for long content to serve the Faith in just one city, she soon made the first of her many teaching trips to other parts of the United States.

In 1899 her niece, Miss Elizabeth Stewart, completed her studies as a nurse in Philadelphia. During that same year Mrs. Brittingham spoke of the Cause to this deeply spiritual girl. Almost immediately convinced of its truth, she only asked her aunt one question: "Are there any martyrs in this Cause?"[1]

On 20th August 1901, just after 'Abdu'l-Bahá had returned to 'Akká from Bahjí, where He had spent the afternoon, the Governor informed Him that He and His brothers, by the decree of Sultán 'Abdu'l-Hamíd, would again be strictly confined within the city limits of 'Akká and would no longer be allowed to walk in the countryside. A few weeks later, in September, Mrs. Brittingham arrived in 'Akká to visit the Master.

In her scholarly, instructive essay, *The Revelation of Bahá'u'lláh*, she has related her experiences there in these words: "Within the walls of the city abides One upon whom the thoughts of the world are centering; some consciously, and others unconsciously. A preparation is going on in all hearts. The vibrations from this great Centre are quickening and vitalizing all intellectual forces and spiritual powers. Having made a great and holy Pilgrimage to that city of spiritual Light, Love, Joy and Peace, it is my privilege to bear the Fragrance of its blessed Consummation unto all." [2]

With deep conviction she stated that 'Abdu'l-Bahá is the Centre of the Covenant of God, that "He knows no station save that of servitude, humility and lowliness to the beloved of El-Baha," that "recognition of this Station is the Life of every soul," and that "in the Holy Hands of Abdul-Baha is the Revelation of Baha'u'llah." [3]

According to her pilgrim notes, someone in 'Akká said to her: "At another time the Blessed Perfection instructed the gardener, Abul Kasim [Abu'l-Qásim], to attend to some business for him, he and the Master both being in the Rizwan. The Master, meeting Abul Kasim just afterward, instructed him to go to Acca and bring them some food for supper.

"The gardener sought Baha'o'llah and asked that he might tell Him of the Master's command. Baha'o'llah said in reply to Abul Kasim: 'That is well. You must go. You must do everything that the Master says. Everything the Master says is just the same as if I said it. He is me and I am he. There is no difference between my commands and the commands of the Master.'" [4]

As a result of her precious meetings with 'Abdu'l-Bahá, and the keen realization that she had gained from being near to Him of the agonizing problems that He had to face every day, on her return to America Mrs. Brittingham served the Cause with even more spirit than before.

In February 1902, the Bahá'í Publishing Society, then located in Chicago, published *The Revelation of Bahá'u'lláh*, from which I have already quoted. In the first chapter of this stimulating, historic work, Mrs. Brittingham explained:

"Jesus Christ used physical illustrations in order to impart the highest knowledge of God. Since our environment is material in character, every Messenger and Prophet from God has made use of material figures in order to convey to our understanding certain spiritual realities. Thus the Appearance of the Founder of each Dispensation is the Sun of Truth, newly arising upon the horizon of the darkened spiritual heavens, and bringing forth a New Day of Light." [5]

In the fourth and last chapter, she concluded: "In this day the veil is to be removed from the entire earth .... Until today the sacred books of all religions have been sealed. Today their seals are broken. Therefore it is the cycle for teaching, and for bringing every religion into a knowledge of and concord with all others." [6]

The Master revealed these words to Mrs. Brittingham about her essay: "Blessed art thou that thou hast compiled in the name of thy Lord, the Clement, a treatise comprising evident proofs regarding the appearance of the Kingdom of God in this sublime age." [7]

Mrs. Brittingham taught constantly. Whenever she succeeded in helping to lead someone into the Cause, she would enclose in a letter which she sent to 'Abdu'l-Bahá that person's declaration of Faith. The Hand of the Cause Hasan Balyuzi records that the Master, much pleased with the results of her efforts, had said laughingly that "Mrs. Brittingham was our Bahá'í-maker ...."[8]

One of Mrs. Brittingham's pupils was the heroic Dr. Susan Moody. She had already attended Bahá'í classes for some years in Chicago, but she did not become a confirmed believer until, during 1903, she made an intensive study of the Faith with Mrs. Brittingham in New York. Dr. Moody, named by the Master Amatu'l-A'alá, the Handmaid of the Most High, and often extolled by the Guardian throughout a long career of heroic Bahá'í service mostly spent in Ṭihrán as a doctor, educator, and bearer of God's Message for this day, often expressed her gratitude to Mrs. Brittingham for her invaluable instruction.

The Master revealed many Tablets for Mrs. Brittingham. In the spring of 1904 He answered one of her numerous questions in these words: "Thou hast written regarding the tests and trials to be manifested in the American countries. Know this, that hardships and misfortune shall increase day by day, and the people will be distressed. The doors of joy and happiness shall be closed upon all sides; terrible wars shall happen. Disappointment and the frustration of hopes shall surround the people from every direction, until they are obliged to turn to God. Then the Lights of great happiness will enlighten the horizons, so that the cry of 'Ya-Baha-El-Abha!' may arise upon all sides. This will happen! (Signed) Abdul-Baha Abbas"[9]

In 1906, shortly after the much-loved Mary J. Revell, a resident of Philadelphia, had come into the Bahá'í community, Mrs. Brittingham spent several months in that city. During part of this time she made the first of her frequent visits to Mrs. Revell's home. Situated very close to the Railway Station, her home was the only one which the Master visited in June 1912, when He spent three days in Philadelphia.

Mrs. Brittingham's husband, James, was a firm, active Bahá'í. He worked in the office of a Railroad Company in New York City. As a result he was unable to accompany his wife on her teaching trips, but he gave her whatever assistance he could.

In 1909 he published *The Message of the Kingdom of God*, a moving, persuasive talk that he had given at a public meeting in New York City. As his wife had done in a more comprehensive work, he related a short history of the Cause and explained with pertinent quotations from both the Old and New Testaments that the promise made by Jesus Christ had now been fulfilled. In a powerful closing passage, he asserted: "The Light of Knowledge hath appeared, before which the darkness of every superstitious fancy will be annihilated. The Hosts of the Supreme Concourse are descending to assist all those who rise up to serve their Lord, to subdue and gain the victory over the city of the hearts; to proclaim the Glad Tidings of the Coming of GOD and to unite the souls of His creatures."[10]

In October 1909 Mrs. Brittingham made her second

pilgrimage to the Holy Land. Although 'Abdu'l-Bahá had been released from the prison house more than a year before as a result of the Young Turk Revolution, and was no longer confined to the city limits, He had not yet moved from 'Akká to Haifa.

Among her notes, she has recorded the following statement by the Master: "Human-kind have come to the world in innumerable numbers, and passed away; their physical bodies and that which belonged to them passed away with them. Their health and disease both passed away. Their rest and hardship both vanished. Their wealth and poverty ended. Their honor and misery terminated. But the reality of man is immortal. The spirit of man is everlasting. It is the spirit to which importance is to be attached. The difference (between spirit and body) is this, that one will enter the realm of enlightenment whereas the other will fall into the world of darkness." [11]

On 10th March 1910, Mrs. Brittingham and her niece, Miss Elizabeth Stewart, were appointed to the newly-established Unity Band. The stimulating task of each member was to correspond every month with one of the twelve Women's Assemblies of the Orient. Mírzá 'Azízu'lláh Khán of Ṭihrán, to whom the women of the West addressed their letters, assured them of the great happiness which these letters gave to "their dear sisters of the East" and earnestly requested the ladies of the West to continue writing to them.

In 1909 Dr. Susan Moody had left the United States to live in Ṭihrán with the purpose of serving the Cause of God there. By now a well trained, skilful doctor, she was able to establish in Ṭihrán a much needed medical practice, particularly among the poor. Two years later she invited Elizabeth Stewart to come there and be her assistant. These two ladies, working under the most difficult circumstances, not only saved hundreds of lives, but helped to bring the Bahá'í Communities of Persia and America more closely together. Mrs. Brittingham and her niece wrote to each other regularly, except when it became impossible during certain periods of the First World War.

In April 1911, while the Master was still visiting Egypt,

and several months before He had begun His travels to the Christian West, He revealed a Tablet for Mrs. Brittingham which included these remarks: "If the believers of God in New York and other cities of America establish, in a befitting manner, union and harmony, with spirit, tongue, heart and body, suddenly they shall find Abdul-Baha in their midst. Unless this union is brought about, the Breath of the Holy Spirit shall not have any effect, for the physical body must find capacity, so that the life of the Spirit may breathe through it." [12]

In a stirring address entitled 'The Turning of the Pages of the Book of the Covenant', which Mrs. Brittingham gave on 5th November 1916, she forcefully reminded her audience of the five great Tablets which 'Abdu'l-Bahá had recently revealed for the North American Community. She described these Tablets as the greatest call that the Master had ever given to the American Bahá'ís, to summon those who are spiritually asleep to the Kingdom of God. In conclusion she urged all of the believers to make a superhuman effort to respond without delay to His great command.

Early in 1917, Mrs. Brittingham spent several months in Arizona. On her arrival in the city of Douglas, a newly declared believer arranged for Mrs. Brittingham to address an open forum of the Young Women's Christian Association. During her visit to Douglas, which lasted for two weeks, she taught individuals and groups at the home of this same believer. These beautiful meetings resulted in the formation in Douglas of the first Spiritual Assembly of Arizona.

During this trip she gave the message to about a hundred and fifty people. She felt, however, that her work had merely broken the ground in Arizona for future teachers to achieve there great results for the Cause.

Early in 1919, Mrs. Brittingham wrote to Albert Vail the following information about herself for inclusion in his article for 'Star of the West' called 'The Teaching Campaign': "Since January 1917, I have raised the call of the Kingdom in Arizona, Southern California, Oregon, Washington, Wyoming, Utah and very briefly in Reno, Nevada. I have given the Message in one church in Arizona and three in

California, to employees of the lunch room of the Great Northern Shipping Dock, Seattle, to army boys at Fort Wright, Spokane, in the State Prison, Salt Lake City, and to Metaphysical, Theosophical and many other gatherings in halls and homes, having thus addressed up to January 1, 1919, one hundred and thirty-three assemblages." [13] She also taught by correspondence receptive individuals whom she could not meet regularly.

Mrs. Brittingham often asked the Master's advice on personal matters, even on such subjects as diet. On the last afternoon of my pilgrimage in January 1955, as we were talking together in her sitting-room, the Hand of the Cause Amelia Collins said to me with much amusement: "Once Mrs. Brittingham came to stay with my husband and myself in California before my husband had met many Bahá'ís. The morning after her arrival I made a particular effort to prepare what I thought would be a delicious breakfast. When she came into the dining-room and looked at the table she said with some distress. 'Oh! but the Master told me to eat apples.' My husband politely suggested to her that perhaps she would be more comfortable in a hotel."

The distinguished Bahá'í writer, Marzieh Gail, has mentioned in a letter that Mrs. Brittingham used to share with the friends this suggestion by the Master: "When you eat an orange eat a little of the peel." [14]

In a Tablet revealed for the dear Revell sisters, Jessie and Ethel, at the end of 1920, the Master asked the sisters to give Mrs. Brittingham this message: "O thou harbinger of the Kingdom of God! If thou hast time and no obstacle exists, thou mayst take a trip to Philadelphia so that thou mayst impart joy to the friends and spread the breaths of God ...." [15]

During one of her last visits to the Revell home in Philadelphia, Mrs. Brittingham gave a series of radio talks on the principles of perfect justice. In a forceful address entitled 'Progress,' she clearly explained, without mentioning the word 'Bahá'í', the only way to establish the divine principles throughout the planet. In part she said: "There must be a Spiritual Wave to assuage the thirst of the hearts of humanity, sensitizing all to the higher Divine Law. This will create the ultimate foundation which, instead of dividing, will lift the denizens of this world to the standard of that reality which will forever discard all that separates! For separateness belongs to impermanent phases of material civilization, while the effulgence of and from God, shining in the hearts, burns away every barrier in that universal, divine establishment which will make of this world another world and convey enduring happiness to all of humankind. It must be the institution of the Kingdom of God upon earth .... Nothing less will bring about the Most Great Peace." [16]

Late in the evening of 28th January 1924 she died at the Revell home. On that very evening she had dictated eleven letters, each one for a believer, to Jessie Revell. Jessie records: "Those who have known Mrs. Brittingham also know her wonderful smile. But the night she went home her smile was one that did not belong to this earth." [17]

A few weeks afterwards a charming photograph of her appeared in 'Star of the West'. As she sits with hands folded resting on her knees, she looks directly in front of her. The calm, thoughtful expression on her kind, sensitive face, and her warm, penetrating eyes surely reflect a great and noble spirit. [18]

In January 1908 'Abdu'l-Bahá said to Helen Goodall and her daughter Ella Goodall Cooper, while they were visiting Him in 'Akká: "Give Mrs. Brittingham my best love and greetings and tell her that her services which she renders to this Cause are always before my eyes. They are written in the Book of the Kingdom, in the Heavenly Books, and will never be forgotten; and before long they will be written in the pages of the world in glorified writing, which shall be read by all people." [19]

Her photograph hangs among those of other eminent Bahá'ís in the Mansion of Bahá'u'lláh at Bahjí. The Guardian has acclaimed her "immortal services," and named her a disciple of 'Abdu'l-Bahá.

Howard and Mabel Ives

HOWARD COLBY IVES, THE YOUNGEST in a family of five children, was born in Brooklyn, New York. After the death of his father in 1869, when Howard was two years old, his mother took the children to Niagara Falls, to live with their grandfather. Although this arrangement proved none too happy, they did not return to Brooklyn until Howard was seventeen. A year later, on the advice of doctors, who were afraid that a low cough from which he suffered might develop into consumption, Howard was sent on an extended trip to Wyoming, where the dry climate and high altitude would surely benefit him.

Howard spent the next two years living on a ranch tending sheep. As he sat by himself in the hills and looked at the stars, he sometimes wrote poetry. Always a passionate "seeker of Truth," he tried to dispel his doubts concerning the existence of God. But although he returned home entirely recovered from his physical illness, he still had not risen from his state of restless agnosticism.

His devoted daughter, Muriel Ives Newhall, has described in a letter to me the following experience which Howard had soon afterwards:

One evening walking home from his job as errand boy on Wall Street he came up the slight rise on to Brooklyn Bridge. It was sunset and Father walked slowly, shelling the peanuts that always filled his pockets and reading Browning. Suddenly he was overwhelmed. Knowledge and certainty exploded within him. He shouted his discovery. "There is a God," he shouted—right there on Brooklyn Bridge. When he told me this story he burst out laughing—and Father had a wonderful laugh, rich, deep and filled with joy. "There was an old apple woman going by" he said, "and she looked scared to death. She thought I was crazy. But I knew I was sane for the first time in my life."

In 1890 Howard married Beth Hoyt, who was four years his senior. At first they lived in Flatbush, a suburb of New York. Their first son, Waldo, died there of pneumonia when he was six months old. Soon after their second son, Whitney, was born, Howard decided to attend Williams College, in Massachusetts. As soon as they had moved to Williamstown, Beth, who was most anxious to help him, opened their house to boarders. One day shortly before Christmas, when Whitney was just three years old and in bed recovering from diphtheria, the boarding house caught fire. Someone wrapped Whitney in blankets and then carried him out of the house, but as a result he had a relapse and died a little more than a week later.

The death of this lovely child was of course a crushing blow to his parents. In March their only daughter, Muriel, was born. By this time Howard had already left College and returned to his former job of selling insurance. During the first three years of Muriel's life, Howard travelled with his wife and daughter to wherever he was working. When Muriel was four, they moved to a small yellow brick house in Philadelphia, and while they were living there Howard and Beth had another son, Douglas. He only lived a few hours.

Howard did not allow such unhappy events to discourage him from his spiritual search. Muriel has written: "One evening in that house while I sat on Mother's lap having my very straight hair turned into ringlets by Mother's twisting it up on rags, Father came to stand in the doorway with a book in his hand. He said, 'Beth, I've found it. I've found what I want to do. I'm going to become a Unitarian minister.' The book was a volume of William Ellery Channing's sermons and Father was radiant with his discovery."

A year later in 1902 he moved with his family to Meadville, Pennsylvania, and entered the Unitarian Theological School. Beth again gave him enormous help. Making portraits of students her speciality, she became a professional photographer. Besides this, each Saturday in her large dining-room she held a sale of Oriental rugs, fabrics, candleshades that she had water-coloured, and her own baked delicacies. During summer holidays, in order to make some extra money, Howard raised funds for a foriegn college run by Americans. Muriel recalls, "Father said to Mother jokingly one day, 'It's no credit to you, Beth, that you're completely unselfish—you're just born that way and there's nothing you could possibly do about it.'"

In 1905, at the age of thirty-eight, Howard graduated from theological school. After the Ives had first spent a year in a small parish with a beautiful church in Brewster, Massachusetts, on Cape Cod, he was called to a parish in New London, Connecticut. There he found that for lack of a church the congregation was meeting in club rooms. During the four years that the Ives stayed in New London, he was responsible not only for building a nice, modest brick church there, but also for greatly increasing the size of his congregation.

In 1907 Howard and Beth adopted an orphaned boy of fourteen from a family of mill workers. They treated the boy like a son and gave him a fine education. Even so he did not turn out well, and became an increasing cause of anxiety to his foster parents until the pathetic end of his short life.

In 1910 the Ives moved again, this time to a parish in Summit, New Jersey, where Howard supervised the building of a church modelled after one by Christopher Wren. Early in 1911, Howard brought together "a group of brothers of the spirit aiming to express their highest ideals in service to struggling humanity."[1] Every Sunday evening this group, which called itself the Brotherhood Church, with Howard as its voluntary guide, gathered in a large Masonic Hall in Jersey City.

Much loved by his congregation, Howard was now a respected minister of the church. His strenuous efforts for it, however, had ceased to give him real satisfaction. In his now classic spiritual autobiography *Portals to Freedom*, first published in 1937, he wrote that during the fall of 1911 he experienced a period of great unhappiness. Although he had never faltered in his love for Jesus of Nazareth, even in his earlier years as an agnostic, he was now plagued with spiritual unrest, and his duties as a paid clergyman were a cause of great frustration to him. Confused, disappointed, and depressed by his daily round of conventional duties, he felt himself on the verge of spiritual bankruptcy and did not know where to turn.

One day in October 1911, he found in a copy of 'Everybody's Magazine' an article which contained the story of 'Abdu'l-Bahá's life, and news of His forthcoming journey to the United States of America. He re-read this illuminating article several times and placed it in his scrap-book. Not long afterwards, Mr. Clarence Moore, a Trustee of the Brotherhood Church for whom he had a deep love and great respect, called his attention to the Bahá'í Cause.

A few months before the Master set sail for New York, Howard attended his first Bahá'í meeting. Attracted by its spirit, he asked the chairman, Mountfort Mills, to address the Brotherhood Church, and a week or two later Mr. Mills gave a moving talk there on 'The Divine Springtime'. Encouraged by this esteemed believer, who devoted a great deal of time to teaching him, Howard began to attend meetings each week. "My heart was in a turmoil and yet incredibly attracted," [3] he later wrote. On 'Abdu'l-Bahá's arrival, Howard expressed his longing to speak to Him alone without even an interpreter in the room, and at nine o'clock in the morning of the Master's second day in New York City, Howard, among a large group of people, visited Him in His suite at the Hotel Ansonia on Upper Broadway. Without even speaking to him first, 'Abdu'l-Bahá granted Howard his heartfelt wish.

In his fascinating and moving book Howard has described this meeting:

I could not speak. We both sat perfectly silent for what seemed a long while, and gradually a great peace came to me. Then 'Abdu'l-Bahá placed His hand upon my breast saying that it was the heart that speaks. Again silence: a long, heart-enthralling silence. No word further was spoken, and all the time I was with

Him not one single sound came from me. But no word was
necessary from me to Him. I knew that, even then, and how I
thanked God it was so.[4]

After this priceless experience, although he was still in
spiritual turmoil, he often consoled himself with this thought:
"At last the desire of my soul is in sight."[5] He yearned to
know what made 'Abdu'l-Bahá so infinitely superior to
everyone else. A few days later, he again met Him, this time
in the beautiful home of the dearly-loved Edward and Carrie
Kinney at 780 West End Avenue, in New York City. Only
after frequent conversations with Him there and in other
places did he slowly begin to understand the perfect answers
of the Master to his eager questions.

According to Muriel, who was fifteen at the time, when her
father used to come home and describe his recent conversations with the Master, "his brown eyes became aflame" as
he told her mother and herself of "the things He had said"
and "the tremendous majestic manner of His saying them."
Beth reacted with cool caution to these accounts.

On Sunday evening 19th May, in response to Howard's
invitation, the Master spoke at the Brotherhood Church. As
he looked at the Master from the audience, he did not find it
"difficult to imagine a world transformed by the spirit of
divine brotherhood. For He Himself was that spirit in-
carnate."[6] The Master concluded His formal talk with these
revealing remarks: "In the future there will be no very rich nor
extremely poor. There will be an equilibrium of interests, and
a condition will be established which will make both rich
and poor comfortable and content. This will be an eternal
and blessed outcome of the glorious twentieth century which
will be realized universally. The significance of it is that the
glad-tidings of great joy revealed in the promises of the holy
books will be fulfilled. Await ye this consummation."[7]

Although Howard was already much criticized by those
close to him, by influential members of his congregation, and
by certain clergymen, for his growing interest in the Cause, he
still had not attained a true understanding of what he was investigating. Only at moments did he find himself relieved from
spiritual confusion by a glimpse of what he felt was the truth.

Over the weekend of August 9th Howard visited the Master at an inn where He was staying in the mountain summer resort of Dublin, New Hampshire. On Sunday morning the Master, with His precious advice and loving encouragement, made Howard realize that he could never rest until he had approached the station to which He was calling him. A few days after he had left Dublin Howard wrote to 'Abdu'l-Bahá to thank Him for His great kindness. The Master replied with His first Tablet to Howard, in part of which He revealed:

A hundred thousand ministers have come and gone: they left behind no trace nor fruit, nor were their lives productive .... I have become hopeful, and prayed that thou mayest attain to another Bounty; seek another Life; ask for another World; draw nearer unto God; become informed of the Mysteries of the Kingdom; attain to Life Eternal and become encircled with the Glory Everlasting.[8]

During the next few months, while he was travelling throughout the Eastern States for his work, Howard read only Bahá'í books in his free time. When he returned home in the autumn, he was forced to close the Brotherhood Church through lack of financial support. The Master counselled him in a second Tablet not to be unhappy but to spend his time in spreading the teachings of Bahá'u'lláh. Every Friday Howard was now attending the already famous study class which the much-loved Juliet Thompson gave in her house at 48 West Tenth Street. She and the other believers whom he got to know there helped him to draw closer to the Faith.

On the evening of 15th November 1912, the Master gave in this house a powerful, comprehensive talk upon "the distinctive characteristics of the Manifestation of BAHA'-U'LLAH" and proved "that from every standpoint His cause is distinguished from all others."[9] Howard has written that as He spoke, "His face was illumined with a radiance not of this world."[10] During the last few days of 'Abdu'l-Bahá's visit Howard seldom left His presence. Not yet aware of the Master's divine station, Howard already believed that

'Abdu'l-Bahá was a perfect man, and he wanted to do whatever he could to be even a little like Him. Two or three months after the Master's departure, however, all of Howard's former doubts and confusions vanished. He realized that Bahá'u'lláh was the Messenger of God for this Day and that His eldest Son, 'Abdu'l-Bahá, was the Centre of the Covenant.

A Tablet which the Master revealed for Howard around this time included the following advice: 'Endeavor as much as thou canst that thou mayest master the Principles of Bahá'u'lláh, promulgate them all over that continent, create love and unity between the believers, guiding the people, awakening the heedless ones and resurrecting the dead." [11]

Soon after his conversion to the Bahá'í Faith, Howard gave up his ministry and resigned from the Church, much to Beth's disappointment. The Ives moved from their house in Summit to a small apartment near Columbia University in New York, and returning to the business world, he chose work that would give him the opportunity to travel and to meet large numbers of people. His job, which was to sell the Alexander Hamilton Business Course, took him away from home for long periods of time. The strain of their new situation which included the return of financial worries became too much for Beth, and she had a series of nervous breakdowns.

On 22nd June 1916, when World War One had reached its most violent stage, the Master revealed His final Tablet for Howard. In part He wrote: "O thou speaker in the Temple of the Kingdom! Praise be to God that most of the time thou art traveling, going from city to city raising the melody of the Kingdom in meetings and churches, and announcing the glad-tidings of Heaven." [12]

Although Beth had always been a devoted, unselfish wife and mother, Howard's ardent services to the Bahá'í Faith greatly disturbed her. She did not see fit to follow the same path. About six years after he had recognized His Lord, Howard and Beth obtained a legal separation, soon followed by a divorce. In 1919 Howard met his future second wife, Mabel Rice-Wray.

Mabel was born in St. Louis, Missouri, in 1878. The grand parents of her father, Albert Simon, came from Germany. Her mother, Caroline McGrew, who was of English descent, had lived in Virginia before her marriage. Mabel's parents, who were old enough to be her grandparents, brought her up in the small town of Kirkwood, Missouri. A hall ran through the length of their attractive, old-fashioned house. "When she was a young girl, Mabel once rode on her donkey down this hall from one end of the house to the other." Decidedly popular, she had great charm, enormous vitality and rare physical beauty. She also possessed a quality seldom found in such an attractive, sought-after girl, a deep interest in spiritual truth. She always examined any teachings that she thought might lead her to what she felt everyone needed. Just before the turn of the century, when she was twenty-one, Mabel heard of the Bahá'í Revelation from Mrs. Doty, of Baltimore, Maryland. Although like other seekers in the West at that time, Mabel had access to only a few selections from the Holy Writings, which included some Tablets of 'Abdu'l-Bahá, she soon recognized the station of Bahá'u'lláh. When someone asked Mabel how she had found it possible to do this, she replied, "I only knew that a Manifestation of God had again walked the earth and that was enough."[13]

In 1903 she married Theron Canfield Rice-Wray. At first they settled in Newark, New Jersey. Within four years they had three children, Edris, Landon Carter, and Colston, the second of whom died when he was a child.

Edris has written to me: "My mother and my father lived in different worlds. He was dynamic, forceful, and brilliant, but very worldly when compared to her. He had high ideals, and a great admiration for 'Abdu'l-Bahá and often said that the standards of his life were based on the words of 'Abdu'l-Bahá, but he never became an active Bahá'í and could not accept the Will and Testament of 'Abdu'l-Bahá."

In 1909 the Rice-Wrays moved to Tropico, later called Glendale, a suburb of Los Angeles. While living there Mabel became a close friend of Kathryn Frankland who, with her husband Alec, had moved to California in 1903 to serve the

Cause. These two distinguished ladies worked hard for the Faith together. Mabel had frequent firesides and study classes in her home. She also found time to be active in certain women's organizations, particularly those which were trying to foster more humane treatment of children, equal rights for women, and world peace.

From around 1911 for the rest of their lives, Mabel's parents, Albert and Caroline Simon, lived with the Rice-Wrays. According to Edris, her father behaved with the same generosity to his wife's parents as he always had to his own family and never complained of this added responsibility.

On 18th October 1912, while Mabel and her family were still living in Tropico, 'Abdu'l-Bahá took the train from San Francisco to Los Angeles, so that He might visit the grave of the steadfast Thornton Chase, the first believer of the West. Just as she was in the midst of moving her family into a new house, Mabel heard the thrilling news that 'Abdu'l-Bahá had already arrived in the city. Leaving her mother in charge of the operation, Mabel quickly dressed Edris and Colston and drove them both to the hotel where the Master was staying. They arrived just as He and a group of believers had entered the lobby. Mabel and her children accompanied Him and the others upstairs to His room and stayed there with Him for over an hour. Edris and Colston have written: "We children did not fully appreciate the importance of this meeting at the time; to us He was as a kind grandfather, but to our mother it was a moment of rededication, a moment of increased awakening. She became inflamed with the deepest longing to serve this Cause, of which He was the authorized Interpreter and Exemplar." [14]

In 1914 the Rice-Wrays and the Simons moved to Detroit, Michigan. Faced with serious marital problems at this time, Mabel learned not to ask God for personal happiness, but rather for the privilege of serving His Cause. Mainly through her strenuous efforts a Bahá'í group was soon established in that city. She did not neglect the Bahá'í education of other people's children or her own. In reply to a letter from her, the Master gave Edris the name Roushan and Colston the name Rouhi, and revealed for them the immortal prayer that begins: "O my Lord! O my Lord! I am a child of tender years. Nourish me from the breast of Thy mercy, train me in the bosom of Thy love ...."[15]

In 1918, much to Mabel's unhappiness, Theron left her, and soon afterwards insisted upon a divorce. She, who had never worked for a living, now took a job as a saleswoman.

Towards the end of his life, her father gave Mabel a most welcome surprise. Edris has written me this delightful description of what he did. "In his sixties he changed his business, in his seventies he changed his politics, and at ninety-five he became a Bahá'í. He changed almost overnight from a crochety old devil to almost an angel. Everyone loved him." The Master revealed these words for Mabel about this precious event: "Convey my greetings to thy honored father. Tell him that entrance into the kingdom .... maketh an old man young and maketh strong the feeble."[16]

In November 1920, a little more than a year after their first meeting, Mabel and Howard were married. With the intention of making enough money to support them in a life wholly devoted to serving the Cause, they settled temporarily in New York City not far from where the noble Bahá'ís, Harlan and Grace Ober, were living. These four became deeply united in their teaching work and closely involved in business. One day in 1921, realizing that their plan to achieve security was not realistic, Howard and Mabel decided to do what might seem to some impossible. With no money saved they left the city without further delay. Mabel recalled how this happened: "So began our long Odyssey. We advertised for some selling proposition for two salesmen who wished to travel, received 21 answers, chose one, and felt ready to go. We sold or gave away all our earthly possessions, reduced all our earthly goods to a trunk or two and a couple of suitcases. When we had bought our train tickets to Pittsburgh, we had just $7.00 between us."[17]

During this visit of six weeks, their first to this city, they held thirty-six Bahá'í meetings. From there they moved from city to city and continued to travel in the eastern, central, and southern parts of the country most of the time for the rest of their lives. In order to support themselves they began by selling show-cards of their own making to small stores. Sometime later they sold a course in adult education.

One winter, when they were again in Pittsburgh, Howard heard that a fortune could be made in rabbit skins and raised hundreds of rabbits. Before he had sold any of them the Depression, which had just begun, caused the fur-market to collapse. As a result he was obliged to sell his rabbits for their meat. Some years later he told Muriel, "with his uproarious laugh, how skilful he had become—he was able to skin a rabbit a minute."

During another stay in that same city the Ives, the Obers, and Willard McKay and his wife Doris, shared a house, did business together, and in wonderful unity taught the Faith with remarkable results.

The Ives often travelled by car. Howard used to paste some of his favourite Bahá'í prayers on the dashboard, and as he drove his wife from place to place he would try to memorize these prayers. This practice of course led to several accidents. Muriel has written:

Father, even without the distracting prayers on his dashboard, was not a good driver—there were too many interesting things to think about. The last accident he had was when he and Rizwanea [as Mabel was sometimes called] were on their way to keep a speaking date. The car got tangled up with a truck, a telegraph pole and another car. Father was taken to a hospital and Rizwanea went off to get a wrecker and salvage anything that was salvageable. There wasn't much. Then she went back to the hospital to find out what the doctors had learned about Father. For all she knew he might be dead. But as she approached the hospital she saw him sitting on the steps waiting for her so that they could be on their way to keep a Bahá'í speaking date."

Howard and Mabel often longed to have a permanent home. This natural inclination, however, always came second to their much stronger desire to proclaim and then to work towards the establishment of the Cause in another city.

In 1934, while they were living in Knoxville, Tennessee, Howard, at sixty-seven, realized that he had a fine gift for writing. The Directors of the Tennessee Valley Authority engaged him to write a series of articles on its vast plan "to build a series of at least eight great dams and from 20 to 30 smaller ones for the control and release of a large part of the potential water power of this region, totaling in the neighborhood of three million horse power."[18] In the hot climate of Tennessee to which he was not accustomed, Howard worked on these articles every day of the late spring and early summer of that year. One morning he had a heart attack and collapsed on the floor beside his bed. Along with his eyesight and his hearing, Howard's always delicate health now became permanently impaired.

In 1936, while they were living with Edris, Howard often described to both ladies his experiences with the Master. Afraid that these precious incidents would never be recorded, Edris insisted that Howard should write a book about them. Although twenty-four years had elapsed since these events had taken place, he felt sure of the exact words that the Master had said to him. For this reason, according to Edris, in the first manuscript of *Portals to Freedom* he quoted the Master directly. Later, however, these quotations were changed to read, "'Abdu'l-Bahá said that ...." followed by His remarks.

This much loved book about the Master's journey to America, and Howard's gradual spiritual awakening through His presence, has already been a source of joyful and inspired instruction to countless sincere seekers and believers alike, and will surely remain the same throughout the coming centuries.

Shortly after he had finished *Portals to Freedom* he wrote a revealing and impressive book-length epic poem entitled *The Song Celestial*. He told Edris: "It came through so fast I could hardly get it down on paper."

In this absorbing work man asks God how to find His Universe. God replies:

The heavens of My Mercy are so vast;
The Oceans of My Bounty so unbound,
That never hath a soul besought unblest,
Nor any seeker but hath surely found.

It is for this that all My Prophets came
That They might lead men thither, and man's claim
To paradise, which like celestial fire
I lighted in his heart, substantiate.[19]

Not yet free of doubt, man now asks God how to recognize these Prophets when they come. In two verses of clear and powerful explanation God says:

They speak not as the scribes, with learned lore
Culled from the out-worn teachings of the past,
Which leave men darker than they were before,
As blind lead blind. They speak not as men speak.
In accents wise and yet sublimely meek
They tell of what I whisper to Their soul.[20]

Man expresses his fear that if he serves God alone selfish people will destroy him. God assures man that His hosts are now building a new World Order to protect him, and that a Chosen Few will lead His hosts to victory. At last convinced that what God has said to him is perfect truth, man says:

Now to myself at last—at last—I die!
And, risen to true Life, armed with Love's sword,
I march beneath Thy banner, nor care when,
Nor where, nor how I meet my shining Lord
Enthroned in Man, for I shall know Him then![21]

In the concluding verse of this uplifting poem, God makes these promises to man:

My Glory rests upon thee. On thy head
My confirmations fall. Before thy tread
All obstacles shall fade and I will lead
Thee to thy heart's desire. I grant release
To thee from bondage; from all fear surcease.

To every soul who followeth Guidance—Peace.[22]

In December 1939, *World Order*, the Bahá'í magazine, published a stimulating essay by Howard on 'The Valley of Astonishment', the sixth valley in *The Seven Valleys*, a mystical masterpiece revealed by Bahá'u'lláh. During this period, besides other interesting Bahá'í articles, Howard wrote a study course that has not yet been published.

When Muriel spoke to her father two or three years before his passing he had already become excited about the prospect of taking the wonderful journey from this world to the next and drawing much closer to God. Howard told her: "There's only one thing I want, one thing I pray for—that I may be conscious and know when I cross the threshold, I want to be aware."

Starting in the fall of 1941, Howard and Mabel visited in succession Memphis, Tennessee, Hot Springs and Little Rock, Arkansas. In this last-named city, where Bahá'ís had never been before, Howard became seriously ill. At the same time the National Teaching Committee, unaware of Howard's critical condition, asked Mabel to help solve a Bahá'í problem in Kentucky. Although she knew that he was dying, they decided as always to consider the Faith first. She returned to Little Rock shortly before his passing.

As he lay in bed constantly in pain, he heard an enquirer who was sitting in the next room ask a question. Without hesitation he left his bed, "stumbled weakly to the door and leaning against it answered the question. He then went back to bed relaxed and content."

A little while before he died, Howard said to Mabel, "Darling, we'll be together through all the worlds of God." [23] She agreed with him that this was so.

Muriel has written this beautiful note about him: "Rizwanea telegraphed me: 'Your father died in great triumph.' When the wire arrived my daughter, Barbara, then fifteen, was with me and I am sure for not more than a half minute we clung to each other. Our sun had darkened. There was no ground under our feet. And then Barbara whispered—quoting a poem of Father's—' Listen to thy heart's whisper—I am here.' And with that all fright, all grief, all sense of loss left us—both of us—and it has never come back. Father is with us—he has never left us for a moment—and we are both convinced that the worlds of God are, as 'Abdu'l-Bahá assures us, truly interwoven, and it is only the imagination of man that separates them."

The funeral service for Howard took place on 23rd June 1941, in Little Rock. On this occasion about fifty friends gathered in a small chapel to show their love for Howard and to offer him their heartfelt prayers. The Guardian cabled this uplifting message: "Profoundly deplore tremendous loss outstanding promoter Faith. Evidences his magnificent labors imperishable. Deepest sympathy. Ardent prayers." [24]

After his passing Mabel resumed her intensive teaching work, convinced of his help from the unseen world. She travelled alone to widely scattered cities, mostly in the southern states, and stayed in each city for several months. Her son and daughter have declared, "It was amazing, during the last two years of her life how she was able to combine both her former qualities and his as a Bahá'í teacher. She could still make contacts, attract people and give lectures, but now she also had his distinct quality of being able to confirm souls and deepen them in the teachings." [25]

While Mabel was serving the Faith in Omaha, Nebraska, she said to a friend, "I have lived longer than you have and so I will tell you this; some day you won't remember when you were happy, you won't remember the times when you were sad, you will only remember the times when you helped the Cause of God." [26]

Early in January of 1943 Mabel travelled from Louisville, Kentucky, across the continent to Albuquerque, New Mexico. During her visit of three weeks to that attractive city she helped both to increase the size of the community and to give it a stronger unity.

Although Mabel was not well at the time, Edris persuaded her to fly to Chicago for the Bahá'í National Convention in Riḍván of 1943. When to her great happiness she met many of her strong and active spiritual children there, she remarked, "How thrilling to see how they grow from year to year." [27] A week after the convention was over, she left for Oklahoma City. Instead of resting there for two weeks as she had planned, when Mabel found that the community was expecting her to start a series of lectures without delay, she left her sick-bed to give the first one. At the end of her third lecture, however, she was obliged to enter a hospital.

In the early evening of 18th June 1943, shortly before Mabel was expected to give her last lecture in Oklahoma City, Edris and Colston were sitting on either side of their mother's bed. "My children", she said. "Yes, we are both here," they answered. After a pause, she went on, "But I have so many children .... and there's so much work to be done."[28] Edris and Colston knew of course that the end had come. When a lovely peace spread over their mother's face, they looked at each other. One of them said, "You know what we have to do." The other said, "Which of us is going to do it?"

After they had quickly decided that Edris should speak in their mother's place, she hurried to the hall, and after first informing the audience that her mother could not come, gave a talk such as she had planned. When Edris had finished, "she quietly and beautifully announced the step her mother had taken the hour before, into the next world of God."

Mabel died just two days less than two years after Howard. She was buried in Oklahoma City's Memorial Park. National institutions of the Faith and eminent Bahá'ís have often praised her magnificent services to the Cause. With his infallible knowledge, the Guardian confirmed these other opinions in this cable:[29] "Profoundly deplore loss self-sacrificing, distinguished teacher Faith Mabel Ives. Manifold contributions teaching activities before and since inception Seven Year Plan outstanding, memorable, highly meritorious. Assure daughter deepest loving sympathy, prayers. Abiding felicity crowning noble labors."

Mariam and Charles Haney

IN AUGUST 1975, AT THE BAHÁ'Í Summer School in Waterford, Ireland, the Hand of the Cause Paul Haney spoke to me about his parents. His mother, a heroic lady, whose maiden name was Mary Ida Parkhurst, was born on 13th November 1872 in New York City. When she was twelve, her parents moved with their two sons and three daughters to Minneapolis, Minnesota. Although kind and ethical, Mr. and Mrs. Parkhurst had little interest in spiritual matters. Mary Ida was quite different from her parents. While still a young girl, she went from church to church looking for what she thought might be the truth. Although her search was unsuccessful until she reached the age of twenty-eight, she was never tempted to settle for a belief that she could only partially accept. In no way discouraged, she was still determined to find the right answer to her questions.

When she was about twenty, Mary Ida first met her future husband, Charles Freeborn Haney, in Minneapolis. Fourteen years her senior, he came from a strict background. His father, the Reverend Richard Haney, a famous minister in the Methodist Church, was one of the founders of Northwestern University in Evanston, near Chicago. He had five daughters and two sons. One of them, following in his father's footsteps, became a clergyman; but Charles refused to do the same. Like Mary Ida, he was a seeker of truth. He practised law for a few years and then worked successfully for several private businesses.

Charles and Mary Ida were married in 1893. During the first seven years of their life together they still could not find the spiritual answer for which they both longed. During a

155

visit of several months to Boston they looked carefully, but with no satisfaction, into Christian Science, as they had into other sects and philosophies.

In January 1900, while they were staying at a small hotel on the west side of Chicago, the Haneys noticed that a charming young married couple was meeting each day with some men in oriental dress. Attracted to this group, the Haneys became curious to know what they were discussing with so much enthusiasm. After the Haneys had introduced themselves to this couple, who were the well-known early Bahá'ís Charles and Elizabeth Greenleaf, they soon found out what they believed. Finding the Haneys unusually receptive, the Greenleafs spoke to them at great length about the Bahá'í Faith. Almost immediately they accepted it as the Word of God for this Day.

On 9th July 1959, from a nursing home in Takoma Park, Maryland, Mrs. Haney wrote to a dear friend, Mrs. Alice Dudley: "A good and wonderful day to be writing to you. The Báb gave up his life for humanity .... that we might live .... for on this day in the square of Tabríz took place that Martyrdom which will shake the world when the people realize the truth. It was the Báb and His life story which acted on me as a magnet to draw me to this Most Great Cause when I was only in the 'twenties'; to be exact .... 59 years ago last January ...."[1]

Not long after they had recognised the station of Bahá'u'lláh, the Haneys moved to New York City. For almost eleven years, until 1911, they divided their time between there and California except for occasional trips to other places. By working hard at his profession Charles was able to provide sufficient means so that his wife could give all her time to the Faith.

Early in her Bahá'í life, 'Abdu'l-Bahá gave Mary Ida the name of Mariam, which from then on she always used.

During her first five years in New York City Mariam worked closely with Mrs. Ellen V. Beecher, called Mother Beecher by 'Abdu'l-Bahá and her friends. According to Mariam, this remarkable Bahá'í, already advanced in years, trained from childhood her granddaughter, the future Hand of the Cause Dorothy Beecher Baker, "and brought her safely into the Bahá'í fold." [2]

An important service that Mariam began at this time when there was little Bahá'í literature translated into English, and which she continued to perform until the ascension of the Master, was to make copies of many precious Tablets which He had revealed for believers and sincere seekers in the West and attend to their distribution throughout the American Bahá'í Community.

In 1902, 'Abdu'l-Bahá asked the "immortal" Lua Moore Getsinger, whom later He called the "Herald of the Covenant," to go to Paris and deliver a powerful petition from Him to the Sháh of Persia, who was visiting that city. The Master pleaded with the Sháh to protect the Bahá'ís of Persia from the fanatical religious leaders who were once again persecuting them in a cruel and horrible fashion. Mariam accompanied Lua to Paris, and stayed there with her for several weeks while she was struggling to obtain an audience with the Sháh, until she had successfully completed this difficult and important mission. In her moving and informative account of this dramatic event, Mariam reported that Lua presented two petitions to the Sháh, the first one to him personally. She also remarked that for several years afterwards the persecutions in Persia greatly diminished. [3]

While these two courageous ladies were still in Paris, Mariam received from the Master a Tablet which included these words: "Verily I read thine eloquent, excellent and graceful letter of wonderful words, and I was rejoiced at its contents which showed thine abundant joy at the appearance of the Kingdom of God, thy great attraction to the Beauty of God, and thine intention to accompany and assist the maid-servant of God, Lua, in diffusing the fragrance of God." [4]

During their first seven and a half years in the Bahá'í community the Haneys often asked the Master for permission to visit Him in 'Akká. He always advised them to postpone their pilgrimage, however. In a Tablet translated on 28th October 1903, the Master explained to Mariam: [5]

"As to the question of thy being granted the favour of

157

visiting the Holy Tomb (i.e. 'Akká): In these days this is very difficult on account of the events and occurrences in Persia and the calumnies of the faithless. For the present, thou shouldst wait and endure patiently. I hope thou wilt make thy pilgrimage in the future. Now, be thou engaged in guiding the people, for this is equivalent to visiting the Holy Tomb.

> Send loving greetings to thy revered husband
> Upon thee be greeting and praise
> (Signed) 'Abdu'l-Bahá 'Abbás."

Late in 1908, after the Haneys had been married for sixteen years and Mariam was at last expecting a child, the Master sent them their longed-for invitation. When they arrived in the Holy Land the following February, the Master was still living within the walled city of 'Akká, although he had been released from confinement almost six months before as a result of the Young Turk Revolution. The Haneys stayed in 'Akká for nine days with Him. A skilful secretary, Mariam took stenographic notes of much that the Master said to them personally and to large groups of which the Haneys were a part. Mariam later reported that after He had read her notes, the Master stated: "These notes are correct. You may print them." [6] According to His instructions the Haneys had these notes published and called them *A Heavenly Feast*.

One day the Master said to the Haneys: "Conveying the Message (or teaching) is accomplished to-day by the Confirmation of the Holy Spirit, and not by any fund of knowledge or by the possession of facts. The confirmations of the Holy Spirit are obtained by attractions of the heart. Without these attractions, the former is unobtainable. The proof of this is evident. The disciples of Christ, with the exception of St. Paul, were not learned men, but they taught the world. By the power of attraction, zeal and conflagration, as well as severance from the world and by the giving of life, they taught. And this proved the magnet attracting the confirmations of the Holy Spirit." [7]

While Charles and Mariam were still with Him, the Master blessed their unborn child. On the day of their departure,

Mariam remained outwardly calm until they had left the Master, and boarded the ship. By this time she could no longer restrain her tears. On their way home the Haneys met most happily with the friends in Egypt, Paris, and London. When they arrived back in America, Mariam found a Tablet waiting for her, in which the Master had revealed: "I was with you when you were weeping on the ship." [8]

Some months after he and his wife had returned to California, Charles received a Tablet from the Master which included these remarks: ".... From the day thou didst go until now thou art in My mind and present in the Assemblage of the Merciful. Thou hast never been forgotten and shalt never be. The sweetness of that meeting and the ecstasy of those conversations are still fresh in the taste of My Spirit.

"Certainly the precepts delivered to thee are remembered by thee and thou art arising to perform them with the utmost endeavor." [9]

On 20th August 1909, while the Haneys were living in Los Angeles, their son Paul was born. Two years afterwards, Charles accepted a good position which Franklin K. Lane, later Secretary of the Interior, had offered him with the Interstate Commerce Commission in Washington, D.C., and he moved there with his family.

In the course of His historic journey throughout North America in 1912, 'Abdu'l-Bahá made two visits to Washington. The Haneys, of course, met with Him whenever possible. The Hand of the Cause Paul Haney told me this touching incident: "While the Master was in Washington, owing to lack of space in certain houses not all the Bahá'ís could be asked to every meeting. One evening when my mother, like some others, was left out, she walked around the house where He was in order to be near Him. Realizing this without being told, the Master came to the window in front of which she was passing, opened the curtain and waved to her."

About two weeks after 'Abdu'l-Bahá left Washington for the second time, a few days before he was due to leave the country, Mariam travelled to New York in her intense longing to be with Him. When, on the morning of December 5th, the Master gave his last spoken message in America on board the steamship *Celtic*, Mariam had the enviable task of recording this beautiful, never-to-be forgotten talk. According to her notes, he said in one passage: "Beware lest ye offend any heart, lest ye speak against any one in his absence, lest ye estrange yourselves from the servants of God. You must consider all His servants as your own family and relations. Direct your whole effort toward the happiness of those who are despondent, bestow food upon the hungry, clothe the needy and glorify the humble. Be a helper to every helpless one and manifest kindness to your fellow creatures in order that ye may attain the good-pleasure of God. This is conducive to the illumination of the world of humanity and eternal felicity for yourselves. I seek from God everlasting glory in your behalf; therefore this is my prayer and exhortation." [10]

The Bahá'í Temple Unity, an administrative body which had been established in 1909 to direct the building of the first House of Worship in America, held its sixth Annual Convention in Chicago, at Riḍvan 1914. As one of two delegates from the local spiritual assembly of Washington, D.C., Mariam gave an encouraging report of Bahá'í progress in that city. Among her remarks were these:

"When Abdul-Baha was in Washington He testified—Praise his holy name!—that the Washington Assembly was a united Assembly..... We decided .... that it should also be an instructive Assembly..... Then, this little band of firm, steadfast, tried and true believers studied the Word, and they are trying to crystallize that Word into their lives..... The seed of Truth of BAHA'O'LLAH has been scattered widely in Washington .... Those seeds are germinating in the hearts, and after a while we shall see the results." [11]

While the Haneys were living in Washington, Charles made frequent business trips to various parts of the country despite his failing health. The eminent Mrs. Isabella D. Brittingham, one of the first Bahá'ís in America and a close friend of the Haneys, wrote that during 1917 she met Charles in Los Angeles, California, Portland, Oregon, and Salt Lake

160

City, Utah. While they were together in this last-named city, they spent many hours "reading and communing upon the holy utterances of God ...." She noted how he had "so clear a vision of divine happiness and great peace under constant physical pain .... The key to all this .... was steadfastness in the Covenant and Testament of God, which the beloved of our hearts has defined as love and obedience to the commands of 'Abdu'l-Bahá." [12]

In 1919, while he and his family were living temporarily in Evanston, Illinois, Charles became critically ill. Although the greatly esteemed Dr. Zia Bagdadi took excellent care of him, Charles died at the age of sixty during the summer of that year. Shortly afterwards, the Master revealed a Tablet for Mariam and Paul. In one part He wrote: ".... O Thou the All-Mighty, the All-Forgiving. Thy servant, Charles Haney, was firm in the Covenant and Testament and burning with the fire of separation. He was a believer. He was assured. He was spiritual. He was radiant. The Lamp of Thy Love was aflame in his heart and the veils of superstition were entirely consumed. He was ill for a long time, yet he was patient and thankful, dignified and heroic. Now he hath been divested of the earthly garment, and hath abandoned the transitory world of dust. He hath ascended to the horizon of the Ancient Glory." [13]

Uncertain of their future plans, Mariam and Paul first moved back to California. While they were living there, a future Hand of the Cause, Corinne Knight True, made her second pilgrimage to the Holy Land. In 1920, she sent to the Haneys her notes, which the Master had signed:

"I told Him (Abdul-Baha) you (Mariam Haney) had friends who wished you to go to California, and others wanted you in Minneapolis and Chicago etc., and that *you* wished to know where *He* wanted you to go. He said, 'Washington, D.C.' I asked Him if that was a good place for Paul's education and He said it was. How glad you will be to go to Washington by the direct Word from our Lord." [14]

On their way to Washington during Ridvan 1920, Mariam and Paul stopped over in New York City to attend the twelfth National Convention of the Bahá'í Temple Unity.

After it was over, the Executive Board of this body invited Mariam to be the secretary of its recently established National Teaching Committee.

In her first letter for this committee, written on 25th May 1920, she informed "all Baha'i sisters and brothers in America" that the committee was already making plans in accordance with the Master's revealed instructions in His *Tablets of the Divine Plan*. She stated: "We feel sure that all hearts will rejoice to know that the work of spreading the glad-tidings of the Kingdom and the teaching service which was so explicitly given to this country and Canada in the *Divine Plan* last year, has been taken up with a renewed energy, with an enthusiasm born of the Spirit and with a greater grasp of its scope and importance." [15] She also remarked that 'Abdu'l-Bahá had given the well-known teacher, Mírzá Asadu'lláh Fáḍil-i-Mázindarání (Jenabe Fazel) instructions to visit all of the states and every assembly in America and Canada, and that the committee's first great responsibility for the year was to make sure that his teaching work was properly organized.

While she was secretary, Mariam complied and edited regular bulletins which contained Tablets and addresses revealed by the Master, and stimulating news about the teaching work in North America.

In Bulletin Number 2, issued on 19th July 1920, she reported on the successful teaching tour of Fáḍil and his party. According to her report, after visits to Chicago, Kenosha, Wisconsin, and Detroit, he and his party "....proceeded to New York City for their second visit. A few heavenly days were spent there .... and the harmonizing effect of the presence of Jenabe Fazel was never more noticeable. He has love, peace, kindness in his own heart, and he radiates these qualities through confirmation from the divine Source." [16]

On 8th December 1920 the Master wrote to Mariam, expressing His pleasure at receiving the Bulletin of the Teaching Committee and asking her to convey His utmost love to the members.

In 1921 Mariam helped Mrs. Agnes Parsons on a most important task. As Mariam later wrote in a touching tribute to her close friend, the Master had instructed Mrs. Parsons when she was on a visit to Haifa in early 1920: "'I want you to arrange a Convention for unity of the colored and white races. You must have people to help you.' After Mrs. Parsons had returned to America she often spoke of this command. In those days 'to arrange a Convention' seemed a tremendous undertaking, but she always said: 'I will be able to do it. I must for it is the Will of 'Abdu'l-Bahá.' And in accordance with the explicit command of the Master she succeeded in gathering around her a helpful, active and earnest Committee." [17]

This convention was held in May 1921 in Washington, D.C., and Mariam, as one of five ladies on the arrangements committee, spent several months of hard work in helping Mrs. Parsons to plan it.

Louis G. Gregory, later the first Negro Hand of the Cause, reported with enthusiasm: "The First Congregational Church, historically famous for its opposition to race prejudice, was opened for these meetings. The speakers, without exception, struck the highest note of duty, justice, freedom, love, understanding, broad sympathy, universal brotherhood, the abandonment of prejudices, surrender of selfish and limited thoughts in obedience to the Will of God. A majority of the speakers were those known as Bahá'ís; but there were others, one in the same spirit, great souls who represented high stations in political, social, business or religious life, and true servants of God and the realm of humanity." [18]

Fáḍil concluded an eloquent address, the last of the Convention, with these stirring remarks: "The Sun of Reality has dawned from the horizon of the world. The Breeze of Generosity is wafting and the Call of the Kingdom has reached the ends of the earth! Ere long there will be great waves of love. The banner of Universal Peace will be hoisted! Gloom will be dispelled. We shall all be as the leaves of one tree and the flowers of one rose-garden, and all the friends of God will embrace each other." [19]

According to Mariam, "Immediately after the close of the Convention Mrs. Parsons sent the following cable to 'Abdu'l-Bahá: 'Convention successful. Meetings crowded. Hearts comforted.' And 'Abdu'l-Bahá replied at once by cable: 'The white-colored Convention produced happiness. Hoping will establish same in all America.' The Tablets of the Master which followed, not only to Mrs. Parsons but to others, indicated that the first Amity Convention was termed by the Master 'the mother convention' from which many Amity Conventions would be born, and in one Tablet He called it a perfect convention."[20]

As the Bahá'í world knows, on 28th November 1921, in the early hours of the morning, 'Abdu'l-Bahá ascended to the Abhá Kingdom. How can anyone adequately describe the devastating grief that believers such as Mariam must have felt when they heard the news of this heart-breaking event? On 16th January 1922, less than two months later, the saintly, beloved sister of 'Abdu'l-Bahá, Bahá'íyyih Khánum, known as the Greatest Holy Leaf, sent the following cable to the Bahá'ís of the world: "In Will Shoghi Effendi appointed Guardian of Cause and Head of House of Justice."[21] As soon as she had heard this joyful news, Mariam turned to the Guardian without hesitation, and throughout the thirty-six years of his ministry she served him with the same devotion and unqualified obedience which she had always shown the Master.

In 1924, the future Hand of the Cause, Horace Holley, at that time Secretary of the American National Spiritual Assembly, suggested that an annual Bahá'í Year Book be compiled. The Guardian encouraged this Assembly to start doing so without delay and offered any assistance that he could give "to make it as comprehensive, as attractive, and as authoritative as possible."[22]

Together with Horace Holley and Albert Windust, Mariam served on the Editorial Committee for the first two volumes of this important book. Greatly pleased with the second volume, which like all future ones bore the title *The Bahá'í World*, the Guardian wrote in a letter of 6th December 1928, addressed to the Bahá'ís in the East and the West: "It stands unexcelled and unapproached by any publication of its kind in the varied literature of our beloved Cause. It will, without the slightest doubt, if generously and vigorously supported,

ALFRED E. LUNT

ISABELLA BRITTINGHAM

MABEL AND HOWARD IVES

MARIAM HANEY
with Lua Getsinger (seated) and two Eastern Bahá'ís

CHARLES HANEY

JOHN ESSLEMONT

QUEEN MARIE OF RUMANIA

GEORGE TOWNSHEND

arouse unprecedented interest among all classes of civilized society." [23]

Early in 1924, the same year that she had begun her work for *Bahá'í World*, Mariam was appointed associate editor (and the eminent teacher and writer, Stanwood Cobb, editor) of the fascinating, informative 'Star of the West' soon to be entitled 'The Baha'i Magazine'. Starting with the issue of May, 1924, she remained in that capacity until its last number was published in March 1935.

Since this magazine first appeared as a pamphlet entitled 'Baha'i News' in 1910, the Master had stressed its importance and encouraged its development. From the start of his ministry the Guardian did the same. On 12th May 1925, he added in his own hand the following message to a letter written to the two editors on his behalf: "Dearly beloved fellow workers: The Star is shining more radiantly than ever before. Its tone is distinctly higher, the range of its articles wider, the treatment of the subject matter fuller and more adequate, its spirit more universal and worthy of the lofty principles of Bahá'u'lláh. May it grow from strength to strength, and achieve its purpose throughout the Bahá'í world. Pressure of work has prevented me from contributing an article to the May issue of the Star, but I assure you that I follow its development with keen interest and will continue to pray for the success of your joint and noble endeavours."

Not content to confine her efforts for either 'Star' or *Bahá'í World* to editorial work, Mariam often wrote inspiring biographies of early believers and stimulating articles on Bahá'í history for both publications.

Her instructive essay, entitled 'Old and New Paths at Green Acre', which first appeared in 'The Bahá'í Magazine' of September 1925, and a year later in the first volume of *Bahá'í World*, gives a vivid sketch of this important Bahá'í centre in Eliot, Maine, from its earliest days.

She wrote a warm tribute to the great Bahá'í heroine, Keith Ransom-Kehler, who died in Persia on 23rd October 1933, while she was working for the protection of the believers there, and whom the Guardian elevated to the station of Hand of the Cause of God after her death. Mariam concluded her essay with these words: "If we wish a concrete example of the power of the word of Bahá'u'lláh to effect a transformation in the life of a distinguished scholar, we have it in the spiritual rise of Keith, as she was affectionately known by Bahá'ís around the world." [24]

In an absorbing essay entitled 'The Passing of Dr. Susan I. Moody', Mariam recorded how this remarkable woman left her country for Persia in 1909 and served the Cause there as a doctor and teacher, except for one short journey home, until her death in Ṭihrán, twenty-five years later at the age of eighty-three. "Enroute to Persia Dr. Moody stopped in the Holy Land to see 'Abdu'l-Bahá. She received from Him the necessary instruction and encouragement which gave her strength for, and joy in, the work ahead of her. At the time of parting He said: 'You will need patience, patience, patience!' She tried never to forget that important injunction." [25]

During the early nineteen forties, Mariam wrote a short, but exciting history of the Bahá'í Faith in America. She started it with the first reference to Bahá'u'lláh in that continent, included in a paper by the Rev. H. H. Jessup which was read on 23rd September 1893 at a session of the Parliament of Religions at the Columbian Exposition in Chicago; and she ended with a sketch of the highly successful Convention for Racial Unity already referred to. In nine brief chapters she described with great spirit many important and dramatic events of this period, in some of which she had herself taken part. These essays appeared in successive issues of 'World Order', starting in February 1945.

In the thrilling second chapter 'Teaching by the Early American Believers', she wrote: "From the very beginning the believers made contact with 'Abdu'l-Bahá through sending a letter to Him indicating their acceptance of the Faith and asking innumerable questions. Tablets were received in reply, and gradually these Tablets assumed very large proportions. The greatest spiritual teaching in all history was accomplished through the receipt and dissemination of these Tablets and the instructions therein, for 'Abdu'l-Bahá not only answered all these questions, but interpreted and elucidated the teachings of His Father Bahá'u'lláh, solved intricate problems and upon His followers showered His divine love and kindness."[26]

In the moving sixth chapter entitled 'Abdu'l-Bahá's Visit to America', she observed: "The people of America, for the most part, were unaware that the Divine Servant of God was in their midst. They did not know that America was on the threshold of living through the most momentous period of the history of the North American Continent, for what event, however great, could possibly be compared with receiving bounties directly from the Holy Messenger Who was the Channel of Guidance for humanity, and Who possessed all the endless resources and power necessary to fulfil the divine mission given to Him by His Father Bahá'u'lláh! The greatest date in American history will be recorded as April 11, 1912, when the breezes of the Holy Spirit began to sweep over this country through 'Abdu'l-Bahá's heavenly magnetic influence."[27]

Although the vital information which her book contains is now available in the works of Bahá'í scholars, whom she never sought to emulate, the fine feeling and deep conviction with which Mariam has written this short history makes it well worth reading, not only for its vivid picture of the first years of the Cause in America, but for what a remarkable woman has, perhaps unconsciously, imparted about herself.

In 1944, the last year of the first Bahá'í century, at the request of the National Spiritual Assembly of the United States, Mariam compiled a record of the Bahá'í teaching that had been carried on in North America since the first believers had embraced the Cause there in 1894. This valuable record occupies an important place in the centenary volume prepared by the National Assembly.

In 1975 Alice Dudley wrote me a delightful letter about her close friend, Mariam. Early in 1951, while Alice was living in Washington, D.C., she and Mariam first met. According to Alice, "Mariam had great presence—a queenly dignity, always dressed very simply in black—no jewelry or ornaments. Just a narrow black velvet ribbon encircled her neck—Her hair was very white, tinged with red; her skin like white velvet .... She was careful of her diet and lived as much as possible in accordance with the Bahá'í Teachings on food and health. She never complained about physical ills .... She spoke often of the Bahá'í meetings in the early days—the great love and spirituality which prevailed among the believers. She had a lovely sense of humor and would sometimes do 'imitations'—just for me privately, not with malicious intent—she never spoke unkindly about anyone."[28]

On 19th March 1954, in a message to the Bahá'í world, Shoghi Effendi cabled: "Announce to all National Assemblies elevation of Paul Haney to rank of Hand of the Cause."[29] One cannot refrain from reflecting for a moment on the great happiness that Mariam must have felt when she heard this joyful news. Almost two months later, the Guardian's secretary wrote on his behalf to Mariam: "He (the Guardian) hopes that dear Paul will ever-increasingly be able to render the Cause important services. Surely you and his father in the Abhá Kingdom must rejoice to see how your cherished hopes are being fulfilled in this beloved son, who is so devoted, and has the interests of the Faith so completely at heart."[30]

A little less than nine months before his tragic passing, the Guardian sent this message to Mariam: "May the Almighty bless your efforts, guide and sustain you always, and aid you to enrich the record of your unforgettable services to His Faith. Your true brother, Shoghi."[31]

On 25th November 1957, the twenty-six Hands of the Cause who were gathered in the Holy Land selected Paul Haney and eight other Hands to act as the "Custodians of the Bahá'í World Faith".[32]

Mr. Haney told me that, although his mother was eighty-five when he was chosen to live in the Holy Land, she unselfishly and without hesitation told him and his wife that they must answer this call to service and leave her in America.

Mariam continued as before to correspond with the believers in various parts of the world. What Bahá'í could have failed to appreciate her rare gift of spiritual friendship? From all accounts this noble, saintly woman, even during her final years of failing health, served the Faith in every way she could.

On 1st September 1965, only a few months before she would have reached her ninety-third birthday, Mariam passed to the worlds beyond. This moving message of assurance which the Universal House of Justice sent to the National Spiritual Assembly of the United States soon afterwards must always be a source of happiness to those who loved her dearly:[33]

"Grieved announce passing Mariam Haney, devoted servant Baháu'lláh, mother beloved Hand Cause Paul Haney. Her total dedication Faith spanning period more than sixty-five years, staunch upholder Covenant earliest days of testing, tireless activities circulating Tablets Master, services National and International level, wholehearted loyalty steadfastness assure loving welcome Abhá Kingdom ...."

John Esslemont

JOHN EBENEZER ESSLEMONT, of a distinguished Scottish family, was the youngest child of his father, who had the same name. He was born on 19th May 1874 at Fairford Cults, Aberdeenshire, Scotland. After Ferryhill private school and Robert Gordon College, he went to Aberdeen University. On his graduation with honours in April 1898, he received not only the degree of Bachelor of Medicine and Surgery, but he also won the first Phillips Research Scholarship. During part of 1899, he did valuable research work at Berne and Strasbourg.

In December 1899, he became assistant to Professor Cash at Aberdeen University. A little more than a year later, he moved to Australia. While living there, on 19th December 1902 he married a brilliant pianist, to whom he had become engaged before leaving Scotland. Not well suited to each other, they soon separated.

John Esslemont was never physically strong, and at the end of two years he returned to Aberdeenshire because of ill health. On finding that the climate there did not improve his health, he went to South Africa and stayed for five years. In 1908 he again returned home and accepted the position of resident medical officer at the Home Sanatorium, Southbourne, Bournemouth.

In 1912 he, along with some other doctors, became interested in a State medical service. Two years later he wrote a paper on this subject and read it before the British Medical Association. The Advisory Committee on Public Health gave his paper careful attention and found it very useful.

A seeker after truth from his earliest years, Dr. Esslemont had not yet found a belief that he could accept. One Sunday in December 1914 he had dinner in London with Dr. Parker, who was also interested in a State medical service, and his wife, Katherine. On this occasion he heard for the first time in his life, from Mrs. Parker, the word 'Bahá'í'. Because of his eager response she gave him the Bahá'í message, and she spoke too of her meeting with 'Abdu'l-Bahá during His historic trip to London in 1911. In answer to his request for literature, she lent him some pamphlets.

This conversation and his reading of the pamphlets led him to make a thorough investigation of the Faith. Without delay he wrote to the Bahá'í Assembly of London for further information and bought all of the Bahá'í books in English that he could find. He studied these books so intensely that soon, in a series of letters to Mrs. Parker, he was making suggestions of books that he thought might interest her.

In February 1916, about fourteen months after he had first heard of the Cause, he wrote a long letter to a believer in Manchester. A touching portion of this letter concludes: "Oh! may people all over the world soon turn to God, as revealed in Bahá'u'lláh, with humble and contrite hearts, begging for His forgiveness and blessing and imploring His mercy and bounty! Then shall His Kingdom come in men's hearts and the whole world become one home and all mankind one family." [1]

Dr. Esslemont became the first Bahá'í in Bournemouth, and His teaching there was largely responsible for the establishment of its first Spiritual Assembly. When in May 1922, the first Spiritual Assembly for England was established, Dr. Esslemont was one of its members, and he continued to serve nationally until he left England for the last time in 1924.

Deeply convinced of the need for an international language, that it must play an important part in the achievement of the unity of mankind, he learned to read, speak and write in Esperanto.

He was anxious to study carefully all the Bahá'í books that he could find. He was not content just to read those available in English, he also took the pains to learn Persian and Arabic. Because of his own difficulty in finding the knowledge that he wanted, he soon became keenly aware of the scarcity of literature in English, and he decided to try and write a book that might help others in their spiritual journey.

At the end of 1918 Dr. Esslemont recieved this Tablet from the Master, translated by Shoghi Effendi:

To his honor Dr. Esslemont—Upon him be greeting and praise! O thou lover of all mankind!

Verily, have I chanted thy verses of praise to God, inasmuch as He hath illumined thine eyes with the light of guidance, the light of the oneness of the world of humanity; so much so that thy heart overflowed with the love of God and thy spirit was attracted by the fragrance of God, and I supplicate divine Providence that thou mayest become a torch to that gathering, so that the light of knowledge might shine out from thee, that thou mayest be confirmed to act in accordance with the significances of the *Hidden Words* and strengthened by God under all circumstances.

Concerning the book you are editing, send me a copy thereof ....

I pray the Lord to support thee in the service of all humankind, irrespective of race or religion. Nay rather, thou shouldst deal with all according to the teachings of BAHA'O'LLAH which are like unto life to this Glorious Age.

Upon thee be greeting and praise!
(Signed) Abdul-Baha Abbas.[2]

One 9th January 1919 Dr. Esslemont sent a copy of this precious Tablet to the editor of 'Star of the West.' In a letter to the editor he wrote: "We are delighted to welcome your President (Woodrow Wilson) to Europe and hope that great good will result from his visit. There will be much unrest and fermentation in Europe for years yet, I expect, but unrest is better than the placid acquiescence with vile conditions—with slums, drunkenness, prostitution, sweated labour, and profligate extravagance; and it seems to me that on the whole, things are moving towards a better state of affairs—towards the Most Great Peace." [3]

Following the Master's request in His Tablet, Dr. Esslemont sent Him a rough draft of the first nine chapters of his book.

After the Master had read them, He invited Dr. Esslemont to visit Him in Haifa and bring the entire manuscript. So during the winter of 1919–1920, Dr. Esslemont spent two months and a half there as the Master's guest. Falling ill soon after his arrival, he was unable to meet with 'Abdu'l-Bahá as much as he had hoped. The Master, of course, showed him every consideration.

Dr. Esslemont has written, "... 'Abdu'l-Bahá discussed the book with me on various occasions. He gave me several valuable suggestions for its improvement and proposed that, when I had revised the manuscript, He would have the whole of it translated into Persian so that He could read it through and amend or correct it where necessary." [4]

In an appealing description of the Master's daily life at that time, when He was nearly seventy-six, Dr. Esslemont has stated: "His unfailing patience, gentleness, kindliness and tact made His presence like a benediction." [5] Rúḥíyyih Khánum has informed us that during this visit Dr. Esslemont not only got to know Shoghi Effendi personally, but also collaborated with him and some other believers in the translation of an important Tablet by the Master.

On his return home Dr. Esslemont completed the revision of his book and sent it to 'Abdu'l-Bahá. After its translation into Persian, the Master was able to correct three and a half chapters (I, II, V, and part of III) before His passing.

In the first part of 1920 Shoghi Effendi came from Haifa to England and entered Oxford University. The friends knew well that his reason for doing this was to gain more knowledge of English so that he would be able to translate with even more facility than before the Tablets of the Master and all the Holy Writings into this language.

Dr. Esslemont was one of the dear friends who welcomed Shoghi Effendi to England with genuine warmth and affection, and Shoghi Effendi visited him more than once at his private sanitorium in Bournemouth. A charming photograph shows them, seated together, relaxed and happy, on the front piazza. [6] Some years later, after the passing of Dr. Esslemont, Shoghi Effendi wrote to a friend, "I shall ever recall the happy and restful days I spent at Bournemouth in the company of our departed friend John Esslemont and I will not forget the pleasant hours we spent together while taking our meals in the sanatorium." [7]

On 29th November 1921, at 9.30 in the morning the following cable reached Major Tudor-Pole in London at his office in St. James's Street. "Cyclometry London. His Holiness 'Abdu'l-Bahá ascended Abhá Kingdom. Inform friends. Greatest Holy Leaf." [8] Urgently asked by Major Tudor-Pole to come to his office, Shoghi Effendi arrived there at midday. After he had read the heart-breaking news he collapsed. Without delay Dr. Esslemont wrote him the following warm and understanding letter: [9]

The Home Sanatorium
Bournemouth

Dearest Shoghi,

It was indeed a "bolt from the blue" when I got Tudor Pole's wire this morning: "Master passed on peacefully Haifa yesterday morning" .... It must be very hard for you, away from your family and even away from all Bahá'í friends. What will you do now? I suppose you will go back to Haifa as soon as possible. Meantime you are most welcome to come here for a few days .... Just send me a wire .... and I shall have a room ready for you .... if I can be of any help to you in any way I shall be so glad. I can well imagine how heart-broken you must feel and how you must long to be at home and what a terrible blank you must feel in your life .... Christ was closer to His loved ones after His ascension than before, and so I pray it may be with the beloved and ourselves. We must do our part to shoulder the responsibility of the Cause and His Spirit and Power will be with us and in us.

Several days later in a letter to a Bahá'í student, Shoghi Effendi wrote, "The friends have insisted on my spending a day or two of rest in this place with Dr. Esslemont after the shock I have sustained and tomorrow I shall start back to London and thence to the Holy Land." [10]

Despite his constant struggle against ill health, Dr. Esslemont not only continued to teach both in person and through letters, and to fulfil his Bahá'í administrative duties, but also to help the newly-established National Spiritual

Assembly prepare his book, which he now called *Bahá'u'lláh and the New Era*, for publication. There was a brief delay while Shoghi Effendi himself reviewed the book.

It is certainly no exaggeration to state that this now rightly famous book, written at a time when there was still a dearth of authentic literature in English, or in any Western language, and published twenty-one years before Shoghi Effendi's own immortal history of the first century of the Bahá'í Erá, *God Passes By*, has already served thousands of grateful believers in many countries as a much needed introduction to the history and teachings of the Bahá'í Cause.

The Guardian has referred to *Bahá'u'lláh and the New Era* as "the textbook of the Faith" and said that it "would inspire generations yet unborn." [11] Marie, Queen of Rumania, the first member of royalty to recognize the station of Bahá'u'lláh, read this book first and felt that others should do the same. She called it "a glorious book of love and goodness ...." [12]

This absorbing and comprehensive book contains such a large number of inspiring passages that it is hard to choose only a few from which to quote. In Chapter I entitled 'The Glad Tidings,' Dr. Esslemont clearly explained: "Bahá'u'lláh asked no one to accept His statements and His tokens blindly. On the contrary, He put in the very forefront of His teachings emphatic warnings against blind acceptance of authority, and urged all to open their eyes and ears, and use their own judgment, independently and fearlessly, in order to ascertain the truth." [13]

In Chapter III, 'Bahá'u'lláh: The Glory of God', first published as a separate pamphlet, he has movingly written: "From His place of confinement in distant 'Akká, Bahá'u'lláh stirred His native land of Persia to its depths; and not only Persia; He stirred and is stirring the world. The spirit that animated Him and His followers was unfailingly gentle, courteous and patient, yet it was a force of astonishing vitality and transcendent power. It achieved the seemingly impossible. It changed human nature. Men who yielded to its influence became new creatures. They were filled with a love, a faith and enthusiasm, compared with which earthly joys and sorrows were but as dust in the balance. They were ready to face life-long suffering or violent death with perfect equanimity, nay, with radiant joy, in the strength of fearless dependence on God." [14]

At the conclusion of Chapter V, 'What Is a Bahá'í?' he wrote in the same vein: "The life to which Bahá'u'lláh calls His followers is surely one of such nobility that in all the vast range of human possibility there is nothing more lofty or beautiful to which man could aspire. Realization of the spiritual self in ourselves means realization of the sublime truth that we are from God and to Him we shall return. This return to God is the glorious goal of the Bahá'í; but to attain this goal the only path is that of obedience to His chosen Messengers, and especially to His Messenger for the time in which we live, Bahá'u'lláh, the Prophet of the New Era." [15]

During the autumn of 1924 a conference on living religions was held in London. Dr. Esslemont wrote both a general pamphlet, *Bahá'u'lláh and His Message,* and a small leaflet, *What Is the Bahá'í Movement?* for this occasion.

In a section of the former entitled, 'The Baffling Modern Problems', he has made clear the need for the coming of a new Prophet to heal the countless social illnesses of this day that the Christian Church has failed even to mitigate.

By the end of 1922 the Guardian's already heavy burden of work had so greatly increased that what he urgently needed was more helpers. In January 1923 he wrote to the London Bahá'ís: "The presence of a competent assistant in my translation work at present in Haifa would be most welcome, and highly desirable and I submit this matter to the members of the Council that they may consider the matter of sending for a time one of the English friends who could attend with me to this all-important work." [16]

During that year the sanitorium in Bournemouth closed owing to the death of the proprietor, and Dr. Esslemont lost his position. In 1924 Shoghi Effendi sent him a warm invitation to spend the winter in Haifa, and early in November he left London. On November 15th from Malta he wrote to the friends in England that he was greatly enjoying his trip and that his health had much improved. While he was spending a day or two at Port Said, he had some happy meetings with the friends. On November 21st he arrived in Haifa. Without delay he began to work for Shoghi Effendi.

The immortal Martha Root has written a touching tribute to Dr. Esslemont. She met him for the first time during April 1925 in Haifa, and she went to see him as did many others in the hospital where he lay ill. Soon after her visit, he became well enough to return to his own room. He lived in a house with some other Bahá'ís near the Guardian's apartment in 'Abdu'l-Bahá's house. The Guardian made sure that Dr. Esslemont received the best possible care. Every evening his Persian teacher used to talk Persian with him for about an hour. In the mornings when Martha came to work with him, he would tell her in Esperanto the thrilling stories about the Bahá'í Cause that his teacher had told him the evening before.

Martha has written, "Our Bahá'í brother was a great scholar. Everything he did bore the mark of extreme efficiency .... In our Esperanto work he was not satisfied just with any word, but sometimes we would discuss a dozen words and search their exact meanings in several dictionaries to find the word that would most brilliantly express the spirit of each thought." [17]

One day when his illness prevented him from working she said to him, "If you do not do anything, you are still doing much work every day, for your book is spreading the Bahá'í Message in every land." [18]

During the last few months of his life among other tasks he was helping to translate his book into German. He spent the summer of 1925 in Germany, both to assist in this work and to try and regain his health. In September he returned to Haifa. On 22nd November 1925 he died of a stroke. Martha, with her usual refreshing simplicity, has written, "Dr. Esslemont's sudden passing into the Eternal Realm brings home to us the importance of appreciating the value of the time. Are we working to the utmost and happily? Is our work efficient? If it is, whether in this world or in the next, we are a joy-bringer to our friends and to all humanity." [19]

In the years after Dr. Esslemont's passing, the Guardian showered honours upon him, naming him as one of the three luminaries of the Cause in the British Isles, and calling him the first of the nineteen disciples of 'Abdu'l-Bahá.[20]

On 30th November 1925 in a deeply moving letter to the believers of the East and West, Shoghi Effendi has described Dr. Esslemont.[21] "To me personally he was the warmest of friends, a trusted counsellor, an indefatigable collaborator, a lovable companion. With tearful eyes I supplicate at the Threshold of Bahá'u'lláh—and request you all to join—in my ardent prayers, for the fuller unfolding in the realms beyond of a soul that has already achieved so high a spiritual standing in this world. For by the beauty of his character, by his knowledge of the Cause, by the conspicuous achievements of his book, he has immortalized his name, and by sheer merit deserved to rank as one of the Hands of the Cause of God."

Queen Marie of Rumania

IN HIS MONUMENTAL HISTORY of the first century of the Bahá'í Era, *God Passes By*, Shoghi Effendi has referred at some length to the conversion of Marie, Queen of Rumania, and her services to the Bahá'í Faith. In other works, too, he has strongly emphasized the great importance of these thrilling events.

Marie was born at Eastwell in Kent, England, on 29th October 1875. Her father Alfred, Duke of Edinburgh, was the second son of Queen Victoria. Her mother, the former Grand Duchess Maria Alexandrovna, was the only daughter of Czar Alexander II. On 10th January 1893, Marie married Prince Ferdinand, nephew of King Carol and Queen Carmen Silva of Rumania.

This young English princess who, until her marriage, had always remained sheltered from the harsh realities of life, naturally went through heart-breaking experiences as the young wife of a foreign prince. At first she had neither close friends nor a suitable occupation. Her unceasing efforts to live as she thought right often provoked the severe disapproval of the Royal Family and the mostly corrupt aristocracy. After the birth of her first child, Prince Carol, however, she began to feel more at home in her new country.

In her autobiography, *The Story of My Life*, appearing first as a serial in the American magazine 'The Saturday Evening Post' in 1934, and a year later published in four volumes, the Queen described her life in some detail from its beginning until the end of the First World War. Although over-long, often repetitious and sometimes badly written, the book shows the greatness of her character and contains many

moving chapters. Possessed of unusual charm and physical
beauty, she had a deep love for people and a sincere desire
to help them. As soon as she was permitted to do so, she
became strenuously involved in humanitarian work.

From the outbreak of the War she was keenly opposed
to the aggressive policies of the German government. Despite
strong opposition from many prominent people in Rumania,
she did not hesitate to make her views entirely clear. Although
a good judge of character, her husband Ferdinand, who had
become King in October 1914, did not share her strong will-
power. At a most critical moment, she helped him to
make the much-needed decision to declare war against
Germany.

Deserted by its close ally, Russia, because of the revolution
in that country, Rumania suffered greatly. With a large
amount of its territory occupied, the situation was desperate
for a period of many months. Marie was sincerely grateful
when King George V offered safe residence in England to
herself, King Ferdinand and their children for the duration
of the war. But she did not accept the offer. Always confident
of ultimate victory for her adopted country, she never for a
moment relaxed in her efforts to help achieve it. Without
fear for her own safety, she visited soldiers in trenches close
to the scene of battle, organized Field Hospitals for the
Red Cross and took care of some of the wounded soldiers
personally.

Professor Seton-Watson in his *History of the Roumanians*
has written the following passage about her courageous
services: "At this point it would be unpardonable to omit
a brief eulogy of the sustained heroism of Queen Marie.
For months she courted danger daily amid the epidemics
of the hospitals and the overcrowded city and set an example
of calm and confident endurance which many Roumanian
women were proud to follow, and which did much to
uphold British prestige in south-east Europe." [1]

In order to raise money for the Rumanian Red Cross in
English-speaking countries, she wrote a book called *My
Country*. Although this book could not truthfully be called a
distinguished literary work, it still describes with fine feeling

the simple peasants of Rumania, its beautiful countryside, and interesting historic buildings. It also touches on the death of her youngest son, Mircea, not yet four years old, on 20th October 1916. She consoled herself with the thought that maybe his death was necessary then, so that he would be in the next world to welcome those brave soldiers who were dying each day for their beloved country.

During the last week of January in 1926, Martha Root, who was already well-known throughout the Bahá'í World as a great teacher, but certainly not known to Queen Marie, who had not yet even heard of the Cause, arrived in Bucharest for a visit of two weeks. Without delay, Martha sent the absorbing and comprehensive text-book *Bahá'u'lláh and the New Era* by the distinguished Dr. J. E. Esslemont, together with a note, to Her Majesty.

The Queen was so impressed with this book that she sat up until three o'clock in the morning reading it. The next day, she invited Martha to call on her on 30th January 1926, at Controceni Palace, situated half an hour by carriage from the centre of the city. Martha has vividly described her journey there along the crowded road until she saw in the distance "the splendidly wooded grounds of the palace .... like a winter fairyland, enchanting with light snow and icicles, half revealing half concealing their forest greens." [2]

After men in livery and the butler had guided her into the palace and "up a wide circular stairway to a drawing room", [3] a lady-in-waiting led her along wide halls into a beautifully furnished music room. The Queen appeared immediately. The lady-in-waiting whispered to Martha, "Her Majesty", and left the room. After a warm greeting, Queen Marie said to Martha, obviously in reference to the contents of the book that she had been sent, "I believe these Teachings are the solution for the world's problems today!" [4]

One cannot help reflecting for a moment on the joy that must have filled Martha's heart when she heard the Queen make this overwhelming statement. As they sat together by the table, the Queen spoke to Martha about the responsibilities that fall upon a king and queen to do all in their power to help develop their country, and explained to her how "when justice has not been found anywhere else, theirs is an ear that can still listen, a hand that can still give, a heart that can still pardon," [5] and that a king and queen can never refuse to see someone who is in need.

The Queen felt that religious intolerance only dissipated human love and that what gave vitality to religion was the spirit, not the form. She asked Martha questions about the Bahá'í plan for world peace, and showed a deep interest in what Bahá'u'lláh has revealed about the progress of the soul. As she was leaving, Martha gave the Queen a copy of *The Seven Valleys*, a short mystical masterpiece by Bahá'u'lláh.

Greatly elated by the Queen's spontaneous acceptance of the Bahá'í teachings, and filled with admiration for her, Martha left the palace with this most inspiring thought: "Though one can hardly vision it with earthbent eyes, those thousand years of peace foretold in the Bibles of the world are to begin in this century!" [6]

As a result of the meeting with Martha and without further prompting, the Queen wrote her first testimony in support of the Bahá'í Revelation in her syndicated series, entitled 'Queen's Counsel,' which appeared in newspapers throughout the United States and Canada. On May 4th of the same year she wrote, "It teaches that all hatreds, intrigues, suspicions, evil words, all aggressive patriotism even, are outside the one essential law of God, and that special beliefs are but surface things whereas the heart that beats with divine love knows no tribe nor race .... It is Christ's message taken up anew, in the same words almost, but adapted to the thousand years and more difference that lies between the year one and today .... If ever the name of Bahá'u'lláh or 'Abdu'l-Bahá comes to your attention, do not put their writings from you. Search out their Books, and let their glorious, peace-bringing, love-creating words and lessons sink into your hearts as they have into mine." [7]

Martha had informed the Guardian about her historic interview with Queen Marie. On 29th May 1926, the day after he received a copy of the Queen's testimony, Shoghi Effendi wrote to Martha that this is "a well deserved and memorable testimony to your remarkable and exemplary

184

endeavours for the spread of our beloved Cause. It has thrilled me and greatly reinforced my spirit and strength; yours is a memorable triumph, hardly surpassed in its significance in the annals of the Cause."[8]

The Guardian wrote to the Queen herself a joyful appreciation of her public testimony. She answered him with an unforgettable letter:[9]

Bran August 27th 1926

Dear Sir,

I was deeply moved on reception of your letter.

Indeed a great light came to me with the message of Bahá'u'lláh and 'Abdu'l-Bahá. It came as all great messages come at an hour of dire grief and inner conflict and distress, so the seed sank deeply.

My youngest daughter finds also great strength and comfort in the teachings of the beloved masters.

We pass on the message from mouth to mouth and all those we give it to see a light suddenly lighting before them and much that was obscure and perplexing becomes simple, luminous and full of hope as never before.

That my open letter was balm to those suffering for the cause, is indeed a great happiness to me, and I take it as a sign that God accepted my humble tribute.

The occasion given me to be able to express myself publicly, was also His Work, for indeed it was a chain of circumstances of which each link led me unwittingly one step further, till suddenly all was clear before my eyes and I understood why it had been.

Thus does He lead us finally to our ultimate destiny.

Some of those of my caste wonder at and disapprove my courage to step forward pronouncing words not habitual for Crowned Heads to pronounce, but I advance by an inner urge I cannot resist.

With bowed head I recognize that I too am but an instrument in greater Hands and rejoice in the knowledge.

Little by little the veil is lifting, grief tore it in two. And grief was also a step leading me ever nearer truth, therefore I do not cry out against grief!

May you and those beneath your guidance be blessed and upheld by the sacred strength of those gone before you.

Marie

Late in the summer of 1926, the Guardian heard that the Queen planned to visit the United States, and his secretary wrote to the National Spiritual Assembly on his behalf: "We read in *The Times* that Queen Marie of Rumania is coming to America. She seems to have obtained a great interest in the Cause. So we must be on our guard lest we do an act which may prejudice her and set her back. Shoghi Effendi desires, that in case she takes this trip, the friends will behave with great reserve and wisdom, and that no initiative be taken on the part of the friends except after consulting the National Assembly." [10]

During her trip the Queen wrote further 'open letters' which appeared respectively on the 27th and 28th September in the same syndicated series as the first one. God ".... is the voice within us that shows us good and evil. But mostly we ignore or misunderstand this voice. Therefore did He choose His elect to come down amongst us upon earth to make clear His word, His real meaning. Therefore the Prophets; therefore Christ, Muhammad, Bahá'u'lláh, for man needs from time to time a voice upon earth to bring God to him, to sharpen the realization of the existence of the true God." [11]

On 7th October 1926, the Guardian wrote a most moving message to the believers of the West concerning Queen Marie's response. He included this statement: "With bowed heads and grateful hearts we recognize in this glowing tribute which royalty has thus paid to the Cause of Bahá'u'lláh an epoch-making pronouncement destined to herald those stirring events which, as 'Abdu'l-Bahá has prophesied, shall in the fulness of time signalize the triumph of God's holy Faith." [12]

On 5th October 1927, Martha Root again visited Bucharest. While there she planned to lecture on the principles of the Bahá'í Cause and to write her customary articles for the newspapers. The main purpose of her visit, however, was to bring the love and sympathy of the Bahá'í world to the Queen, in mourning for King Ferdinand, who had died less than three months before.

Although the Queen was not receiving visitors, she made an exception for Martha. A lady-in-waiting invited Martha to visit the Queen on October 8th at Pelisor, one of two palaces in the town of Sinaia. After spending the night there, Martha walked to the Palace in the morning, partly to enjoy the charming town and the beautiful country around it, but also because "deep in her heart, too, was the longing to go on foot and humbly to the first Queen of the whole world who had publicly written of Bahá'u'lláh's great Principles for this universal cycle." [13]

She met the Queen in her drawing-room. Bahá'í books lay on the table and sofa next to it. The Queen had just been reading in them certain passages about eternal life, and she spoke of these passages to Martha. To her message of love from the Bahá'ís, the Queen replied with one to Shoghi Effendi, to 'Abdu'l-Bahá's sister, called the Greatest Holy Leaf, and to His widow, the Holy Mother; the Queen hoped some day to visit them and to pray at the Holy Shrines.

Martha told the Queen that her public testimonies had been translated into many languages and that "ten million people in one continent alone had read them. She explained, too, what a balm they had been to those suffering persecution for the Cause. This gracious Queen replied: 'I am very thankful; I take it as a sign that God accepted my humble tribute.'" [14]

The Queen felt that everyone should teach the Cause humbly. She admired "the spirit of selflessness found in the Teachings .... She said: 'With bowed head I recognize that I, too, am but a channel and I rejoice in the Knowledge.'" [15]

Queen Marie thought that the Bahá'ís should start to teach the younger generation. She felt that the best book for everyone to read first was Dr. Esslemont's *Bahá'u'lláh and the New Era*.

Martha then gave the Queen an illumined sheet, inscribed with a prayer of Bahá'u'lláh and with a lock of His hair placed in the centre, a sacred gift from the Bahá'ís of Mashhad in Persia. The Queen was so delighted with this gift that she decided to have a special frame designed for it, and placed in it, also, a small photograph of 'Abdu'l-Bahá'.

After the Queen had spoken of doing this, Princess Ileana

and her young brother, Prince Nicolas, entered the room. The Princess invited Martha to come downstairs for a talk in her sitting-room. On her table there was a tiny photograph of 'Abdu'l-Bahá, and included in her library were most of the books of Bahá'u'lláh and 'Abdu'l-Bahá so far published in English. She planned to translate two Bahá'í booklets into Rumanian. She had already given *Bahá'u'lláh and the New Era* to a friend of hers at Court and had received from him a fine response. Martha thought that the princess not only possessed rare charm and beauty, but, more important, had a deep interest in spiritual matters.

On 25th October 1927, in a letter to Martha, Shoghi Effendi expressed the great happiness that the news of her meeting with the Queen and princess had given him and concluded by asking Martha to extend his warm invitation to them both to visit him in the Holy Land.

Travelling from Greece, Martha arrived in Belgrade, the capital of Jugoslavia, on 18th January 1928. She had heard from Princess Ileana that she and her mother would be visiting the Queen's son-in-law, King Alexander I, and her daughter, Queen Marie Mignon, in Belgrade, to be there for the birth of her second child.

Two days after this event, Martha received a note from the palace, "Mama and I would be so glad to have you take tea with us at half past four, Ileana." [16] Queen Marie spoke of the meaning of God and true religion, and she made this beautiful statement: "The ultimate dream which we shall realize is that the Bahá'í channel of thought has such strength, it will serve little by little to become a light to all those searching for the real expression of Truth." [17]

Many years before she had heard about the Bahá'í Cause, the Queen's royal relatives in Russia had given her a precious brooch. It consisted of "two little wings of wrought gold and silver, set with tiny diamond chips and joined together with one large pearl." [18] As she picked up this brooch and held it in her hand, Her Majesty said to Martha, "Always you are giving gifts to others, and I am going to give you a gift from me." [19] With obvious delight, the Queen clasped the brooch onto Martha's dress.

Martha sent the brooch to Wilmette, Illinois, as a gift to the first Bahá'í Temple of the West. At the National Bahá'í Convention in Riḍván of that year this question came up: 'was it right to sell this brooch that had belonged to the first Queen who had served the Faith of Bahá'u'lláh?' After some consideration it was decided that, because of the urgent need of money to continue building the Temple, it would not be wrong to sell the brooch. Mr. Willard Hatch of Los Angeles, a devoted believer for many years, bought this precious brooch. In 1931 he took it with him when he went on pilgrimage to the Holy Land and, after first obtaining the Guardian's approval of course, presented it for the archives on Mount Carmel to remain there always.

In April 1928 Queen Marie and her daughter Ileana visited Cyprus. Although the newspapers had mentioned that they also planned to visit Haifa, they did not arrive. In a letter to Martha, the Guardian expressed his fear that if the Queen and her daughter had intended to make the pilgrimage, "these premature disclosures"[20] might have made it impossible.

In October 1929, Martha had another historic meeting with Queen Marie and Princess Ileana, this time at Her Majesty's attractive summer palace called Tehna-Yuva, a Turkish phrase meaning "a solitary nest". Designed by the Queen herself, this palace with small houses around it was situated at Balcîc on the edge of the Black Sea. Martha was one of several guests at lunch. After the meal was over, the Queen and Princess asked Martha upstairs for a talk in a delightful sitting-room which overlooked the murmuring sea. Martha gave Queen Marie warm greetings from Shoghi Effendi and devoted good wishes from the Bahá'ís everywhere. The Queen said that she wanted very much to visit the Holy Land, to meet Shoghi Effendi and Bahá'íyyih Khánum, the Greatest Holy Leaf, to pray at the Shrines of Bahá'u'lláh and 'Abdu'l-Bahá, and at the Most Great Prison where the Holy Family had lived for many years. Martha quoted the Queen as saying, "Ileana and I will go to Egypt and Palestine this winter after the New Year and we shall surely go to Haifa."[21] The Princess said that she was always looking forward to visiting Haifa.

Her mother spoke of the difficult tasks that she gave Ileana to do and the brave spirit with which she accomplished them. Again struck by her charm and spirituality, Martha felt even more strongly than before that the great interest of this princess was to serve her country.

As Martha was leaving, the Queen took out a fine photograph of herself with a message written on it of love and faith. She asked Martha to send this photograph to Shoghi Effendi, who thanked the Queen for it in the following splendid letter:[22]

Haifa, Palestine,
December 3, 1929

Your Majesty

I have received through the intermediary of my dear Bahá'í sister Miss Martha Root, the autograph portrait of Your Majesty, bearing in simple and moving terms, the message which Your Majesty has graciously been pleased to write in person. I shall treasure this most excellent portrait, and I assure you, that the Greatest Holy Leaf and the Family of 'Abdu'l-Bahá share to the full my feelings of lively satisfaction at receiving so strikingly beautiful a photograph of a Queen whom we have learned to love and admire.

I have followed during the past few years with profound sympathy the disturbed course of various happenings in your beloved country, which I feel must have caused you much pain and concern. But whatever the vicissitudes and perplexities which beset Your Majesty's earthly path, I am certain that even in your saddest hours, you have derived abundant sustenance and joy from the thought of having, through your glowing and historic utterances on the Bahá'í Faith as well as by your subsequent evidences of gracious solicitude for its welfare, brought abiding solace and strength to the multitude of its faithful and long suffering adherents throughout the East. Yours surely, dearly beloved Queen, is the station ordained by Bahá'u'lláh in the realms beyond to which the strivings of no earthly power can ever hope to attain.

I have immediately upon the publication of the second volume of the Bahá'í World, by the American Bahá'í Publishing Committee, forwarded directly to Bucarest, to the address of Your Majesty and that of Her Royal Highness Princess Ileana, copies of this most recent and comprehensive of Bahá'í publications. I will take the liberty of presenting in the course of the coming year the III

Volume of this same publication which I trust will prove of interest to Your Majesty.

May I, in closing, reiterate the expression of profound appreciation and joy which the Family of 'Abdu'l-Bahá and Bahá'ís in every land universally feel for the powerful impetus which Your Majesty's outspoken and noble words have lent to the onward march of their beloved Faith.

The Family also join me in extending to Your Majesty, as well as to Her Royal Highness Princess Ileana, a most cordial welcome should Your Majesty ever purpose to visit the Holy Land to 'Abdu'l-Bahá's home in Haifa as well as to those scenes rendered so hallowed and memorable by the heroic lives and deeds of Bahá'u'lláh and 'Abdu'l-Bahá.

Shoghi

Not long after she had received this letter, while travelling through the Near East with Princess Ileana, the Queen made known her intention of visiting the Holy Land. In the keen hope that she would do so, Shoghi Effendi saw to the careful preparation of a gift for her—the Tablet that Bahá'u'lláh had sent to her grandmother, Queen Victoria, "copied in fine Persian calligraphy, and illuminated in Tehran."[23]

Failing to receive news from the Queen when she was in Egypt, on March 8th the Guardian sent her a personal cable in which he warmly renewed his invitation and stressed not only the historic importance of such a visit, but also the joy and hope that it would bring "to the silent sufferers of the Faith throughout the East".[24] Still not hearing from her, on March 26th he cabled her another invitation and concluded, "Deeply regret unauthorized publicity given by the Press."[25] As he later informed Martha, "Reporters who called on me representing the United Press of America telegraphed to their newspapers just the opposite I told them. They perverted the truth."[26]

Shoghi Effendi had learned that the Queen had actually sailed for Haifa. For this reason he was, of course, encouraged to think that she would succeed in making her pilgrimage. Two days after this second cable, the Rumanian minister in Cairo answered: "Her Majesty regrets that not passing

through Palestine she will not be able to visit you."[27] He was not telling the truth. The Queen and Princess Ileana actually arrived in Haifa on their boat, but they had been met at the dock, cruelly forbidden to stay in Haifa even for a few moments, led to an automobile and quickly driven away. In the meantime, the Greatest Holy Leaf had waited for many hours in the Master's house for the Queen and her daughter who never came.

On 2nd April 1930, in a letter to Martha, the Guardian explained fully the unhappy events that had ruined the Queen's plan for her pilgrimage and suggested to Martha that she write to the Queen explaining the situation and assuring her of his great disappointment. He concluded, "I cherish the hope that these unfortunate developments will serve only to intensify the faith and love of the Queen and will reinforce her determination to arise and spread the Cause."[28]

On 28th June 1931, the Queen wrote to Martha, "Both Ileana and I were cruelly disappointed at having been prevented going to the holy shrines and of meeting Shoghi Effendi, but at that time were going through a cruel crisis and every movement I made was being turned against me and being politically exploited in an unkind way. It caused me a good deal of suffering and curtailed my liberty most unkindly .... But the beauty of truth remains and I cling to it through all the vicissitudes of a life become rather sad."[29]

Rúhíyyih Khánum has pointed out, "This letter ends with a sentence, after Her Majesty's signature, that was perhaps more significant of her attitude and character than anything else: 'I enclose a few words which may be used in your Year Book.'"[30]

On 8th August 1932, and again in February 1933, the Queen and her daughter, Ileana, now Archduchess Anton Mödling, received Martha at Ileana's home near Vienna. Her Majesty made a now famous statement quoted as the frontispiece of the *Bahá'í World*, Volume IV. "The Baha'i teaching brings peace and understanding. It is like a wide embrace gathering together all those who have long searched for words of hope. It accepts all great prophets gone before, it destroys no other creeds and leaves all doors open. Saddened by the continual strife amongst believers of many confessions and wearied of their intolerance towards each other, I discovered in the Baha'i teaching the real spirit of Christ so often denied and misunderstood: Unity instead of strife, Hope instead of condemnation, Love instead of hate, and a great reassurance for all men."

Deeply moved by Her Majesty's sustained interest in the Cause of Bahá'u'lláh, despite the ever increasing tragic events to which her country was being subjected, and her own advancing years, on the 23rd January 1934 Shoghi Effendi wrote her a letter which expressed his "heartfelt and abiding gratitude",[31] for a new appreciation that she had just written for the *Bahá'í World*.

A few weeks later on February 16th the Queen received Martha again at Controceni Palace in Bucharest. Martha has written, "How beautiful she looked that afternoon—as always—for her loving eyes mirror her mighty spirit; a most unusual Queen is she, a consummate artist, a lover of beauty and wherever she is there is glory .... She received me in her private library where a cheerful fire glowed in the quaint, built-in fireplace, tea was served on a low table, the gold service set being wrought in flowers."[32]

Chapters of the Queen's autobiography, *The Story of My Life*, had begun to appear each week in 'The Saturday Evening Post'. She was deeply touched by the many letters that she had received in appreciation of her book from all strata of society in the United States of America and from people in many other countries. Martha remarked that these people recognized the deep humanity of Her Majesty's character. The Queen said that while she was in Hamburg on the way to Iceland during the previous year, as she was driving through the streets in her motor car a charming girl tossed a note to her. It said: "I am so happy to see you in Hamburg, because you are a Bahá'í." Then she added, "In my heart I am entirely Bahá'í."[33] She also made this beautiful statement in *Bahá'í World*: "The Baha'i Teaching brings peace to the soul and hope to the heart. To those in search of assurance the Words of the Father are as a fountain in the desert after long wandering."[34]

On 4th February 1936, Martha had her last meeting with Queen Marie. It took place again in her softly lighted library at the Controceni Palace, this time at six o'clock in the afternoon. "The fire in the grate beamed a welcome with its yellow-glowing fragrant pine boughs, large bowls of yellow tulips adorned the apartment." [35]

Deeply concerned over the many sad events that had taken place in the world at large in the two years since she had last seen Martha, the Queen wished that she could do more to bring about the unity of hearts. She spoke about several Bahá'í books that she had been reading, and referred to the depths of the *Kitáb-i-Íqán* and the wonderful *Gleanings from the Writings of Bahá'u'lláh*. About the latter she remarked, "Even doubters would find a powerful strength in it, if they would read it alone and would give her souls the time to expand." [36]

Before Martha left, the Queen promised to write a special appreciation as a frontispiece for *Bahá'í World*, Volume VI, and sent it to Martha a few days later. "More than ever today when the world is facing such a crisis of bewilderment and unrest, must we stand firm in Faith seeking that which binds together instead of tearing asunder. To those searching for light, the Baha'i Teachings offer a star which will lead them to deeper understanding, to assurance, peace and good will with all men. Marie, 1936."

During this last interview, the Queen spoke with much feeling about a dear friend of hers since childhood, Lilian McNeill. They had both recognized the station of Bahá'u'lláh at about the same time. Mrs. McNeill was now living near 'Akká in the Mansion of Mazra'ih, where Bahá'u'lláh had once resided.

During the last few years of her life Queen Marie often wrote letters to Mrs. McNeill in 'Akká. In one of the last she said: "I lead a very quiet life, my household has become small, but I have the feeling of being well loved in the country. My people and I are old associates, we have shared good and bad through forty-three years, and that counts!

"I wonder if I shall ever travel your way again? For the present I have no plans, I sit still and watch the black clouds, and pray for peace. With love and blessing, Marie." [37]

The two old friends had hoped to have a reunion in Haifa during 1938, but because of the Queen's failing health and the unsettled condition of Palestine, such a plan became impossible. After a painful illness that lasted many months, Queen Marie died in July 1938. Lilian McNeill wrote, "The world is the poorer for the passing of such a noble lady, and a blank, impossible to fill, is left in the lives of those who knew her personally." [38]

The Hand of the Cause George Townshend has made this moving comment: "Her death and obsequies were attended with all the ceremonial that befits the passing of a Queen. But who can tell what was the greeting that awaited her on the other side where she learned in an instant how true had been her intuitions of the Manifestation of God and where she saw unobscured now by any mortal veil the white eternal splendour of the Truth that she, alone among the earth's queens, had risen to acclaim." [39]

The Guardian has further assured us: "Queen Marie's acknowledgment of the Divine Message stands as the first fruits of the vision which Bahá'u'lláh had seen long before in His captivity, and had announced in His Kitáb-i-Aqdas. 'How great', He wrote, 'the blessedness that awaits the King who will arise to aid My Cause in My Kingdom, who will detach himself from all else but Me!'" [40]

George Townshend

NOT SINCE MY EARLY BOYHOOD in New York City, when I used to listen to Dr. Henry Sloan Coffin at the Madison Avenue Presbyterian Church, did I receive real satisfaction or assistance from what any clergyman had said or written until I first became acquainted with the writing of George Townshend, sometime Canon of St. Patrick's Cathedral, Dublin, and Archdeacon of Clonfert, County Galway in Eire.

I had this experience in Los Angeles, when I was just thirty-nine, a few months after I had begun to investigate the Bahá'í Faith. I saw for sale in the library of the local Ḥaẓíratu'l-Quds a book by George Townshend called *The Promise of All Ages*. Someone explained to me, "At the age of seventy George Townshend gave up a secure and greatly respected position in the Church of Ireland to join the Bahá'í community."

I felt sure that in so doing he faced not only much criticism from the bishops, the clergy and members of his congregation, but probably ridicule, too, from many. Filled with admiration for him, I wanted immediately to read his book.

Often quoting from the *Kitáb-i-Íqán* revealed by Bahá'u'-lláh, sometimes from *Some Answered Questions* by 'Abdu'l-Bahá and other Holy Writings, Mr. Townshend has written a clear and most convincing explanation of progressive revelation.

In Chapter IV, 'The Mission of the Lord Christ', he wrote about Him: "His Dispensation stands apart from all before it in that it crowns the period of preparation and opens directly into that Age of God for which all previous Messengers had made ready the way .... The central message of Jesus was his promise and his warning that before long (at the end of one more Era, the Era then begun) God would in deed and in fact establish the Kingdom upon earth; its foundations would be laid in the hearts of men, and those who were found to be unworthy would be destroyed. The Event of which poets had dreamed, which seers had descried, which prophets had predicted, was soon to be no more a dream or a hope or a forecast but an accomplished fact of history." [1]

This book includes not only a moving history of the Bahá'í Faith, but also a penetrating, scholarly analysis of its holy writings, laws and aims. In a brilliant foreword he wrote, "The spiritual ideals and noble peace-aims that now increasingly find utterance in western lands are as uprushes from a hidden fire, glimpses of that ordered and balanced scheme for world reform which was wrought out and promulgated by Bahá'u'-lláh in prison some seventy years ago." [2] In conclusion he asked, "Will not the religious leaders and thinkers of the West examine thoroughly and without prejudice, the high claims of Bahá'u'lláh? And will they not, discerning the true Source and spiritual nature of this supreme Epoch of Transition, lead their churches into the heavenly Jerusalem, so that all Christendom may arise for the regeneration of mankind?" [3]

While still investigating the Faith, the next book that I read by George Townshend was *The Heart of the Gospel* in the first edition of 1939. A careful study of the *Kitáb-i-Íqán* and a realization of its great power had led Townshend to a fresh examination of the Bible and then to the writing of *The Heart of the Gospel*. As in *The Promise of All Ages*, progressive revelation is the theme.

In Chapter III, 'Man's Destiny and Man's Effort', he wrote: "The whole Bible gave voice to God's demand from man of this increasing spiritual effort, but no one else sets the demand so high nor insists upon it with such sternness as the Lord Christ. Every other effort, He urges, and every other aim is to be subordinated to this. Every other loyalty is to be postponed to it. None is to allow any danger to deter him nor any difficulty to discourage him. If need be, pain, persecution, shame and even death must be faced: at any cost, the effort to walk in God's way and to follow after righteousness must be maintained. No other effort is so richly rewarded; and neglect of this effort brings its own dire retribution." [4]

In the concluding paragraph of Chapter VI, 'The Power of Christ', we read: "Christ not only reveals new realms of experience and knowledge otherwise inaccessible, but He rouses to activity dormant powers in man, higher faculties as yet unused and undeveloped. He enlarges human consciousness. He shows creative power as the Word of God. He lifts to a new and loftier plane men's conceptions of life and duty. He opens new purposes in life, new fields of human endeavour. And by the exercise of such powers He proves Himself to be, as Christians have always held and as He Himself asserted, a Vicegerent of the Lord of Evolution, a Being altogether apart from anyone else in His Dispensation."[5]

In both books he wrote with much power about his great love for and deep belief in Jesus Christ. Particularly in *The Heart of the Gospel*, where Mr. Townshend devotes many inspiring chapters to Him, does the reader perhaps have a chance to know and love Jesus in a way that he had not done before. Never deterred by conflicting doctrines of the church and the many man-made interpretations of scripture, Mr. Townshend was able to see beyond these to the Reality of Jesus Christ. Without going through periods of doubt and agnosticism, Mr. Townshend made a beautiful transition, denied to many of Christian background, from firm belief in Jesus to an unqualified acceptance of Bahá'u'lláh also.

With increasing interest in the Bahá'í Faith I read his impressive introduction to Shoghi Effendi's *God Passes By*, first published in 1944. In only eight pages Mr. Townshend stated and explained with clarity and force certain important facts about this overwhelming history of the first Bahá'í century. To those of us still unaccustomed to Shoghi Effendi's dynamic, evocative and majestic style, this introduction is particularly helpful. It starts with a paragraph surely capable of arousing much interest in the prospective reader.

Mr. Townshend wrote: "Here is a history of our times written on an unfamiliar theme—a history filled with love and happiness and vision and strength, telling of triumphs gained and wider triumphs yet to come: and whatever it holds of darkest tragedy it leaves mankind at its close not facing a grim inhospitable future but marching out from the shadows on the high road of an inevitable destiny towards the opened gates of the Promised City of Eternal Peace." [6]

Shortly after I had become a member of the Bahá'í community, I read with much interest his most instructive and challenging pamphlet, entitled *The Old Churches and The New World-Faith*. Written directly after his resignation from the Church of Ireland, he addressed all Christian people in general, but more especially the bishops and clergy of his former Church and pleaded with them to investigate fairly the Revelation of Bahá'u'lláh. This pamphlet was sent to ten thousand men of influence in various professions throughout the British Isles. Much to his disappointment he received only one response and that in the negative.

In it he wrote: "To them who have recognized Christ's voice again in this Age has been given in renewed freshness and beauty the vision of the Kingdom of God as Jesus and the Book of Revelation gave it—the same vision, but clearer now and on a larger scale and in more detail." [7]

When I was on pilgrimage during January 1955, I asked the Guardian, "Why do so few of the clergy, many of whom are certainly sincere .... ?" He stopped me and said, not impatiently, "I have heard this question before. They do not come into the Faith because their understanding of Christianity is superficial." I mentioned to the Guardian an essay that I had liked written by a distinguished Bahá'í scholar who had helped lead me into the Faith. "Yes," he said, "but it is not in the same category as George Townshend's work, the best of the Bahá'í writers."

*   *   *

Painstaking historians of the future will undoubtedly write in great detail about the life of George Townshend. His family is listed in Burke's *Landed Gentry of Ireland*. Born at Hatley, Burlington Road, Dublin, on 14th June 1876, George Townshend went to school at Uppingham and to Hertford College, Oxford. Fond of tennis and cross-country running, he did both well in College. After he had graduated from College in 1899, he returned to Dublin and studied for the Irish Bar. During part of this time he was a leader writer for

'The Irish Times'. Called to the Bar in 1903, he was apparently not satisfied with his profession or with life in Ireland. After a year his father sent him to the United States of America.

In 1906 he became a Minister of the Protestant Episcopal Church in Salt Lake City, Utah. Placed in charge of a Mission in Provo for the next four years he worked among the Mormons and American Indians. In 1910 he accepted an appointment to the staff of the University of the South, Sewanee, Tennessee. Two years later he was made Assistant Professor of English. Although he had become an American citizen in July 1916, on a trip back to Ireland he decided to live there again. He shortly afterwards started to work as a curate at Booterstown, County Dublin.

A year after his return to Ireland he received from a friend in America a few pamphlets with quotations from the writings of 'Abdu'l-Bahá. As a result of reading them George Townshend was never to be the same again. Appointed Rector of Ahascragh, County Galway, in January 1919, several months after his marriage, he and his wife Nancy moved there to live in a large Georgian house overlooking an attractive landscape. Soon after they had settled there he first wrote to 'Abdu'l-Bahá. He replied with this Tablet:[8]

To his honour Mr. George Townshend, Galway, Ireland; Upon him be greeting and praise.

HE IS GOD!

O thou who art thirsty for the fountain of Truth!

Thy letter was received and the account of thy life has been known. Praise be to God that thou hast ever, like unto the nightingale, sought the divine rose garden and like unto the verdure of the meadow yearned for the outpourings of the cloud of guidance. That is why thou hast been transferred from one condition to another until ultimately thou hast attained unto the fountain of Truth, hast illuminated thy sight, hast revived and animated thy heart, hast chanted verses of guidance and hast turned thy face toward the enkindled fire on the Mount of Sinai.

At present, I pray on thy behalf.... Upon thee be Bahá'u'l-Abhá.

(Signed) 'Abdu'l-Bahá 'Abbás

July 24 1919.

During 1920 Mr. Townshend wrote a deeply-moving poem, consisting of six short verses, to 'Abdu'l-Bahá. It shows deep love for Him and recognition of His station.

To
'ABDU'L-BAHÁ

HAIL to Thee, Scion of Glory, Whose utterance poureth abroad
The joy of the heavenly knowledge and the light of the greatest of days!
Poet of mysteries chanting in rapture the beauty of God,
    Unto Thee be thanksgiving and praise!

Child of the darkness that wandered in gloom but dreamed of the light,
Lo! I have seen Thy splendour ablaze in the heavens afar
Showering gladness and glory and shattering the shadows of night,
    And seen no other star.

Thy words are to me as fragrances borne from the garden of heaven,
Beams of a lamp that is hid in the height of a holier world,
Arrows of fire that pierce and destroy with the might of the levin
    Into our midnight hurled.

Sword of the Father! none other can rend the dark veil from my eyes,
None other can beat from my limbs with the shearing blade of God's might
The sins I am fettered withal and give me the power to rise
    And come forth to the fullness of light.

Lo! Thou hast breathed on my sorrow the sweetness of faith and of hope,
Thou hast chanted high paeans of joy that my heart's echoes ever repeat,
And the path to the knowledge of God begins to glimmer and ope
    Before my faltering feet.

Weak and unworthy my praise. Yet, as from its throbbing
   throat
Some lone bird pours its song to the flaming infinite sky,
So unto Thee in the zenith I lift from a depth remote
   This broken human cry.

'Abdu'l-Bahá replied with this Tablet:[9]

His honour the Rev. George Townshend, Ireland. Unto him be
Bahá'u'lláh-el Abhá!

HE IS GOD!

O Thou illumined heavenly soul and revered personage in the
Kingdom!

Thy letter has been received. Every word indicated the progress
and upliftment of thy spirit and conscience. These heavenly
susceptibilities of thine form a magnet which attracts the confirmation of the Kingdom of God; and so the doors of realities
and meanings will be open unto thee, and the confirmations of the
Kingdom of God will envelop thee.

The heart of man is like unto a nest, and the Teachings of His
Holiness Bahá'u'lláh like unto a sweet singing bird. Unquestionably
from this nest the melody of the Kingdom will be transmitted to
the ears, bestowing heavenly susceptibilities upon the souls and
quickening upon the spirits.

It is my hope that thy church will come under the Heavenly
Jerusalem.

... Be assured thou art under the favors of His Holiness Bahá'u'lláh.

Unto thee be the glory of Abhá!

(Signed) 'Abdu'l-Bahá 'Abbás
December 19, 1920.

In 1933 his fellow clergymen elected George Townshend,
among eight others, a Canon of St. Patrick's Cathedral in
Dublin. A year later he became Archdeacon of Clonfert.
Some time after this he twice refused a bishopric. In 1936
the Guardian was asked to represent the Faith at the World
Fellowship of Faiths in London. In his place he sent George
Townshend to read a paper. He went there in his clerical
vestments. But the abdication of King Edward VIII on the
next day kept his paper from attracting much attention.

During my first two years in Ireland I often talked to Brian Townshend about his father. Once he told me: "When he was giving a sermon as a Canon at St. Patrick's Cathedral, just after the fall of France in 1940, my father said, 'There is only one person who can heal the world of its present ills. His name is Bahá'u'lláh.' After the service my father asked me, 'Did you hear what I said?' I said, 'Yes.' Father said, 'That is the first time that anyone has mentioned Bahá'u'lláh publicly in Ireland.'"

This enormous Cathedral of St. Patrick deserves further mention. It was begun in 1220 and finished in 1260, built on the site of a succession of earlier churches. A tradition links the Irish Saint Patrick to a holy well, near the site of the Cathedral. The interior has an atmosphere of belonging to another age; " .... on a sunny day, when brilliant shafts of light slant down from above making the dark corners of this great massive building even more than usually silent and mysterious, St. Patrick's can evoke the most convincing illusion of peace and security,"[10] wrote Desmond Guinness in his *Portrait of Dublin*.

I recall a visit to this Cathedral, accompanied by the Hand of the Cause of God A. Q. Faizi and Adib Taherzadeh. Upon entering they slowly walked around it, each saying a prayer, doubtless as Mr. Townshend had prayed countless times in these same places, that the congregation and people would dispel their illusive veils and be enabled to recognize the Spirit of Truth. Mr. Faizi mentioned that the Master had prayed that Mr. Townshend's congregation would follow him into the Faith.

In 1947 a clergyman of the Church of England in India wrote to the Archbishop of Canterbury that George Townshend's books were converting people to the Bahá'í Faith. The Archbishop sent this letter to the Archbishop of Ireland. The Dean of St. Patrick's Cathedral, who was a friend of Mr. Townshend's, took him into a private room and said that he must either refute what he had written or resign. At this time the Guardian cabled to the National Spiritual Assembly of the Bahá'ís of the British Isles that it was imperative that George Townshend should leave the Church.

He resigned from the Church, moved with his family from Galway to Dublin, and became a member of the first Spiritual Assembly of Dublin. His wife Nancy was at first opposed to this, but when he was asked to refute what he had written she stood by his decision and followed him into the Bahá'í Faith. He naturally lost his house and pension.

Mr. Townshend's first book *The Altar on the Hearth*, published in 1926, is mostly composed of prayers, meditations and poems. In an introductory essay entitled 'Of Religion, of Happiness and of the Modern Home', Mr. Townshend wrote: "The purpose of this book is to bear witness to the truth that the power of God is now abroad among men in its fulness, and that happiness in the home (and elsewhere) is to be attained only through conscious communion with that power." [11]

His search for spiritual truth is very moving, as in this prayer and the meditation that follows it:

O My Lord!
I have sought Thee all my life, yet I still wander in a chequered world of light and shadow. Oh, lift me at last into the pure splendour of Thy Truth beyond the reach of any darkness that I may behold Thee as Thou art, and live in Thy continual presence evermore.

————————

The darkness changes and pales, but no light breaks. Error grows intolerable, but Truth still is hidden out of sight. I rest not, but I never reach my goal.

Yet, do I not ask anything, but to journey onward and onward. My path is of Thy making, and Thou leadest me on the way. I ask no more, and I desire no more. [12]

In 'A Vision of God's Triumph', he described with much power his awakening, and concluded: "There shall be no more death nor oppression nor tears. God has ascended His throne. He has taken possession of the hearts of men. Therefore from the darkness with hymns of light I greet the Source of Light, and from the depths give answer to the heights." [13]

The inspiring contents of this book show a devoted churchman progressing from an acceptance of orthodox doctrines, first to a realization that a New Age of God has come, and finally to a realization that Bahá'u'lláh is its Lord. In a vivid and touching tribute to his father, Brian has quoted the Guardian's letter about this book: "The enclosures you have sent me I will treasure, particularly the little book which I conceive as an exquisite expression of lofty thoughts impregnated throughout with the Bahá'í Spirit." [14]

In 1930, the Talbot Press published a short book of stimulating essays by Mr. Townshend, entitled after one of them *The Genius of Ireland*. The essay 'A Kingship in Genius: The English Poet-Prophets,' concerns Tennyson, Browning, Shelley and Blake.

Mr. Townshend wrote of Blake, "More than a century ago a great Poet-Prophet (himself of Irish stock) uplifted in England a strange new Song of Victory and Triumph, and foretold the approach of an age when hypocrisy and tyranny would be dethroned and when man would recognize at last the hidden truth about himself and the world in which he lives and would enjoy the rights of a law-abiding Citizen of the Universe .... He deliberately bent all his powers to aid in that tremendous struggle which must precede the final victory of the Powers of Good on earth." [15]

Mr. Townshend concluded that these poets " .... saw drawing near to a negligent and unbelieving world an Era of Justice and Freedom, of Unity and constructive Peace." [16]

Greatly impressed with the noble genius of certain idealistic writers in the United States, he devoted most of his essay 'The Language of the Commonwealth' to them. He wrote: "The work—in prose or verse—of Emerson, Whitman, Longfellow, Lanier, Whittier and Hawthorne runs through many moods; but if there be one noble trait which in each and all stands out more boldly it is this idealistic attitude of mind." [17]

In his essays, 'The Beauty of Ireland' and 'Irish Humour,' although he makes plain his opinion that the cities of Ireland are not worthy of an earth so lovely and majestic and that the Irish have not learned once more to laugh together, he still describes with much love his country, its beauty, the enormous charm of its people, and their most delightful humour. Of this he wrote: "The real distinction of Irish humour is to be found less in its character than its super-abundance. It is not found chiefly in this class nor chiefly in this locality, but belongs to all the people in all sections." [18]

Mr. Townshend did not refer to Bahá'u'lláh in any of these essays. Although both these books are out of print, many of the essays, prayers, meditations and poems included in them appear in a new, rich and fascinating collection, *The Mission of Bahá'u'lláh*, which was published in 1952.

By this time Mr. Townshend had revised his essay 'The Genius of Ireland' and explained that ignorance of the coming of Bahá'u'lláh and consequent blindness to the Reality of the New Age had been a cause of serious limitation in even the great Irish poets. After careful reflection about the past spirituality of the Irish, he became " .... filled with hope that Ireland may not be slow to catch the vision of the New Day, of the coming of the Kingdom of God, and that she may do for mankind now such service as she did for the world long ago in the hour of its darkness and its need." [19] Mr. Townshend transformed what was once only a charming essay into a most powerful one.

All the essays in this book are precious gems worthy of most thorough study. The first, already mentioned, after which the title is named, served as a masterful introduction to *God Passes By* by Shoghi Effendi. In his deeply moving account and penetrating analysis of Nabíl's history of the Báb, Mr. Townshend wrote of the Bábís, "They did not trust human wisdom nor find as we have done that it betrayed them. They trusted God wholly and for love's sake gave up all they had and were, that they might serve His Truth." [20]

A most touching portrait, 'Abdu'l-Bahá, a Study of a Christlike Character', shows his deep reverence and over-whelming love for the Master. In a precious essay, 'Queen Marie of Roumania and the Bahá'í Faith,' he stresses the great importance of the service that the incomparable Bahá'í teacher, Martha Root, had given in leading a member of Royalty to the Cause of God.

This book further includes an inspiring meditation, 'The Call to God'; a scholarly comment on the letters of

'Abdu'l-Bahá, described as "a fountain of heavenly love and joy, of wisdom and power;"[21] and a beautiful essay, 'The Wellspring of Happiness'.

In September 1937, World Order Magazine published a moving reflection by Mr. Townshend on *The Hidden Words of Bahá'u'lláh*. He calls this book "a love-song". It has for its background the romance of all the ages—the Love of God and Man, of the Creator and His creatures. "Its theme is God's faithfulness and the unfaithfulness of Man."[22] Four months later the same magazine brought out a precious meditation by him on Bahá'u'lláh's work *The Seven Valleys*, and in July 1945, an essay by Mr. Townshend, both touching and informative, on Bahá'í marriage called 'Joined By God'. In 1949 he wrote an introduction and notes to *The Glad Tidings of Bahá'u'lláh*, the volume which represented the Bahá'í Faith in 'The Wisdom of the East Series', published by John Murray. This book is made up of George Townshend's very characteristic selection of a number of passages from the Bahá'í Sacred Writings which wonderfully show that the mission of Bahá'u'lláh was to bring spiritual unity to all of mankind, and so to establish a world civilisation. This work must certainly have brought knowledge of the Bahá'í Faith to many who otherwise might not have heard of it.

After he had left the Church and come into the Bahá'í community, Mr. Townshend saw fit to revise both *The Promise of All Ages*, and *The Heart of the Gospel*. In the case of the latter he did extensive rewriting. As a result this book is even more persuasive than before.

In the same way, his introduction to *The Hidden Words*, included in the edition published by the American Bahá'í Publishing Trust in 1954, is even more impressive than his reflection on them previously mentioned. He wrote, "The *Hidden Words* is not a digest, nor an ordered statement. It is a new creation. It is a distillation of Sacred Fragrances. It is a focus in which all the Great Lights of the past are joined into one Light, and all God's Yesterdays become Today." His conclusion has such power that it would be hard for a serious reader to resist an immediate study of the book.

"The *Hidden Words* stands as a sign of God's victory and of the fulfilment of His ancient purpose for mankind. No book radiant with such intensity of light has ever been given or could have been given to mankind before. It contains the whole sum of all Revelations rounding to their completeness, renewed in power and brought to the perfection of unity by the crowning words of Bahá'u'lláh. It is the Badge of the oneness of all the Prophets of East and West from the beginning until now; the Badge of that Universal Faith on which shall be built the Most Great Peace."

After a long life of exacting scholarship and writing, well over thirty years after he had recognized the station of His Lord, George Townshend started to write what Shoghi Effendi has described as "his crowning achievement," *Christ and Bahá'u'lláh*.

He used to work on the book early in the morning when his household was quiet. At the age of seventy-seven he fell from his bicycle. From that time on he had difficulty in using his hands to write. "Conceived while the most difficult and the final years of his life approached, this remarkable work, cogent, forceful, based on Biblical and Quranic texts and the known facts of history, was written under conditions of increasing hardship. He also contracted Parkinson's disease and had to move to a nursing home where he daily whispered the text to his son or daughter who would write it out and bring it for his approval. His mental faculties never declined, seemed rather to grow sharper, while his spirit blazed forth in joy and triumph to all who visited him. Had his physical means matched his will and inspiration the book would have been very much longer. His 'crowning achievement' it undoubtedly is, yet it presents little more than the partially developed themes of his notes. The complete plan is there, the order, the facts, and above all his vision of the grand kaleidoscope of history unrolling God's plan, through successive revelations of His Word, for the beautification of humanity and its entry into the Kingdom, but the body of the work is not filled in. It remains a 'mother book', the source of countless themes to be pursued by others." [23]

In it he has explained most logically the reason for the

tragic predicament of mankind to-day. If the author does assign blame to anyone it is to the clergy who have always misinterpreted the true meaning of Holy Scripture.

In Chapter I, 'God's Call to the Christians', we read: "This book is written lest Christian men and women, confused by past errors and falsities, should neglect to observe the newness of the age, to heed the warnings of Christ and should fall into the snare of which He told them all so often and so emphatically. Let them not, through lack of discernment or courage, play into the hands of those who are bringing destruction." [24]

In the concluding paragraph of Chapter VI, called 'Muḥammad and The Christians', he wrote: "So kindly were the relations between the two Faiths and so strong the spiritual influence of Muḥammad that the Christian masses were disposed to accept the Faith of the Arabian Prophet. The Báb indeed says that they were only prevented from doing so by the failure of the clergy 'for if these had believed, they would have been followed by the mass of their countrymen.' Had it not been for the unfortunate divisive counsel of these Christian priests, history would have been different, indeed." [25]

In Chapter XIII George Townshend explained that in 1864 Bahá'u'lláh summoned all the kings and the ecclesiastical rulers of the world to turn to Him and follow His dictates. In His first tablet to them He warned of the terrible calamities that would descend upon them if they disobeyed Him. Even so, they neglected his advice. "By an act of forgiveness Bahá'u'lláh made to the Christian kings of Europe a further offer. He addressed to the Emperor Napoleon III of France, to Pope Pius IX, to Queen Victoria and to Czar Alexander, individual letters in which He asked of them their aid in establishing God's Kingdom among the nations." [26] None of the Christian rulers or ecclesiastical authorities, including the Pope, to whom Bahá'u'lláh addressed these tablets turned to Him or paid any attention to His advice.

In spite of this, George Townshend has affirmed that, "Bahá'u'lláh's trust in the Christians and in their support of His teachings never weakened. Towards the end of His life He wrote the Holy Tablet [*Lawḥ-i-Aqdas*], an important work addressed to them in which He rebukes them for their slowness in recognizing Him, promises He will be faithful and pours forth a succession of enthusiastic beatitudes on the Christians who will turn to Him with loving hearts and serve His Faith." [27]

In the epilogue of his book he made this most moving appeal: "O, Christian believers! for your own sakes and for the sake of the Churches, for the sake of all mankind, for the sake of the Kingdom, cast away your conflicting dogmas and interpretations which have caused such disunity and led us to the verge of wholesale self-destruction. Recognize the age of Truth. Recognize Christ in the glory and power of the Father and, heart and soul, throw yourselves into His Cause." [28]

Simply written with the deep conviction of passionate belief, this book is obviously of major importance. It has already helped to lead many people into the Bahá'í Community. As increasing numbers of dissatisfied people leave the Church and many more even than to-day suffer from the unhappiness and worldly anxieties that agnosticism is sure to bring, certainly this book and all his other writings will find an enormous public.

Shoghi Effendi thought so well of George Townshend's writing that for years he sent his translations and manuscripts to him. He greatly admired his command and knowledge of English. In a letter to him the Guardian wrote, "I am deeply grateful to you for the very valuable, detailed and careful suggestions you have given me ...." [29] During the Second World War the Guardian sent his history of the Faith, *God Passes By*, to him, one chapter at a time for fear that it might not get there because of the torpedoes. George and his wife Nancy spent a happy winter reading it. The title of this book was George Townshend's own choice.

Other distinguished writers in the Faith also consulted George Townshend about their work. For example, the Hand of the Cause John Ferraby sent him the manuscript of his book *All Things Made New* for criticism.

Despite his rare gifts George Townshend had great humility. He could hardly believe it when he received a cable from the Guardian that conferred upon him the station of Hand of the Cause of God. In December 1951, the much-loved believer, Juliet Thompson, told me with great enthusiasm, "The Guardian has appointed the first contingent of Hands," and mentioned that George Townshend was one of the three for Europe. She read to me, a newly-declared Bahá'í, a statement by 'Abdu'l-Bahá in His Will and Testament. "The obligations of the Hands of the Cause of God are to diffuse the Divine Fragrances, to edify the souls of men, to promote learning, to improve the character of all men and to be, at all times and under all conditions, sanctified and detached from earthly things. They must manifest the fear of God by their conduct, their manners, their deeds and their words." [30]

As a Bahá'í teacher Mr. Townshend had a deep understanding of other people. Lisbeth Greeves, a believer from Belfast, once told me, "When I first came into the Bahá'í community I felt very strange, and said so to George Townshend. He said to me, 'You would not feel at all strange if you knew how much we love you.'" Jane Villiers-Stuart, a believer from Northern Ireland, recalls: "When I first met him in Belfast before I became a Bahá'í, I was particularly impressed with his directness. I asked him questions and he would answer me the exact question that I had asked, not some question that I had not asked, like some believers did. I said to him once—'If I were a Bahá'í ....' He stopped me and said, 'Yes, but you're not a Bahá'í.' I invited him for tea because I wanted his help. He said to me, 'Why do you keep asking the same questions over and over again? You are going around in a circle. You are neglecting your spiritual life. You must pray and meditate. If you do this, you will receive the answer to many of your questions.' When he left me that afternoon, I felt that he had turned away from me sadly as if to say, 'I am afraid that I have put you off.' On the contrary he had given me enormous help. I do not think that I would have become a Bahá'í without him."

Once when they were visiting Ireland, Mr. Townshend's close friends David and Marion Hofman spoke about him to a small gathering. Marion said, "I think to read the volume of essays called *The Mission of Bahá'u'lláh* is to learn what a Hand of the Cause is really like." David Hofman added, "I think that George's outstanding quality was his love of God."

The last few years of his life were filled with difficulties. He did not ask for an easy, secure life. He prayed to God to make him suffer, so long as that suffering brought him closer to God. He said to the clergy, "The day of grace is over. The day of wrath has come." After he joined the Bahá'í Community some people would not even speak to him on the street.

Soon after I moved to Ireland in 1963, I drove to the cemetery of the Church of Ireland in the village of Enniskerry to visit George Townshend's grave. The cemetery lies next to the church overlooking the charming village and near to the grounds of the great house, Powerscourt. On the grave stone is written a quotation from the Book of Revelation, "And I saw a new heaven and a new earth."

I have made many rewarding visits to that grave. Sometimes, when I stand beside or sit near it, I think of future years and see many people coming to it every day from Ireland and from all over the world to pray and meditate at this holy spot. Sometimes, after leaving the grave, I walk for a while down roads and through fields in the hills of Wicklow. Perhaps while George Townshend was walking in country like this, he wrote this moving prayer:

Make my heart, O God, as this unshadowed mountain lake that sets its face forever toward heaven, and in its calm depths reflects the peace of Thy remote vast worlds of light.[31]

As I look at the well-known photograph of George Townshend, his face strikes me as kind, gentle, deeply sensitive, and filled with charm. His expression, among other appealing qualities, conveys to me a rare sense of humour. In a moving tribute David Hofman wrote of him, "A high, domed forehead, sharp high nose, blue eyes of the mildest temper and gentle mouth from which his speech emerged with the faintest Irish brogue, always in a moderate tone no matter how direct and forceful the thoughts expressed, were the visible temple of this great soul."[32]

In *The Hidden Words*, Bahá'u'lláh has revealed: "O SON OF MAN! Humble thyself before Me, that I may graciously visit thee. Arise for the triumph of My Cause that while yet on earth thou mayest obtain the victory."

The Guardian's cablegram sent to the National Spiritual Assembly of the British Isles at the time of George Townshend's passing gives perfect evidence of what he had achieved.[33]

27th March, 1957.
Deeply mourn passing dearly loved, much admired, greatly gifted, outstanding Hand Cause George Townshend. His death morrow publication his crowning achievement robs British followers Bahá'u'lláh their most distinguished collaborator and Faith itself one of its stoutest defenders. His sterling qualities, his scholarship, his challenging writings, his high ecclesiastical position unrivalled any Bahá'í Western world, entitle him rank with Thomas Breakwell, Dr. Esslemont, one of three luminaries shedding brilliant lustre annals Irish, English, Scottish Bahá'í communities. His fearless championship Cause he loved so dearly, served so valiantly, constitutes significant landmark British Bahá'í history. So enviable position calls for national tribute his memory by assembled delegates, visitors, forthcoming British Bahá'í Convention. Assure relatives deepest loving sympathy grievous loss. Confident his reward inestimable Abhá Kingdom.

Notes and References

Full bibliographical details are given on the first mention of a work, apart from the following titles which have been used throughout. The abbreviated title used in the Notes and References is given in brackets.

'ABDU'L-BAHÁ by H. M. Balyuzi. Oxford: George Ronald, 1973

BAHÁ'Í WORLD, THE. An international record, published periodically since 1926 from New York and Wilmette by Bahá'í Publishing Trust, and since 1970 for Haifa by The Universal House of Justice.

GOD PASSES BY by Shoghi Effendi. Wilmette, Illinois: Bahá'í Publishing Trust, 1944

THE PRICELESS PEARL by Rúḥíyyih Rabbani. London: Bahá'í Publishing Trust, 1969 (Priceless Pearl)

THE PROMULGATION OF UNIVERSAL PEACE. Discourses by 'Abdu'l-Bahá during his visit to the United States in 1912. Vol. I, Chicago: Executive Board of Bahai Temple Unity, 1922. Vol. II, Chicago: Baha'i Publishing Committee, 1925. (Promulgation)

STAR OF THE WEST. The Bahá'í Magazine, published between 1910 and 1933 from Chicago and Washington, D.C., by official Bahá'í agencies variously titled. (Star)

WORLD ORDER MAGAZINE. Published in two series since 1933, from New York and Chicago by official Bahá'í agencies. (World Order)

THORNTON CHASE

1. *World Order*, vol. XI, no. 5, article by Carl Scheffler, 'Thornton Chase: First American Bahá'í,' p. 152
2. ibid.
3. ibid. p. 153
4. *Star*, vol. 5, no. 17, p. 263
5. ibid.
6. ibid.
7. *World Order*, Fall 1971, p. 35
8. ibid. pp. 35–36
9. Thornton Chase, *In Galilee*, Chicago: Bahai Publishing Society, 1908, p. 27
10. ibid. pp. 33–34

11. ibid. p. 55
12. ibid. p. 39
13. ibid. p. 66
14. *World Order*, vol. XI, no. 5, p. 157
15. *In Galilee*, p. 69
16. *'Abdu'l-Bahá*, p. 67
17. Thornton Chase, *The Bahá'í Revelation*, New York: Bahá'í Publishing Committee, no date, p. 61
18. ibid. p. 20
19. ibid. p. 22
20. ibid. p. 28
21. ibid. p. 29
22. ibid. p. 32
23. ibid. pp. 123, 125
24. ibid. p. 127
25. ibid. pp. 173–174
26. *Star*, vol. 21, no. 9, p. 267
27. *Star*, vol. 4, no. 11, p. 188
28. *World Order*, Fall 1971, p. 37
29. ibid.
30. *Star*, vol. 4, no. 11, p. 189
31. ibid.
32. ibid. p. 190
33. *Star*, vol. 4, no. 13, p. 225
34. ibid. p. 226
35. *Star*, vol. 16, no. 1, p. 403
36. ibid. p. 404

PHOEBE HEARST and ROBERT TURNER

1. W. A. Swanberg, *Citizen Hearst*, London: Longmans, 1962, p. 8
2. ibid. p. 14
3. ibid. p. 16
4. W. Black, *The Life & Personality of Phoebe Apperson Hearst*, San Francisco: Bonfils, 1928, p. 58
5. *World Order*, vol. XII, no. 1, p. 28
6. *God Passes By*, p. 259
7. Lady Blomfield, *The Chosen Highway* London: Bahá'í Publishing Trust, 1940, p. 235
8. *World Order*, vol. XII, no. 1, p. 28
9. May Maxwell, *An Early Pilgrimage*, Oxford: George Ronald, 1974, p. 20
10. *World Order*, vol. XII, no. 1, p. 29
11. *Bahá'í World*, vol. VII, pp. 801–802
12. *God Passes By*, p. 259
13. *World Order*, vol. XII, no. 1, p. 29
14. ibid.

NOTES AND REFERENCES

15. *'Abdu'l-Bahá*, p. 307
16. Swanberg, *op. cit.* p. 8
17. *Star*, vol. 11, no. 7, p. 112

HELEN GOODALL and ELLA COOPER

1. *Star*, vol. 23, no. 7, p. 202
2. *Priceless Pearl*, p. 6
3. Helen S. Goodall and Ella Goodall Cooper, *Daily Lessons Received at Acca, January, 1908* Chicago: Bahai Publishing Society 1908, p. 97
4. ibid. p. 9
5. ibid. pp. 13–14
6. ibid. p. 17
7. ibid. pp. 21–22
8. ibid. p. 23
9. ibid. p. 23
10. ibid. pp. 39–40
11. ibid. p. 44
12. ibid. p. 49
13. ibid. p. 84
14. *Star*, vol. 13, no. 8, p. 204
15. ibid. p. 205
16. *Star*, vol. 4, no. 11, p. 194
17. ibid. no. 12, p. 209
18. ibid. p. 204
19. *Star*, vol. 3, no. 13, p. 12
20. *Star*, vol. 13, no. 8, p. 206
21. ibid.
22. *Star*, vol. 6, no. 5, p. 35
23. ibid. pp. 36–37
24. *Star*, vol. 7, no. 11, p. 101
25. *Star*, vol. 10, no. 1, pp. 8–9
26. *Star*, vol. 13, no. 8, p. 194
27. ibid. p. 206
28. ibid. p. 207
29. Shoghi Effendi, *Citadel of Faith*, Wilmette, Illinois: Bahá'í Publishing Trust, 1965, p. 162

HOWARD MacNUTT

1. *God Passes By*, p. 275
2. Julia M. Grundy, *Ten Days in the Light of Acca*, Chicago, Illinois: Bahai Publishing Society, no date, p. 72
3. ibid. p. 74
4. ibid.
5. ibid. p. 76
6. ibid. p. 77
7. Howard MacNutt, *Unity Through Love*, Chicago, Illinois: Bahai Publishing Society, 1906, p. 3

8. ibid. p. 16
9. ibid. p. 27
10. *Star*, vol. 2, nos. 7 & 8, p. 13
11. 'Abdu'l-Bahá, *Promulgation*, Vol. I, p. 2
12. *Star*, vol. 4, no. 12, p. 210
13. ibid.
14. *Star*, vol. 3, no. 10, p. 3
15. *Promulgation*, Vol. I, p. 191
16. *Star*, vol. 19, no. 8, p. 253
17. *Star*, vol. 3, no. 10, p. 3
18. ibid. p. 4
19. *Star*, vol. 10, no. 8, p. 153
20. *Promulgation*, Vol. I, vii
21. ibid. ii
22. ibid. vi–vii
23. *Star*, vol. 17, no. 10, p. 289
24. Shoghi Effendi, *The World Order of Bahá'u'lláh*, Wilmette, Illinois: Bahá'í Publishing Committee, 1938, rev. edn. 1955, p. 81

EDWARD and CARRIE KINNEY

1. *Bahá'í World*, vol. XII, p. 677
2. Letter to the author from Donald Kinney, 24th April 1973
3. *Bahá'í World*, vol. XII, p. 678
4. Juliet Thompson, *Abdul Baha's First Days in America*. From the Diary of Juliet Thompson. East Aurora, New York: The Roycrofters (no date), p. 5
5. *Promulgation*, Vol. I, p. 1
6. Letter from Donald Kinney cited above
7. Howard Colby Ives, *Portals to Freedom*, Oxford: George Ronald, 1974 (1st edition 1937), p. 36
8. Letter from Donald Kinney cited above
9. *Bahá'í World*, vol. XII, pp. 678–679
10. *Star*, vol. 10, no. 19, p. 350
11. ibid.
Unattributed quotations are as remembered by the author.

ETHEL ROSENBERG

1. *The Chosen Highway*, p. 236
2. From Ethel Rosenberg's pilgrim notes, taken in 'Akká and Haifa during February and March 1901, now in the British Bahá'í Archives in London, pp. 2–3
3. ibid. p. 30
4. Ethel J. Rosenberg, *A Brief Account of the Bahai Movement*, London: The Priory Press, 1911, p. 16
5. *Star*, vol. 7, no. 11, p. 108
6. *Star*, vol. 9, no. 19, p. 222
7. *Star*, vol. 7, no. 11, p. 107

8. Rosenberg papers, see 2 above
9. Rosenberg, *op. cit.*, p. 14
10. ibid. p. 16
11. *The Chosen Highway*, p. 165
12. *Abdul-Baha in London*, Addresses, and Notes of Conversations, Chicago: Bahai Publishing Society, 1921, p. 34
13. *Star*, vol. 5, no. 19, p. 293
14. ibid. p. 294
15. From J. E. Esslemont's unpublished diary of his first pilgrimage in 1919, now in the British Bahá'í Archives, page not numbered
16. *Star*, vol. 12, no. 19, pp. 300–301
17. ibid. p. 301
18. *Star*, vol. 14, no. 9, p. 276
19. ibid.
20. *Star*, vol. 22, no. 4, p. 117
21. *Bahá'í World*, vol. IV, p. 262
22. ibid.
23. ibid. p. 263

THOMAS BREAKWELL

1. May Maxwell, *An Early Pilgrimage*, Oxford: George Ronald, 1953 (first published 1917), pp. 12–13
2. *Star*, vol. 5, no. 19, p. 298
3. *Bahá'í World*, vol. VII, p. 707
4. *Star*, vol. 5, no. 19, p. 298
5. *Bahá'í World*, vol. VII, p. 709
6. *Star*, vol. 5, no. 19, p. 298
7. ibid.
8. *Bahá'í World*, vol. VII, p. 709
9. ibid.
10. *Star*, vol. 4, no. 15, p. 256
11. *Priceless Pearl*, p. 150
12. *Bahá'í World*, vol. VII, p. 709
13. ibid.
14. ibid. p. 710
15. *'Abdu'l-Bahá*, p. 77
16. *Bahá'í World*, vol. VII, p. 709
17. ibid. p. 710
18. ibid.
19. A. Q. Faizi, "A Precious Gift", *Bahá'í Journal*, London: N.S.A. of the Bahá'ís of the British Isles, November 1969, p. 2
20. ibid.
21. *'Abdu'l-Bahá*, p. 78
22. ibid. p. 78
23. *Bahá'í World*, vol. VII, pp. 710–711
24. *'Abdu'l-Bahá*, p. 80
25. A. Q. Faizi, op. cit. p. 3

26. *'Abdu'l-Bahá*, p. 80
27. *God Passes By*, p. 259
28. *Bahá'í World*, vol. XIII, p. 845
The reader is referred particularly to the article by May Maxwell in
Bahá'í World, vol. VII.

JULIET THOMPSON

1. *World Order*, Fall 1971, pp. 52–53
2. ibid. pp. 54–55
3. *Promulgation*, Vol. I, p. 9
4. *World Order*, Fall 1971, p. 57
5. ibid.
6. ibid. pp. 61–62
7. *Promulgation*, Vol. II, p. 426
8. *Star*, vol. 10, no. 4, p. 80
9. ibid. no. 11, p. 222
10. ibid. no. 6, p. 109
11. Juliet Thompson, *I, Mary Magdalen*, New York: Delphic Studios, 1940, p. 5
12. ibid. p. 12
13. ibid. p. 30
14. *World Order*, vol. V, no. 5, p. 163
15. *World Order*, vol. VII, no. 12, pp. 422–423
16. *Citadel of Faith*, p. 170

ROY WILHELM

1. *Bahá'í World*, vol. VII, p. 539
2. ibid.
3. ibid.
4. ibid. p. 540
5. *Bahá'í World*, vol. IX, p. 803
6. ibid. p. 805
7. ibid.
8. ibid. p. 806
9. ibid. p. 807
10. *Bahá'í World*, vol. VII, p. 540
11. *Promulgation*, Vol. I, p. 201
12. *Star*, vol. 12, no. 6, pp. 157–158
13. *Promulgation*, Vol. I, pp. 208–210
14. *Star*, vol. 4, no. 14, p. 240
15. *Bahá'í World*, vol. XII, p. 664
16. *Star*, vol. 7, no. 7, p. 60
17. *Star*, vol. 9, no. 14, p. 164
18. *Star*, vol. 8, no. 9, p. 108
19. *Star*, vol. 10, no. 1, p. 10
20. *Star*, vol. 11, no. 9, p. 148
21. Letter from A. K. Kalantar to Marzieh Gail, 20th February 1975

22. *Star*, vol. 11, no. 15, p. 257
23. ibid.
24. *Priceless Pearl*, p.49
25. ibid.
26. *'Abdu'l-Bahá*, p. 451
27. ibid. p. 455
28. *Priceless Pearl*, p. 56
29. *Star*, vol. 13, no. 4, p. 69
30. Shoghi Effendi, *Bahá'í Administration*, Wilmette, Illinois: Bahá'í Publishing Committee, rev. edn. 1945, p. 24
31. ibid. p. 29
32. *Star*, vol. 13, no. 12, p. 329
33. *Bahá'í World*, vol. VII, p. 541
34. *Bahá'í World*, vol. XII, p. 663
35. ibid. p. 664
36. ibid. p. 662

LADY BLOMFIELD

1. Lady Blomfield, *The Chosen Highway* London: Bahá'í Publishing Trust, 1940, p. 1
2. ibid.
3. *Bahá'í World*, vol. VIII, p. 651
4. *Chosen Highway*, p. 149
5. ibid. pp. 149–150
6. ibid. pp. 171–172
7. 'Abdu'l-Bahá, *Paris Talks*, London: Bahá'í Publishing Trust, 1912, pp. 27–8
8. *'Abdu'l-Bahá*, p. 350
9. *Chosen Highway*, p. 155
10. *Bahá'í World*, vol. VIII, p. 652
11. *Chosen Highway*, p. 219
12. ibid.
13. ibid. p. 220
14. *'Abdu'l-Bahá*, p. 436
15. ibid.
16. *Bahá'í World*, vol. VIII, p. 653
17. Quoted in *Bahá'í World*, vol. I, pp. 21 & 23
18. *Priceless Pearl*, p. 57
19. *Bahá'í World*, vol. VIII, p. 653
20. *Chosen Highway*, v
21. *Bahá'í World*, vol. VIII, p. 656

FRED MORTENSEN and ALBERT HEATH HALL

1. *Star*, vol. 11, no. 19, p. 323
2. *Bahá'í News* Chicago: 1910, vol. 1, no. 4, p. 10
3. *Promulgation*, Vol. II, p. 322
4. *Star*, vol. 4, no. 8, pp. 136–137

5. *Star*, vol. 9, no. 14, pp. 155 & 164
6. *Star*, vol. 8, no. 9, p. 109
7. *Star*, vol. 11, no. 19, p. 322
8. ibid. p. 323
9. ibid. p. 321
10. *Star*, vol. 14, no. 12, p. 366
11. ibid.
12. ibid.
13. ibid. The following account of Fred Mortensen's visit to 'Abdu'l-Bahá at Green Acre is drawn from this article.
14. *Star*, vol. 7, no. 17, pp. 167–168
15. *Star*, vol. 10, no. 1, p. 6
16. *Star*, vol. 15, no. 12, pp. 356–357
17. ibid. p. 358
18. *Bahá'í World*, vol. XI, p. 486
19. ibid.
20. ibid.

ALFRED E. LUNT

1. *'Abdu'l-Bahá*, p. 241
2. *Bahá'í World*, vol. VII, p. 533
3. *Promulgation*, Vol. II, pp. 233–234
4. *Star*, vol. 5, no. 4, p. 53
5. *Star*, vol. 6, no. 17, p. 149
6. *Star*, vol. 7, no. 7, p. 60
7. ibid. no. 16, p. 160
8. *Star*, vol. 8, no. 9, p. 106
9. ibid.
10. *Star*, vol. 10, no. 18, pp. 329–330
11. *Star*, vol. 16, no. 4, p. 481
12. *Star*, vol. 16, no. 8, p. 7
13. *Star*, vol. 24, no. 2, pp. 53 & 56
14. *World Order*, vol. III, no. 2, pp. 71–72
15. *Bahá'í World*, vol. VII, p. 533
16. ibid. p. 531

ISABELLA BRITTINGHAM

1. *Star*, vol. 17, no. 8, p. 263
2. Isabella Brittingham, *The Revelation of Bahá-ulláh*, Chicago: The Bahai Publishing Society, 1902, p. 25
3. ibid.
4. *Star*, vol. 8, no. 15, p. 206
5. Isabella Brittingham, op. cit., p. 1
6. ibid. p. 32
7. *Star*, vol. 14, no. 12, p. 376
8. *'Abdu'l-Bahá*, p. 96
9. *Star*, vol. 12, no. 8, p. 148

NOTES AND REFERENCES

10. James F. Brittingham, *The Message of the Kingdom of God*, 1909, p. 13
11. *Star*, vol. 14, no. 1, p. 11
12. *Star*, vol. 2, no. 5, p. 13
13. *Star*, vol. 10, no. 1, pp. 5–6
14. Letter from Marzieh Gail to the author, 10th September 1974
15. *Star*, vol. 12, no. 12, p. 201
16. *Star*, vol. 16, no. 3, pp. 460–461
17. *Star*, vol. 14, no. 12, p. 376
18. ibid. p. 354
19. ibid. pp. 376–377

HOWARD and MABEL IVES

1. Howard Colby Ives, *Portals to Freedom*, Oxford: George Ronald, 1974 (first published 1937), pp. 22–23
2. ibid. p. 20
3. ibid. p. 26
4. ibid. p. 33
5. ibid. p. 35
6. ibid. p. 86
7. *Promulgation*, Vol. I, p. 128
8. *Portals to Freedom*, pp. 130–131
9. *Promulgation*, Vol. II, p. 426
10. *Portals to Freedom*, p. 147
11. ibid. pp. 232–233
12. ibid. p. 248
13. *Bahá'í World*, vol. IX, p. 617
14. ibid. p. 618
15. *Bahá'í Prayers*, Wilmette, Illinois: Bahá.í Publishing Trust, 1973, p. 16
16. From an unpublished Tablet to Mrs. Mabel Rice-Wray, translated by Shoghi Rabbani, Haifa, 19th January 1919.
17. *Bahá'í World*, vol. IX, p. 619
18. *Star*, vol. 25, no. 2, p. 59
19. Howard Colby Ives, *The Song Celestial*, Chicago: The London Press, 1938, p. 8
20. ibid. pp. 23–24
21. ibid. p. 61
22. ibid. p. 62
23. *Bahá'í World*, vol. IX, p. 618
24. ibid. p. 613
25. ibid. p. 620
26. ibid. p. 622
27. ibid.
28. ibid.
29. ibid.

Unattributed quotations from Muriel Ives Newhall and Edris Rice-Wray are from letters written to the author during 1975.

MARIAM and CHARLES HANEY

Some of the Tablets of 'Abdu'l-Bahá quoted in this essay have not been previously published. The originals are held at the National Bahá'í Archives, Wilmette, Illinois.

1. Letter from Mariam Haney to Mrs. Alice Dudley, 9th July 1959.
2. *Bahá'í World*, vol. XII, p. 671
3. *Star*, vol. 15, no. 8, pp. 230–234
4. Tablet from 'Abdu'l-Bahá for Mariam Haney, received in Paris, 20th September 1902, and translated by Ali-Kuli Khan, New York City, 10th October 1902.
5. Tablet from 'Abdu'l-Bahá for Mariam Haney, translated by Ali-Kuli Khan, Washington, D.C., 28th October 1903.
6. Letter from Paul Haney to the author, 29th September 1975.
7. *A Heavenly Feast*, Some Utterances of Abdu'l-Baha to Two American Pilgrims (Charles and Mariam Haney) in Acca, Syria, February 1909: printed privately, no date; p. 28
8. *Bahá'í World*, vol. XIV, p. 344
9. Tablet from 'Abdu'l-Bahá for Charles Haney, translated by Dr. Ameen Fareed, Haifa, 29th May 1909.
10. *Promulgation*, Vol. II, p. 465
11. *Star*, vol. 5, no. 10, p. 149
12. *Star*, vol. 10, no. 19, p. 347
13. Tablet from 'Abdu'l-Bahá for Mariam and Paul Haney, translated by Dr. Zia M. Bagdadi, New York, 9th November 1919.
14. Notes taken at 'Akká by Mrs. Corinne True, signed by 'Abdu'l-Bahá, 1920
15. *Star*, vol. 11, no. 6, pp. 101–102
16. ibid. p. 146
17. *Bahá'í World*, vol. V, p. 413
18. *Star*, vol. 12, no. 6, p. 115
19. ibid. p. 124
20. *Bahá'í World*, vol. V, pp. 413–414
21. *'Abdu'l-Bahá*, p. 482
22. Shoghi Effendi, *Bahá'í Administration*, p. 74
23. ibid. p. 157
24. *Star*, vol. 24, no. 9, p. 269
25. *Star*, vol. 25, no. 12, p. 376
26. *World Order*, vol. XI, no. 1, pp. 24–25
27. ibid. no. 7, p. 216
28. Letter from Mrs. Alice Dudley to the author, 11th September 1975
29. Shoghi Effendi, *Messages to the Bahá'í World 1950–1957*, Wilmette, Illinois: Bahá'í Publishing Trust, 1958, p. 57
30. Letter written on behalf of Shoghi Effendi to Mariam Haney, Haifa, 8th May 1954
31. Postscript by Shoghi Effendi added to a letter written on his behalf to Mariam Haney, Haifa, 15th February 1957

32. *Bahá'í World*, vol. XIII, p. 345
33. *Bahá'í World*, vol. XIV, p. 346

JOHN ESSLEMONT

1. *Star*, vol. 16, no. 11, p. 715
2. *Star*, vol. 9, no. 17, p. 196
3. ibid. p. 197
4. J. E. Esslemont, *Bahá'u'lláh and the New Era*, London: Bahá'í Publishing Trust, rev. edn. 1974, ix
5. ibid. p. 61
6. *Priceless Pearl*, opposite p. 265
7. ibid. p. 34
8. ibid. p. 39
9. ibid. p. 40
10. ibid. p. 41
11. ibid. pp. 102, 91
12. *God Passes By*, p. 382
13. *Bahá'u'lláh and the New Era*, p. 7
14. ibid. p. 46
15. ibid. p. 83
16. *Priceless Pearl*, p. 91
17. *Star*, vol. 16, no. 11, p. 718
18. ibid.
19. ibid. p. 719
20. *Bahá'í World*, vol. III, pp. 84–85
21. Shoghi Effendi, *Bahá'í Administration*, p. 98

QUEEN MARIE OF RUMANIA

1. R. W. Seton-Watson, *A History of the Roumanians*, Cambridge: The University Press, 1934
2. *Star*, vol. 17, no. 3, p. 84
3. ibid.
4. *World Order*, vol. II, no. 3, p. 99
5. *Star*, vol. 17, no. 3, p. 85
6. ibid. p. 87
7. *Bahá'í World*, vol. XII, p. 618
8. *Priceless Pearl*, p. 109
9. ibid. p. 108
10. ibid. p. 107
11. *Bahá'í World*, vol. XII, pp. 619–620
12. Shoghi Effendi, *Bahá'í Administration*, p. 111
13. *Star*, vol. 18, no. 12, p. 367
14. ibid.
15. ibid. p. 369
16. *Star*, vol. 19, no. 6, p. 170
17. ibid. p. 172
18. *God Passes By*, p. 394

19. ibid.
20. *Priceless Pearl*, p. 112
21. *Star*, vol. 20, no. 11, p. 334
22. *Priceless Pearl*, pp. 112–113
23. ibid. p. 113
24. ibid. p. 114
25. ibid.
26. ibid.
27. ibid.
28. ibid.
29. ibid. p. 115
30. ibid.
31. ibid. p. 116; also *Bahá'í World*, vol. IV, frontispiece
32. *World Order*, vol. II, no. 3, pp. 101–102
33. *World Order*, vol. II, no. 3, p. 102
34. ibid.
35. ibid. p. 103
36. ibid.
37. *World Order*, vol. IV, no. 10, p. 385
38. ibid. pp. 384–385
39. George Townshend, *The Mission of Bahá'u'lláh*, Oxford: George Ronald, 1952, p. 63
40. *God Passes By*, p. 395

GEORGE TOWNSHEND

1. *The Promise of All Ages*, (3rd revised ed.) Oxford: George Ronald, 1972, pp. 61–62
2. ibid. ix
3. ibid. p. 171
4. *The Heart of the Gospel*, (3rd revised ed.) Oxford: George Ronald, 1972, p. 34
5. ibid. p. 67
6. *God Passes By*, iii
7. *The Old Churches and the New World-Faith* London: N.S.A. of the Bahá'ís of the British Isles, p. 17
8. *Bahá'í World*, vol. XIII, p. 842
9. ibid. Also *Bahá'í Journal*, London: N.S.A. of the Bahá'ís of the British Isles, August 1957, no. 133
10. Desmond Guiness, *Portrait of Dublin*, London: B. T. Batsford, 1967, p. 26
11. *The Altar on the Hearth*, Dublin: The Talbot Press, 1926, p. 9
12. *The Mission of Bahá'u'lláh*, p. 123
13. ibid. p. 131
14. *Bahá'í World*, vol. XIII, p. 843
15. *The Genius of Ireland*, Dublin: The Talbot Press, 1930, pp. 52 & 57
16. ibid. p. 71
17. ibid. p. 79

NOTES AND REFERENCES

18. ibid. p. 16
19. *The Mission of Bahá'u'lláh*, p. 120
20. ibid. p. 44
21. ibid. p. 77
22. *World Order*, vol. III, no. 6, p. 210
23. Quoted from a biography of George Townshend by David Hofman, not yet (1976) published.
24. *Christ and Bahá'u'lláh*, (revised ed.) Oxford: George Ronald, 1967, pp. 12–13
25. ibid. p. 42
26. ibid. p. 81
27. ibid. p. 84
28. ibid. p. 116
29. *Priceless Pearl*, p. 204
30. Shoghi Effendi, *Bahá'í Administration*, pp. 8–9
31. *The Mission of Bahá'u'lláh*, p. 130
32. *Bahá'í Journal op. cit.*
33. *Bahá'í World*, vol. XIII, p. 845